CISTERCIAN STUDIES SERIES: NUMBER TWENTY-ONE

CONTEMPLATIVE COMMUNITY

CISTERCIAN STUDIES SERIES

CISTERCIAN STUDIES SERIES: NUMBER TWENTY-ONE

Contemplative Community

An Interdisciplinary Symposium

edited by

M. Basil Pennington ocso

CISTERCIAN PUBLICATIONS
CONSORTIUM PRESS
Washington, D.C.
1972

Cistercian Studies Series ISBN 0–87907–800–6
This Volume   ISBN 0–87907–821–9

Library of Congress Catalog Card Number: 70–184548

© Copyright, Cistercian Publications, Inc. 1972

Ecclesiastical permission to publish this book has been received from
Bernard Flanagan, Bishop of Worcester, September 23, 1971.

Printed in the Republic of Ireland by
Cahill & Co. Limited, Parkgate Printing Works, Dublin 8

CONTENTS

INTRODUCTION

THE THIRD CISTERCIAN SYMPOSIUM had two distinct phases. First there was the preparation and exchange of the twelve papers published in this volume. Then there was the week-long meeting at the Abbey of Notre Dame du Lac, August 30—September 6, 1971 which produced the conclusions to be found at the end of this book.

The two were directly connected. The fifty participants[1] had the opportunity to study the papers prior to the meeting. At the opening sessions each author briefly indicated the principal insights he felt his study had to offer and the pertinent questions that were yet to be answered. And, quite naturally, the contents of the papers flowed into and greatly influenced the discussion and conclusions.

The purpose of the Symposium was expressed thus:

> To see more clearly the problems in the life-situation when men[2] freely gather together and commit themselves to live together in a Christian community for the precise purpose of obtaining for each one the maximal freedom to respond to God in prayer and

1. The participants included not only Cistercians—monks and nuns, abbots and abbesses and novices—but also Benedictines and other religious, members of experimental communities and laity. See the List of Participants at the end of the volume, pp. 347

2. It perhaps does not need to be said that when we speak of men we do not intend to exclude the women. There was a good representation of women at the Symposium and they made a very significant contribution.

7

contemplation and of fostering each one's growth in this, and to seek out genuinely practical responses to these problems.

In more concrete terms:

I am a Cistercian. I live in community. I am trying to be a man of prayer. I want to be fully responsive to my community, each man in it and the community as a whole. At the same time I want to live an intense prayer life and attain to the deepest possible union with God and experience of him. In view of this twofold concern what are the difficulties and tensions I am running into and how practically can we best resolve them?

Two things are immediately evident. First of all, the concern here is with a Christian contemplative community. Secondly, before proper solutions can be discerned it is necessary to have a clear understanding of the nature of Christian contemplative community.

Fr Francis Martin, in the first paper in this volume, indicates what, according to the inspired Scriptures, are the essential notes of a *Christian* community as it is idealized in the Acts of the Apostles. And Fr Tarcisius Conner offers a penetrating theological exploration of these Christian aspects. An anthropologist, Br David Steindl-Rast, pinpoints in his very brief but fascinating contribution, the qualities which distinguish the *contemplative* community. It remained for the meeting, and this proved to be its principal task and accomplishment, to bring these elements together in the formulation of a "definition" of *Christian Contemplative Community*. The one arrived at[3] especially shows how the Christian element transforms and transfinalizes a phenomenon that has been common to almost all well-developed human cultures.

The contemplative attitude is one of *openness* to the transcendent. A way of life can properly be called "contemplative" when *every detail* in it is ordered toward fostering this "mindfulness of the Transcendent." Men gather in "contemplative communities" to help each other to live this kind of life. For the Christian this openness means receiving attentively the transforming Word. The

3. See below, pp. 340–341.

community formed mediates the Word and shares in the vital organic unity that comes from being baptized into the one Christ, forming his living Body.

The various historical studies bring out how some of the great leaders and spokesmen of Christian contemplative communities, Gregory of Nyssa, Bernard of Clairvaux, Aelred of Rievaulx and Guerric of Igny, envisioned their ideal and guided their disciples toward its realization. These studies obviously have a particular significance for the Cistercian. They are complemented by a later witness from the Anglican Church. By contrast, Fr Cyprian Davis' study in failure, where men do not live up to the ideal, not only clarifies some of the perennial problems, but offers an opportunity to learn from past mistakes.

Fr Chrysogonus Waddell in considering the liturgical life of the contemplative community emphasizes the fact that such a community needs to express itself, in this case in regards to the liturgy, in a contemplative way, and as a Christian community, in an essentially Christian way. Fr Dominic Salman in his study of the psychological aspects reemphasizes this on a much broader scale, speaking of the community's whole ecological environment. He then goes on to approach more immediately the contemplative's problem of integrating his response to his brethren with his contemplative response to God, offering an extensive consideration of the modes and types of communication within the contemplative community.[4]

Fr Valentine Walgrave also comes to grips with this problem when he treats of "Transcendent Commitment and Community Life" and "Virginity of Heart and Fraternity."[5] Father's very penetrating study also brings out the basic importance of man's contemplative dimension, and how essential it is that this be operative in Christian renewal. Thus he highlights the precise role of the contemplative community at this time as a "regulating factor" in the Church. This is a paper that requires careful reading, but the effort is amply rewarded.

Each paper makes its respective contribution toward an adequate

4. See below, pp. 318–337.
5. See below, pp. 258–261 and 282–284.

response to the problems of integral contemplative life. At the same time, while making these contributions, the papers also develop some of the underlying principles, offer valuable insights and open challenging vistas.

The meeting itself in large measure drew on the principles offered by the various papers, explored them more deeply in a remarkable interdisciplinary effort and formulated the descriptive definition to be found in the Conclusion. In regard to the problem which gave rise to the Symposium, namely, the difficulties and tensions that can arise as a contemplative seeks to respond, as a contemplative, to God and to his brothers, the group seemed to feel that each individual had to find his own solution using the principles provided, a solution that would vary with his particular commitments and responsibilities and his evolving life-experience.[6] Each man has his own idea and experience of God and, under grace, each senses a call to respond to him in a particular way. This way may place more emphasis on solitude or it may place more emphasis on sharing. Both will be present, and always with a certain tension.

The community can best help relieve this tension by fully recognizing the validity of the different emphases within the limits of its tradition and basic commitment and fostering a climate that allows the individual to find and live out his particular solution. Thus the meeting turned its attention to pluralism and to that unity and experience of unity that gives birth to and fosters pluralism.

The unity of a community rests on the commitment of the members to a common goal and shared means. The common goal of the Christian contemplative community is to help each other to grow in love and responsiveness to God, adopting a form of life, in accord with its own proper traditions, that expresses and fosters this love and responsiveness in every detail of daily living. Since however each member has his own particular perception of God and therefore his own particular response to a particular "call,"

6. Thus, for example, a member of a Cistercian contemplative community would have to work out his solution taking into account the guidelines for Cistercian life, Cistercian tradition and spirituality and his role in his community.

commitment to the common goal of the contemplative community implies a commitment to pluralism.

A community will feel free to allow and foster such pluralism only when it has a secure sense of its unity. Therefore it is essential that the members of a contemplative community successfully convey to one another their sincere commitment to their common goal, to their traditional monastic means and to one another. It was for this reason that the meeting gave some particular attention to the ways in which the members of a monastic community could employ their traditional monastic practices as well as new forms to mediate to one another the revelation of God as a faith experience, and thus convey their common commitment, share their experience and so support one another. A number of these ways are enumerated in the conclusions.[7]

In this way the Symposium will hopefully foster more intense contemplative living, greater unity in contemplative communities and consequently that pluralism which will facilitate the individual's resolution of the tensions inherent in communal contemplative life.

I would like to add a word of sincere thanks to all who made the Symposium possible and collaborated so generously in the work. The contribution made by the authors of the papers will be appreciated by all who read this volume. There were others who joined with them in making very significant contributions in the course of the meeting: Fr Ghislain Lafont, the Benedictine theologian from Pierre-qui-vire, Dom Armand Veilleux, the editor of *Liturgie*, Fr John Eudes Bamberger, Secretary General of the Cistercian Order, psychiatrist and patrologist, Sr William Boudreau, who won the acclaim of all for the gracious way she moderated the sessions, and so many others. The wonderful contemplative community of

---

7. "Some of the ways in which this is done are through common prayer, praise and Eucharist, through sharing a common spirituality, through accepting the common leadership of an abbot, through example, through participation in common exercises, mutual service and community support, through the charity of fraternal correction, through a common sharing of the responsibility to work toward unity, and through interpersonal encounter in which the brethren share deeply what God is accomplishing in their lives. Their very oneness in Christ makes them essentially sharers."—See below, p. 345.

Notre Dame du Lac not only provided a most generous and open hospitality but an ideal context within which to celebrate this particular Symposium. To all these and to our God from whom all blessings flow, thank you.

M. Basil Pennington ocso

St Joseph's Abbey, Spencer
Feast of the Maternity of the Blessed Virgin Mary
October 11, 1971

MONASTIC COMMUNITY AND THE SUMMARY STATEMENTS IN ACTS

FRANCIS MARTIN*

YVES CONGAR ONCE REMARKED, "The texts of Acts 4:32 and 2:42–47, dominate and inspire all beginnings or reforms of the religious life."[1] The same can be said in regard to all those religiously inspired communitarian ventures which characterized Eastern Europe in the Sixteenth Century and which have proliferated in the United States right down to our own times.[2] The purpose of this paper is to study the three longer summaries in Acts, but most especially the first two, in an effort to determine what it is that is being described there; the themes that are clustered together in this description; and the theological procedure by which Luke gives a word-dimension to what was lived by the early Christian community in Jerusalem. The more one ponders these

*Fr Francis Martin, a member of the Madonna House Institute, has ust returned to Rome to complete work on his doctorate in Sacred Scripture. He has an SSL from the Pontifical Institute of the Biblicum and an STL from the Pontifical University of Thomas Aquinas (Angelicum). He has published numerous articles on Sacred Scripture and on monasticism and has been lecturing widely. He is Professor of Sacred Scripture at Madonna House.

1. "Quod omnes tangit, ab omnibus tractari et approbari debet," *Revue Historique de droit français et étranger* 36 (1958) 228–229.
2. For a survey of the early period, see: Bestor, A. E., *Backwoods Utopias: The Sectarian and Owenite Phases of Communitarian Socialism in America 1663–1829* (U. of Penn. Press, 1950); Robertson, C. N., *Oneida Community: An Autobiography 1851–1876* (Syracuse U. Press, 1970) esp. c. 3, "What They Thought." For a modern assessment see: Fairfield, D., (ed.), *Communes U.S.A.* (The Modern Utopian: San Francisco, 1971).

brief statements and the incessant and varied use made of them in the whole history of Christianity, the more one becomes fascinated by the evocative power of this image of people living together "of one heart and one soul no one calling anything his own."

We are faced here with a very particular instance of the inter-action between history and myth. The ideal described by Acts was more characteristic of certain currents of Hellenistic thought and practice than it was of the mainstream of Hebrew spirituality, yet the community life of the believers is attributed explicitly to the power of the Spirit of the risen Jesus. The early pre-monastic communities of Syria, Cappadocia and especially Egypt appealed to these texts in Acts for their justification and self-explanation, combining legend and theology in a context of historical narrative. It is hoped that a study of Luke's manner of utilizing, composing and situating the material we now find in these summaries will provide some light on the way the early Christians used them. This in turn may help us in our reflection on these texts and our efforts to bring the healing power of the Gospel to the renewed aspiration which we experience today among Christians and non-Christians alike, for an authentic common life.

This study will include three parts. First, we will analyze the themes that are present in the summary statements, touching only lightly on the question of Luke's sources. Secondly, we will study the common heritage within Jewish Christianity and Hellenistic thought which is reflected there. Thirdly, we will adduce some early texts from the first five centuries of Christianity which use Luke's description as a literary and theological *topos*.

THE THEMES IN THE SUMMARY STATEMENTS

For the sake of convenience we will give here the three summary statements from the first five chapters of Acts and will then proceed to abstract their main themes:

Acts 2:42–47: They devoted themselves to the apostles' instruction (*didache*) and the communal life (*koinonia*), to the breaking of bread and the prayers. A reverent fear overtook them all, for many wonders and signs were performed by the apostles. Those who believed (*pisteusantes*) were together (*epi to auto*) and held all things in common (*koina*); they would sell their property and goods, dividing everything on the basis of each one's need. Every day assiduously they went to the temple with one accord (*omothumadon*), and in their homes they broke bread together sharing their food in great joy and simplicity of heart; they praised God and were looked up to by everyone. Day by day the Lord joined together those who were being saved.

Acts 4:32–35: The assembly of believers (*plethous ton pisteusanton*) was of one heart and mind and none of them ever claimed anything as his own, rather everything was held in common (*koina*). With great power the apostles bore witness to the resurrection of the Lord Jesus, and great respect was paid to them all. None was needy among them, for all who owned property or houses sold them and donated the proceeds, laying them at the feet of the apostles to be distributed to everyone according to his need.

Acts 5:(11) 12–16: Great fear came on the whole church (*ekklesia*) and on all who heard of it. Through the hands of the apostles many signs and wonders occurred among the people (*laō*). With one accord (*omothumadon*) they used to meet in Solomon's Portico. No one else dared join them but the people held them in great esteem. Nevertheless more and more believers (*pisteuontes*), men and women in great numbers, were continually added to the Lord so much so that the people carried the sick into the streets and laid them on cots and mattresses so that when Peter passed by at least his shadow might fall on them. Crowds from the towns around Jerusalem would gather too, bringing their sick and those who were troubled by unclean spirits, all of whom were cured.

The two major themes in these texts are: unity or communion, and the Resurrection-witness, especially of the apostles. The unity of this early community is explicitly linked to faith: in all three descriptions the members of the community are described as believers (*pisteuontes*). Their communion is manifested in the sharing of material goods and their common accord in prayer.

In regard to the Resurrection, Acts 4:33 explicitly refers to the apostolic witness to the Resurrection describing it as transpiring "with great power" (*dunamei megalē*). Acts 2:43 uses the classic formula "wonders and signs" while Acts 5:12 not only speaks of "many signs and wonders" but goes on to give a dramatic description of the healing power of Peter and the others.

It is interesting to note the terminology used by Luke and his sources when describing the group of believers and their unity. There are eight different words to be found in the summaries: "community" (*koinonia* 2:42), "in common" (*koina* 2:44; 4:32), "assembly" (*plethos* 4:32—the occurrences in 5:14, 16 are not technical), "together" (*epi to auto* 2:44, 47), "of one heart and soul" (4:32); "of one accord" (*omothumadon* 2:46, 5:12), "church" (*ekklesia* 5:11), "the people" (*laos* 5:12; 5:13 seems to refer to the inhabitants of Jerusalem).

Not all of the above words are equally operative in Luke's theology, but as we will see, their presence in these summaries is significant for the light it throws on the background of the thinking and self-description of the early community. Luke seems to be referring at one and the same time to the religious context of the Old Testament already given a certain slant by the Essene community at Qumran and elsewhere, and to the Hellenistic ideal of friendship and equality of goods proposed by the neo-pythagoreans and others. Before returning to this let us look briefly at how Luke describes the community of goods and the common prayer practiced at Jerusalem.

In regard to community of goods we find these phrases: "held all things in common"; "none of them ever claimed anything as his own"; "everything was held in common"; "sell their property and goods"; "sold their property and houses and donated the proceeds"; "sharing their food"; "dividing everything on the basis of each one's need"; "to be distributed to everyone according to his need." In regard to prayer we find: "the prayers"; "of one accord in the temple"; "praising God"; "they were all of one accord at the Portico of Solomon."

The activity of the apostles is described as: "teaching"; "performing wonders and signs"; "witnessing to the Resurrection with great power"; again, "performing signs and wonders"; healing and casting out unclean spirits; administering the goods of the community (implied in 2:45 and 4:35).

All of this reality is placed in a context of sacred awe by Luke's use of the word "fear" (*phobos*); "there was fear in every soul"; (2:43—there are a whole series of variants for this verse which speak of "a fear generated through the apostles which was great and upon all"; "great fear came on the whole church and on all who heard of it"). In the Lucan writings this term occurs twelve times and in every instance it is the reaction of people to a manifestation of the divine presence and power. Luke seems then to be using this word here in order to sustain the impression of an experience pervading the whole community as the result of a special action of God. This atmosphere is reflected also in the location of the summary statements. The first is the conclusion of the Pentecost event. The second is found between two series of events: Peter's healing of the lame man, the subsequent persecution of Peter and John, the prayer of the community which resulted in "the whole place shaking and everyone being filled with the Holy Spirit and proclaiming the word of God with boldness," and, the incidents of Barnabas, Ananias, and Sapphira. The third links together these last two incidents and the second persecution by the Jerusalem authorities. The other emotion described by Luke is that of "joy and simplicity of heart" (2:46) and he is also careful to note the respect in which the early community was held by all (2:47; 5:13; cf also 4:33).

It might be possible to sum up our findings so far under the four headings given by Luke in 2:42. There he refers to the "teaching of the apostles" which could be expanded to include their power and miraculous witnessing to the Resurrection. The next term he uses there is "*koinonia*" and we could interpret this to imply primarily to a sharing of goods as well as a sharing of life and common praise of God. The next term "the breaking of bread" has exercised commentators for centuries. It is, admittedly, a common phrase for the Eucharist. It most probably has that meaning here while not excluding the total meal-context in which the Eucharist took place. The last term, "the prayers" refers to the meetings of the early Christians at the temple, but also to meetings for prayer such as

B

described in 4:23–31. The only factor in our analysis which is not explicitly included in Luke's four-fold description is that of reverent awe and the term "believer."[3]

Before passing on to a consideration of the larger context out of which Luke is drawing his information and terminology it might be well to pause briefly to locate some of the above key ideas within the rest of the Lucan writings and the New Testament. The two basic themes, as we have said, are that of "communion" and "Resurrection." The theme of communion is expressed in words linked to the root *koinos*, in a description of the sharing of goods and unity at prayer. The theme of Resurrection is touched upon in the words "witness," "wonders and signs," "great power," "fear," "believers" and in the description of healing.

Dom Jacques Dupont, in a recent article on "The Union Among Christians in Acts"[4] has treated most of the unity themes to which reference has just been made. Basing ourselves on his study, on the wealth of material devoted to the term *koinonia*,[5] as well as on the recent attention given to the notion of the Church as communion,[6] we may note by way of example the following aspects of unity evoked by Luke's description in the summary statements. First, we should observe that within the Lucan corpus, the theme of unity is not restricted to the summary statements in Acts. We find besides the insistence on resolving "disputes" through humility, which is constantly reiterated in the third Gospel (cf Lk 9:46ff, 22:24ff, 12:37, etc.), the theme of repairing the division at Babel worked

3. For a consideration of the summary statements in Acts, see H. Zimmermann, "Die Sammelberichte der Apostelgeschichte," *Bib Zeit* 5 (1961) 71–82.

4. "L'union entre les premiers chrétiens dans les Actes des Apôtres," *Nouv Rev Theol* 91 (1969) 897–915.

5. J. Y. Campbell, "Koinonia and its Cognates in the New Testament" in *Three New Testament Studies* (Leiden:Brill, 1965) 1–28. Also the article on *koinonia* in *Theological Dictionary of the New Testament*, vol. 3 (Eerdmans: Grand Rapids, 1968) 789–809.

6. J. Hamer, *L'Eglise est une Communion* (Paris, 1962); Y. Congar, "Conscience ecclésiologique en Orient et en Occident," *Istina* 6 (1959) 187–236; M. J. Guillou, "Eglise et 'Communion.' Essai d'ecclésiologie comparée," *Istina* 6 (1959) 33–82.

through the Pentecost event. We also find expressions such as: "together they devoted themselves to constant prayer" (Acts 1:14); "and when the day of Pentecost came it found them gathered in one place" (Acts 2:1); "all were filled with the Holy Spirit" (Acts 2:4; cf 4:31); etc. The Pauline preoccupation with unity and his teaching that the oneness of the Church derives from the oneness of God is well known. This is also reflected in Matthew's explicit teaching regarding the unity necessary among the disciples before their prayer can be heard (cf Mt 5:23; 6:14; 18:19–20, 35, etc.).

Luke's use of *omothumadon* reflects the Pauline use of such phrases as "think the same thing" (cf Phil 4:2; 2Cor 13:11; Rom 12:16; 15:5) and is summed up in Phil 2:2 "Fill up my joy by thinking the same thing (*to auto phronēte*), having the same love, being of one soul (*synpsychoi*), thinking as one (*to en phronountes*)." This latter exhortation is followed by Paul's use of a liturgical hymn to put forth the humility of Christ as the model and condition for Christian unity.

Dom Dupont has already noted that Luke's *epi to auto* is used forty-five times in the Bible to translate adverbs made from the root *yahad*. The phrase in Acts 2:47; "day by day the Lord joined together (*prosetithei . . . epi to auto*) those who were being saved," finds its echo in the Qumran phrase "join the community" (*'asp leyahad*; cf 1QS 5:7; 8:19, etc.). We will return to this later when studying the background of the summary statements.

The only instance of *koinonia* and the two occurrences of *koinos* in Acts are found in the summary statements. The use of this root in the context of sharing material goods is found in many places in the New Testament. There are, for instance, the four passages in the Pauline letters where Paul is discussing the collection to be taken up for the "poor" (Gal 2:10, perhaps also Rom 15:26) or "the saints" (Rom 15:25–26; 1Cor 16:1; 2Cor 8:4; 9:1, 12) at Jerusalem. In three instances this *koinonia* or sharing is linked to the word *diakonia* (Rom 15:25–26; 2Cor 8:4; 9:12–13). Another text where *koinonia* bears the meaning "the sharing of goods" and has liturgical overtones is in Heb 13:16: "Do not neglect good deeds and *koinonia*. God is pleased with such sacrifices." In Acts 11:29 we find the collection taken up as a result of the prophecy of Agabus described as a *diakonia*. In Rom 15:27 Paul describes the collection as an exchange of *sarkika* for the *pneumatika* conferred by the mother church. He uses the same image in describing the sharing (*koinein*) by which the Philippians gave him something for what they had received (Phil 4:15; see also Gal 6:6).

All of these references throw light on the Lucan use of *koinonia* and its cognates in the summary statements but they do not exhaust its resonances. There is first of all the ideal of common life alluded to in some of the descriptions of the disciples gathered around Jesus. They held a common purse (Jn 12:6; 13:29); travelled together and were helped by some women of the company (see Lk 8:3); the disciples looked upon themselves as gathered around Jesus, their Rabbi. Besides the Lucan insistence upon leaving all to follow Jesus (Lk 5:11, 28-29; 18:28) there is the characteristic Lucan phrase in 14:33: "None of you can be my disciple if he does not renounce all his possessions" (see also 12:33a). However, as is well known, the deeper aspects of communion of which the sharing of material goods is an external expression are described by Paul in terms of sharing the sufferings of Christ (Phil 3:10); sharing in the body and blood of Christ (1Cor 10:16); the *koinonia* of the Holy Spirit (2Cor 13:13; Phil 2:1). These are echoed in the phrases in the First Letter of John in which *koinonia* describes a communion with Christ (1Jn 1:6), "with the Father and the Son" (1Jn 1:3) and, "with each other" (1Jn 1:3, 7). All of these overtones are exploited when in the early monastic writings reference is made to the "holy and true *koinonia* whose founder, after the apostles, is the Apa Pachomius." It is difficult to imagine that Luke is unaware of these overtones himself when he uses the term *koinonia* to describe the early Christian community.

We should observe in passing that the first use of the term *ekklèsia* in Acts occurs in 5:11 which, whether or not it is considered part of the summary statement, is consciously used in parallel with the other terms denoting the group of believers, *koinonia*, *plethos*, *epi to auto* etc., found in the first two summary statements.

The closest parallel to the Lucan use of the term "signs and wonders" in the summary statements and his description of the healing miracles, is found in the so-called longer ending to the Marcan gospel: "Signs like these will accompany those who have professed their faith" (*pisteusasin*). "They will use my name to expel demons. They will speak new tongues, they will be able to handle serpents, they will be able to drink deadly poison without harm and the sick upon whom they lay their hands will recover" (Mk 16:17). Then, there are undoubted resurrection overtones in the Letter of James which speaks of the presbyters praying over a sick man "anointing him with oil in the Name. This prayer of faith (*pisteōs*) will save (*sōsei*) the sick man and the Lord will raise him up (*egerei*)" (Jas 5:15).

The use of *dynamis* to describe the apostolic preaching is a commonplace in Paul (cf 1 Thes 1:5; 2 Cor 2:4–5; etc.). As is well known, this same term has resurrection overtones throughout the Pauline letters (Rom 1:4; 2 Cor 12:12, 9; etc.). The presence in the summary statements of the terms "signs," "wonders," "power" as well as the word "fear" reflect the whole atmosphere created by Paul's description of himself in 2 Cor. "Indeed I have performed among you with great patience the signs that show the apostle, signs and wonders and deeds of power" (2 Cor 12:12).

To sum up then, the summary statements in Acts present three tableaux in which the early community at Jerusalem is described as experiencing the presence of the risen Christ in a reverential awe begotten of faith and witnessed to by the signs and power and the apostolic witness as well as by their experience of union with one another; a union strengthened and expressed by their common prayer and the pleasing sacrifice of their material sharing.

THE LARGER CONTEXT OF THE LUCAN DESCRIPTION

Historians are quick to point out that the *vita communis* described in Acts could not have been a complete communism: there would have been no need to describe Barnabas' act of generosity in Acts 4:36–37 if such a gesture were necessary for entrance into the community, and at least some of the disciples in Jerusalem must have still owned homes which they placed at the disposal of the community (Acts 12:12). Then too, the common life of Jesus and the early disciples does not seem to have excluded the fact that well on into the apostolic ministry the disciples still had access to boats and that the beloved disciple had some wherewithal to take care of Mary, the Mother of Jesus. (See Jn 19:27).

When we ask the question as to the elements at work in forming the community life at Jerusalem we are confronted with two facts: the undoubted presence of Qumran influences in the terminology and structure of the community, and the careful Lucan use of words which depict the Christian Church as the fulfillment of the Greek ideal of friendship.

The excellent studies by Fitzmeyer and Johnson[7] in regard to the relation between Qumran and Acts leave no doubt that the early Christians were conscious of the spirituality and practices of the Qumran community. Not only does the phrase *epi to auto* reflect the root *yahad*, as we have seen, but the word *koinonia* itself seems related to the Qumran description of itself as a community. Both groups describe themselves as "the Way" (Acts 9:2; 19:9, 23; 22:4; etc., 1QS 9:17–18; 10:21; etc.). The term *plēthos* in Acts 4:32 should be translated as "full assembly" or "congregation" as also in Acts 6:5; 15:30 and possibly 15:12. At Qumran the term *harabbím*, "the Many," has the same connotation (cf 1QS 61:7–9, CD 13:7; etc.). The term refers to a plenary meeting of the group in order to decide important matters (cf Acts 6.2).[8]

The Qumran practice of sharing wealth is well known. It is certain that, for full membership, at least in the group governed by the Manual of Discipline, complete renunciation of property was

7. J. Fitzmeyer, "Jewish Christianity in Acts in Light of the Qumran Scrolls" in Keck, L., Martyn, J. (ed.), *Studies in Luke-Acts* (New York, 1966) pp. 233–257; S. Johnson, "The Dead Sea Manual of Discipline and Jerusalem Church of Acts" in Stendahl, K., (ed.). *The Scrolls and the New Testament* (New York, 1957) pp. 129–142.

8. See H. Huppenbauer, "*rbym, rwh, rb* in der Sektenregel," *Theol Zeit* 13 (1957) 136–137. There also is an excellent discussion in H. Ringgren, *The Faith of Qumran* (Philadelphia, 1963) p 211ff.

strictly required and infractions or fraud were severely punished. Near the very beginning of the Manual of Discipline we read these lines: "All those who freely devote themselves to his truth shall bring all their knowledge, powers, and possessions into the Community of God, that they may purify their knowledge in the truth of God's precepts and order their powers according to his ways of perfection and all their possessions according to his righteous counsel" (1QS 1:11–13). In practice this meant first of all some solemn expression of desire to enter the Community. This was followed by a year of waiting during which the novice took no part in the official functions of the Community and retained the possession of his own goods. During this time his "spirit and deeds were examined" (1QS 6:14–17). "Then, when he has completed one year within the Community, the Congregation shall deliberate his case with regard to his understanding and observance of the Law." If he is accepted, he enters into the life of the Community, though he does not as yet take part in their sacred meals and his goods are in the care of the "supervisor" (*mᵉbagger*) who, however, "shall not spend it for the Congregation" (6, 18–20). After a second full year, "he shall be examined," and if he is accepted, "he shall be inscribed among his brethren in the order of his rank for the Law, and for justice, and for the pure Meal; *his property shall be merged* and he shall offer his counsel and judgment to the Community" (6, 21–23 *italics added*).

It is difficult to determine exactly to what extent the community at Qumran was poor. The fact of shared wealth is not synonymous with communal poverty. Pliny the Elder in his *Historia Naturalis* (5:17) describes the Essenes as "without women, without love, without money," but he is probably going on hearsay. The community often designated itself as "poor" (*'anî*) or "needy" (*'ebyôn*), but this terminology derives as much from the vocabulary of the Old Testament, especially the Psalter, as it does from any self-conscious desire to be poor. There are, however, enough textual and archaeological indications to warrant the conclusion that the community at Qumran was not wealthy and did not seek wealth. The sectarians did not seek "the wealth of violence" (1 QS 10:19) and were convinced that "no riches equal your Truth" (1 QH 15:22).

We have seen how the summary statements in Acts specifically mention that the community of goods saw to it that "none was needy among them" (Acts 4:34). There are provisions among these connected with Qumran for the same type of aid. Philo explicitly mentions the care the Essenes took of the sick and the aged, and Josephus, in his famous description of the Essenes in his *Wars of the Jews* (II, 8) praises their care for one another and their hospitality. In the *Damascus Rule* we read the following provisions:

> This is the rule for the Congregation by which it shall provide for all its needs: They shall place the earnings of at least two days out of every month into the hands of the Supervisor (*mᵉbagger*) and the Judges, and from it they give to the fatherless, and from it they shall succor the poor and the needy, the aged sick and the homeless, the captive taken by a foreign people, the virgin with no near kin, and the maid for whom no man cares, the orphaned children, and every one of the brethren whose house in one way or another is threatened with danger (CD 14:11–17).

These stipulations reflect perhaps the condition of those who did not live at Qumran. They married and retained their property while accepting the spirituality and outlook of the congregation. It is about these that the Damascus Rule speaks in 7:6–8: "And if they live in Camps according to the order of the earth (as it was from ancient times) marrying (according to the custom of the Law) and begetting children, they shall walk according to the Law and according to the statute concerning binding vows. . . ." The word "Camps" seems to refer in the documents to gatherings of the sect, how well organized we do not know, who lived outside the main Community in the desert. Some of the prescriptions of the Damascus Rule, and perhaps even of the Manual of Discipline, and other documents seem to be principally concerned with them: regarding groups of ten (1QS 1:8–10); contributions for the poor (CD 18:13–17); etc. Now, if we add to this the descriptions given by Philo and Josephus of the Essenes living in the towns of Palestine and numbering in all about 4,000 we have a picture of a sect scattered throughout the country who were easily recognized by their strict and characteristic observance of the Law and by their connection with a communal, frugal, and celibate ideal which they practiced in varying degrees.[9]

We have seen above how the Qumran community described itself as "poor," reflecting there an Old Testament ideal more than a financial condition. This same outlook is echoed in regard to the Jerusalem community by Paul who, as we have seen, refers to the Christians in Jerusalem as "the poor" or "the saints." When we combine this with the reverential way in which Paul speaks of the Jerusalem church as the "church of God" for whom he took up a collection, we can see that the originator of that special place in the Christian imagination held by the Jerusalem community because of its fervent life of poverty and unity was Paul himself (cf 1Thess 2:14, 1Cor 15:9, Gal 1:13, 1Cor 10:32, 11:16).

In his treatise on friendship in the Nichomean Ethics (8:8–11), Aristotle quotes the proverbs *Koina ta philōn*, "Between friends all things are in common" and *en koinonia ē philia* "Friendship is in sharing." There were also current expressions such as, *philōn ouden idion*, "Among friends nothing is private." These phrases echoed frequently in the neo-pythagorean theories about communal ownership and friendship. These philosophers often quoted Plato in the *Republic*.[10] In the first century BC Philostratus in his life of Apollonius of Tyana is also engaged in a similar effort to portray an ideal human life. There seem to be echoes of some of these phrases in the well known description of the Essenes given by Josephus and Philo. The presence within Hellenistic culture of these ideas and terminology can hardly be ignored when we read in Acts that the early Christians held "everything in common" ((*a*) *panta koina*), and also that "no one called anything private"

9. For a more supple analysis of the celibate ideal at Qumran see H. Hübner "Zölibat in Qumran?" *New Test Stud* 17 (1971) 153–167.

10. For references see the article by Dupont (n. 4) and the article *Koinonia* (n. 5). There is an interesting article on *koinonia* and friendship by Sister A. Maris, "Koinia: Its Biblical Meaning and Use in Monastic Life," *Am Ben Rev* 18 (1967) 189–212.

(*idion*). We will see Cassian link Greek theories about friendship with the text in Acts 4:32 and in so doing he undoubtedly is faithful to Luke's intention in describing the common life at Jerusalem whose structures and shared wealth may have come more consciously from Qumran but whose life in the Resurrected Lord fulfilled the aspirations of Greek culture.

THE USE OF THE SUMMARY STATEMENTS IN ACTS IN EARLY CHRISTIAN
LITERATURE

In assessing the influence of the summary statements in Acts upon the early communities throughout the Christian world, we must take two factors into account. One is the Hellenistic and Judaeo-Christian influence at work in these communities, and the other is the description in Acts of how these influences coalesced to produce the ideal community at Jerusalem. It is impossible to determine exactly in most instances which came first, but one thing is certain, there sprung up very early within the bosom of the local churches small groups of ascetics who spontaneously bound themselves together without losing their communion with the larger context in which they found themselves and who, independently of one another, began to lead a life which we would term today "pre-monastic." The existence of such groups has been verified in Syria by Voöbus who finds such communities at Odessa and Osrhoene as early as the year one hundred.[11] These communities and their spirituality had an influence upon Eustathius of Sebaste and Basil of Cappadocia, and indirectly influenced some dimensions of the same type of life in Egypt.[12]

In Syria we find a strong ascetic ideal which ultimately resulted in the Messalian heresy, but whose early beginnings should not be viewed as dimly as does Voöbus. There are many indications that

11. A. Voöbus, *History of Asceticism in the Syrian Orient* (Louvain, 1958, 1960).

12. See J. Gribomont, "Le Monachisme au Sein de l'Eglise en Syrie et en Cappadoce," SM 7 (1965) 7-24.

the spirituality of Qumran influenced these early ascetics. They called themselves the "Sons/daughters of the Covenant" (*gyâma*) which Beck[13] describes as a "confraternity" and which he maintains designates an ecclesiastical state: *un ordre d'ascètes célibataires vivant dans les conditions d'un état ecclésiastique.* The term *gyâma* is often translated by the Hebrew *berit*, and there is an undoubted reference to the desert ideal in this phrase. De Vaux and others[14] have already spoken of the desert ideal of the Qumran community who described themselves in such terms as a "community of eternal covenant" (1QS 5:4) and also speak of a "covenant of eternal community" (11QS 3:11) and of those who "enter a new covenant" (CD 6:19). Black undoubtedly goes too far when he reduces the celibate ideals of Syria to the Holy War concepts of Qumran but he is probably correct in linking some aspects of celibacy to the concept of priestly holiness reflected in the Scrolls.[15] It is significant in this regard that the Gospel of Thomas uses the word *monachos* in four logia (4, 16, 49, 75) in one of which the expected *parthenoi* of Mt 25:10 is replaced by *monachi*. This, according to Quispel, reflects the same type of Judaeo-Christian influence that we find in the Syriac use of the word *ibidaja*, also deriving from the root meaning "one" or "alone."[16]

The ever present mystery of the *therapeutae* described by Philo (*Vita cont.* 21–90) in Egypt is another instance of Judaeo-Christian influence but again it is difficult to assess what historical part they played in the development of community life in Egypt despite the

13. E. Beck "Ascétisme et Monachisme chez Saint Ephrem," *L'Orient Syrien* 3 (1958) 280–281.

14. R. de Vaux, *"Les institutions de l'ancien Testament* (Editions du Cerf: Paris, 1958) 30ff.

15. M. Black, "The Tradition of Hasidaean-Essene Asceticism: Its Origins and Influence," *Aspects du Judéo-Christianisme. Colloque de Strasbourg, 1964* (P.U.F.: Paris, 1965) 19–32.

16. G. Quispel, "L'Evangile selon Thomas et les origines de l'ascèse chrétienne," *Aspects du Judéo-Christianisme, op. cit.* 34–52. Some aspects of logia 49 and 75 have been studied by Marguerite Harl, "A propos des logia de Jésus: le sens du mot *monachos*," *Revue des Etudes Grecques* 78 (1960) 464–474.

assertions of Eusebius in his *Ecclesiastical History* (2:5). Milik
describes the way of life of the *therapeutae* as being "analagous to
that of the Essenes" and concludes:

> So from its modest beginnings in the second century BC the
> Essene movement spread widely throughout the Jewish world.
> At least four different branches are known to us, the celibates of
> Qumrân (solitaries and cenobites), the married Essenes living in
> isolated Jewish villages of southern Syria (he may wish to
> modify this in view of the new understanding of "Damascus"),
> the Palestinian "Tertiaries," and the Therapeutae, Egyptian
> Jewish hermits.[17]

Research in the area of actual historical connection between
Essenian piety and Christian asceticism has only begun, while the
relation to other forms of Jewish spirituality, such as that characterized by the Hasidim and others, is still too uncertain to be
relied upon. We must restrict our study here to the communal
dimension of that type of life which appealed to the summary
statements in Acts for its model. Studies by Gribomont, Armand
Veilleux, E. Beck, L. Leloir,[18] and others have established the fact
that there was a pre- or proto-monastic stage to be found in
communities of Christians who formed themselves within the
structure of the local church, who dedicated themselves to a life of
asceticism and service, who in some places were closely associated
with the local clergy, and who governed themselves by a variety
of simple and supple arrangements. Rather than attempt here to
summarize the work of the above-mentioned scholars, I refer the
reader to the excellent summary to be found in the early part of the
article by Veilleux.[19] Certain aspects of that summary should,

---

17. J. Milik, *Ten Years of Discovery in the Wilderness of Judaea,* Stud. Bibl.
Theol. No. 26 (London, 1959) p 92.

18. Article by Gribomont cf n 12. Article by Beck, n 3. See L. Leloir,
"Saint Ephrem, moine et pasteur," *Théologie de la Vie Monastique,* Théologie,
49 (Paris, 1961) 85–97. The two works of Armand Veilleux which are pertinent
here are: *La Liturgie dans le Cénobitisme Pachômien au Quatrième Siècle,* Studia
Anselmiana 57 (Rome, 1968); "The Abbatial Office in Cenobitic Life,"
MS 6 (1968) 3–45.

19. Article in MS.

however, be mentioned here because of their relevance to the theme of this paper.

1) There were two currents within early Christian asceticism: "The one stemmed from Judaeo-Christian encratism and led to the first communities of ascetics, whether of the urban or desert type, the other led from the urban schools of spiritual training to the school of the desert." (p 6)

2) The Judaeo-Christian type of community asceticism made its influence felt, not only in those churches of similar linguistic and cultural orientation, such as in Syria, but also was responsible for the movements associated with Eustathius of Sebaste, Basil in Cappadocia, and Pachomius in Egypt. (p 7)

3) Obedience in this type of community can be described in these words which Dom Gribomont uses in regard to the Basilian communities: "Obedience is defined as perfect conformity to the commandments of God as revealed in Scripture; this is incumbent upon all and does not imply any necessary reference to an abbot. It finds its norm, when one is called for, in the needs and opinions of others, and favors the advice of those who have a particular charism for discerning the will of God." (p 10, translation by Veilleux)

What characterized the premonastic movement of Judaeo-Christian origin was, among other things, that they formed *communities* of people who were drawn together by a common desire to carry out their baptismal promises to the full. In this they differed from those groups who, along the lines of the catechetical schools (especially Alexandria), gathered around a master. This distinction cannot be maintained as ironclad. Many communities undoubtedly began around some charismatic leader, and indeed, for whatever influence it might have had the Qumran community itself was, if not founded, then at least strengthened by the coming of the Teacher of Righteousness. Still, there is a very great difference between a school, even a school of spirituality, and a community. The former embodies an ecclesiastical function and contains an important aspect of the Church; the latter in its being is a realization of Church.

Some Early Texts

If we turn from an attempt to establish historical connections between Jewish and Hellenistic piety, and Christian community life to consider textual allusions to the summary statements in Acts, we find that some areas of the early Church seem to have been much more attuned to the apostolic ideal of communal life than others.

1. The *Didache*

No matter how we assess the Jewish background of the first six chapters of the *Didache*, it is obvious that the doctrine stems from those currents of thought in which interaction between Judaism and Hellenism had already taken place. We read in *Did.* 4:8: "Do not turn away (*apostrepho*) the one who is in need. Rather you should share (*sugkoinōnēseis*) everything with your brother and not call anything your own (*idia*). For if you are sharers (*koinōnoi*) in what is immortal how much more in that which is mortal." There are terminological correspondences in this phrase to Mt 5:42 (*apostrepho*), Heb 13:16 and Acts 4:32. The basic presupposition of this instruction is a life in common. Audet links this atmosphere to the same context as *adelphotēs* of 1Pet 5:9.[20]

Because of its relationship to the *Didache* we will list here the passage from the *Letter of Barnabas:* "You should share (*koinōnēseis*) in everything with your neighbour and not call anything your own (*idia*). For if you are sharers (*koinonoi*) in what is uncorruptible how much more in that which is corruptible."[21]

2. St Ephrem

The *Didache* may reflect, if we accept its Syrian origins, an earlier expression of the same spirituality we find in Ephrem. The most overt communal overtones evident in the spirituality of Syria are to be found in the use of phrases like "sons/daughters of the Covenant."

---

20. J. P. Audet, *La Didachè. Instructions des Apôtres* (Paris, 1958) p 333.

21. For a new assessment of the Letter of Barnabas, see E. Robillard, "L'épitre de Barnabé: trois époques, trois théologies, trois rédacteurs," *Rev Bib* 69 (1971) 184-209.

In hymns whose authenticity may be questioned, but whose antiquity is well established, we find that the apostolic life is conceived mostly in terms of asceticism without the same emphasis on communal life we will find in Egypt. In a hymn in honor of Abraham Kidunaia we find this description:

> With the eyes of your soul you gazed on the Apostles and Prophets, and etched them in your members. Whoever looked on you saw them in you. Their chastity was depicted in you, their uprightness was shown forth in you; you clothed yourself with their ascetic life, clothing your body with their fasts, and from your mouth their prayers burst forth.[22]

An interesting interpretation of the "apostles and prophets" of Eph 2:20 is found in this hymn in honor of Julianus Sabba:

> He carried the Beatitudes in all his faculties, and in his members he bore their power. He gazed on the Prophets and Apostles; his two eyes loved the two beauties, and his two ears listened to the unity of the two Covenants.[23]

3. Egypt

The Egyptian origins of what is now termed "monasticism" are still shrouded in mystery. It is difficult for the modern historian to assess exactly the role of Anthony and Pachomius, those two giants around whom have been clustered the attributes of many of their predecessors. The intuitive genius of Pachomius is only beginning to be appreciated in our own day and he appears to have been not the organizer-soldier of a pre-existing movement so much as the true father of the *koinonia*. It is in the literature emanating from Pachomius and his immediate disciples that we find the most explicit developments of the theology contained in the summary statements of Acts, but before we analyze this literature it is worth noting the interesting allusion to Acts 4:32ff found in St Athanasius' account of Anthony's conversion: "As he was walking along,

22. T. J. Lamy, *Sancti Ephraemi Syri Hymni et Sermones* (Malines, 1899–1902) 3:758.

23. Lamy, 3:870.

he collected his thoughts and reflected how the Apostles left
everything and followed the Savior, also how the people in Acts
sold what they had and laid it at the feet of the Apostles for distribution among the needy, and what great hope is laid up in heaven
for such as these" (*Vita Ant.* c2).[24]

We learn from the life of Pachomius that an angel told him:
"It is the will of God that you serve men in order to call them to
him."[25] In the same life of Pachomius we read that as the first
brethren started to gather around him he gave each one his
appointed task and took care of whatever money they possessed or
earned. They trusted him because they knew him to be "an honest
man and because, after God, he was their father. This arrangement
which he had established with them could be adjusted in keeping
with their weakness as the apostle says: 'I became weak with the
weak in order to gain the weak' (1Cor 9:22). . . . he proceeded in
this way because he saw that they were not ready yet to bind
themselves together in that perfect community as it is described in
the Acts in regard to the believers: 'They were of one heart and
one soul and all goods were in common and no one said of the
things that belonged to him 'this is mine.' " (Another manuscript
of the same life of Pachomius adds at this point the text from Heb
13:16: "Do not neglect good works and *koinonia*. Sacrifices of this
kind are pleasing to God.")[26]

In the boharic life of Pachomius we read of three men who came
to Pachomius and, "having entered the holy *koinonia*, they were
exercised in many ascetic practices. They saw him working alone

24. Tr of the *Vita Antonii* is basically that of R. Meyer, *The Life of St
Antony*, ACW 10 (Westminster, Md.: Newman, 1950). The use of Mt 19:21
in early monastic literature is extensive. See for example, *Liber Orsiesii* 27;
Cassian, *Inst* 7:16, 27; *Conf* 3:4, 7; 8:3; St Basil, *Longer Rules* 8, 9; *Shorter
Rules* 101, 205. St Augustine was meditating on this incident in the life of
Anthony when he had his own dramatic conversion based on Rom 13:13–14
(*Conf* 8:12) and Mt 19:21 figures in the account of St Francis' vocation (See
the *Vita* by St Bonaventure, c 3).

25. For a discussion of this text, cf Veilleux, *La Liturgie (op. cit.)* p 169, n 9.

26. L-.T. Lefort, *Les Vies coptes de Saint Pachôme et de ses premiers successeurs*
(Louvain, 1943) S (1) p 3, 12–32; S(3) p 65, 31–33.

in all the departments of the monastery, cultivating the vegetables, preparing food, answering the door when someone knocked; and if someone were sick, he used to take care of him. For he used to say in his heart, of the three who lived with him, 'They are neophytes and they have not arrived yet at that maturity by which they can serve others.' In fact, he used to exempt them from all duties saying 'That to which you are called, strive to achieve.' " (1Tim 6:12; 1Cor 9:24.)[27]

This notion of mutual service as being the mature fruit of the apostolic life in the *"holy and true koinonia"* is the most characteristic aspect of Pachomian spirituality. Pachomius had been told to serve men and in the service he offered to those who lived near him and were in need or to those who came to him and needed his patience as he waited for them to mature, he honored "the agreement he had made with God."[28]

This lesson was not lost on the disciples of Pachomius. In the famous *Third Catechesis of Theodore* we read: "We are the children of the holy vocation of the *koinonia*"; and in the *Liber Orsiesii* we find: "We should love one another and show that we are truly servants of the Lord Jesus Christ and sons of Pachomius and disciples of the *koinonia*."[29] We find applied to Pachomius phrases such as "Our father by whom the life of cenobites was founded."[30] "Our father who first established coenobia."[31] Finally, we have this text, again in the *Third Catechesis of Theodore:* "We thank God, the Father of Our Lord Jesus Christ, for having made us able to forget our pains and distresses (cf 2Cor 1:2–4) by the sweet fragrance of the submission and solidity in faith of the law of the holy and true *koinonia* whose author, after the apostles, is Apa Pachomius."[32]

27. L.-T. Lefort, *S. Pachomii vita boharica scripta* (CSCO 107, Louvain, 1936) p 15, 9–25.

28. Lefort, *Les vies* S(1) p 4, 6–7.

29. *Lib. Ors.* 23. L.-T. Lefort, *Oeuvres de s. Pachôme et de ses disciples* (CSCO 160, Louvain, 1956) p 125, 9–11.

30. Letter of Theodore: A. Boon, *Pachomiana latina* (Louvain, 1932) p 105.

31. *Lib. Ors.* (Boon, p 116).

32. Lefort, *Oeuvres* p 41, 20–24.

C

Perhaps the one text in Pachomian literature which embodies nearly all of the resonances set up by the word *koinonia* in this early period is found in the *Liber Orsiesii:*

> That this coming together of ours and our communion (lat. *communio*, prob. *koinonia*) by which we are joined together is of God the apostle teaches us when he says: "Do not forget good works and sharing; God is pleased by sacrifices of that kind" (Heb 13:16). And then we read in the Acts of the Apostles: "The multitude of believers was of one heart and soul, and no one called anything his own; rather they held everything in common. The apostles gave witness to the Resurrection of the Lord Jesus with great power" (Acts 4:32–33). The Psalmist agrees to these words when he says: "Behold how good and pleasant it is for brothers to dwell as one" (Ps 132:1). So those of us who live in coenobia and are joined to one another by mutual love, should be zealous for discovering how, in this life, we may have fellowship with the holy Fathers so that in the future life we may share in their lot; knowing that the Cross is the source of our doctrine, and that we must suffer along with Christ (Rom 8:17) and experience the fact that without tribulations and sufferings no one attains the victory.[33]

The theme of the *koinonia* extending to all those who have preceded them is a commonplace in Pachomian literature and explains why all the Old Testament and New Testament images used of the Church are applied with such facility to the *koinonia*.[34] It also helps us to understand how the Old Testament saints were looked upon not only as models but as sharers in this same holy and true *koinonia* and as unique realizations of that same charism of the Holy Spirit which moved in Egypt and throughout the Church. This same type of spirituality is reflected in this passage from Athanasius' letter to Dracontium (4):[35] "It is necessary for us to walk by the standard of the saints and the fathers and imitate them,

33. *Lib. Ors.* 50 (Boon, p. 142, 14–29).

34. See P. Tamburrino, "Les Saints de l'Ancien Testament dans le 1er Catéchèse de saint Pachôme," *Melto* 4 (1968) 33–44.

35. Quoted in S. Benko, *The Meaning of Sanctorum Communio* (London, 1964) p. 81.

knowing that, if we depart from them, we become aliens from their communion (*koinonia*)."

We read in Col 1:24: "Now I rejoice in my sufferings for you. . . ." This dimension of the apostolic life is also a realization of that sharing by which the *koinonia* is established. "Carry the burdens of one another and thus you will fulfill the law of Christ" (Gal 6:2). Alluding once again to Acts 4:32 we find these words in the *Third Catechesis of Theodore*:

> Being all of one heart, suffering one for another, practicing fraternal love, mercy and humility according to the injunction of the Apostle Peter (1Pet 3:8), following one and the same voice and putting into practice its words in all our acts with the conviction of faith knowing that in thus listening we make ourselves servants for Jesus about whom we have heard in the Gospels the voice of the Father declare "This is my beloved Son in whom I take delight. Listen to him."[36]

4. St Basil

Basil's preferences for cenobitic life over the eremitic life are well attested. In the two "Rules of St Basil" the first two summary statements of Acts are cited twelve times.[37] It is interesting to note that few of these make any explicit reference to the theme that the *koinonia* of these urban groups of ascetics was a continuation of the church at Jerusalem. The witness is perhaps all the stronger in that relationship is presupposed between the two communities, and regulations for Christians in Cappadocia can be derived from descriptions of Christians at Jerusalem. Also, Basil's view of these communities is very similar to that institution in the Syrian church which, as we have seen bears the name "sons/daughters of the Covenant."

In Basil's *Eighth Homily on the Famine* he refers to the generosity of the "three thousand" who right after Pentecost shared all their goods. He then goes on to point to the example of the common

36. Lefort, *Oeuvres* pp. 51–52.

37. Relying on the index in *Saint Basile. Les Règles Monastiques*. Intr. et Trad. par L. Lèbe (Maredsous, 1969).

life of some pagans who hold nothing as private and whose nobility makes the avariciousness of many Christians all the more deplorable.[38]

5. St Augustine

Augustine's preoccupation with the common life began in earnest after his appointment as Bishop of Hippo. The most fascinating part of the summary statements in Acts for him was the phrase "one heart and one soul," but he does not ignore the economic aspect of life in common. Father Melchior Verheijen has consecrated an article to the study of Augustine's use of Acts 4:32–35.[39] There are at least fifty occurrences in the writings of St Augustine where this text is theologically operative. It will suffice to quote but a few here:

(i) . . . the souls of many men, after they had received the Holy Spirit and in a certain way had been welded together by the fire of love, made up but one soul . . . so many hearts, so many thousands of hearts, the love of the Holy Spirit made into one heart; so many thousands of souls the Holy Spirit calls one soul because he had made them but one soul.[40]

(ii) He who wishes to make a place for the Lord should rejoice, not in private joy, but in the joy of all (*gaudio communi*).[41]

(iii) If, as they drew near to God, those many souls became, in the power of love, but one soul and these many hearts but one heart, what must the very source of love effect between the Father and the Son? Is not the Trinity for even greater reasons, but one God? . . . If the love of God poured forth in our hearts by the Holy Spirit, who is given to us, is able to make of many souls but one soul and of many hearts but one heart, how much more are the Father and the Son and Holy Spirit but one God, one Light, one Principle?[42]

(iv) First of all, because you are gathered together in one that you

38. Cited by Giet in *Les Idées et l'Action Sociales de Saint Basile* (Paris, 1941) 112–113.

39. *Théol de la Vie Mon* (n 16) 201–112.

40. *Coll. Max. Ar.*, Ep 12, PL 42:715.

41. *In Ps 131*, PL 37:1718.

42. *In Joann.* 39:5, CC 36:347f.

might live harmoniously (*unanimes*) and that there be one soul and one heart toward God, you should not call anything your own.[43] (*Rule*; PL 32:13–77)

(v) And you should not call anything your own but let all things be common to you and distributed to each one of you according to need.[44] (*Rule*; PL 32:13–79)

6. Cassian

In the writings of Cassian we encounter for the first time a conscious and reflexive use of the summary statements in Acts put at the service of theological and ecclesiastical presuppositions. Dom de Vogüé has pointed out the two "versions" of the account of the church at Jerusalem which Cassian presses into service.[45] Cassian is under pressure and is trying to solidify and reform monasticism in Gaul. He appeals to Egyptian monasticism as the authentic and authoritative source of all monastic tradition. His problem then is to justify this authority by linking it to apostolic tradition.

In the *Institutiones* (2:5) we find the tradition of the twelve psalms to be said at the morning and evening Office. Cassian, wishing to establish the authority of this practice, attributes it not only to angelic intervention but also to the earliest centuries of the Church in Alexandria. There is no doubt that Cassian is depending here upon Pachomian sources, notably the "Rule of the Angel," but he is unable to so much as mention Pachomius because of his need to justify the tradition by direct linear descent from the apostles. The story runs this way: The disciples of St Mark at Alexandria were living like true monks, withdrawn from the city and engaged in a life of severe asceticism. Their Synaxis consisted of fifty or sixty psalms. In order to temper their zeal and enable their followers to keep up, an angel appeared and prescribed twelve psalms for the morning and evening prayer. Cassian then goes on to note that not only did the Christians of Alexandria

43. Rule, PL 32:13, 77.

44. *Ibid.* 79.

45. "Monachisme et Eglise dans la Pensée de Cassien" in *Théol. de la Vie Mon.* pp. 213–240.

exceed those of Jerusalem by the fervor and length of their prayers, but they also added to the community of goods described in Acts an asceticism which was heroic. So much for what Dom de Vogüé calls the "Alexandrian version" of Cassian's use of Acts.

In the *Collationes* (18:5–8), in the conference of Abbas Piamun we have what Dom de Vogüé calls the "Jerusalem version." Cassian creates here a sort of "historical romance" by linking Acts 4:32–35 with the account in Acts 15 of the meeting at Jerusalem. After the compromising made necessary by the influx of many gentiles and witnessed to by the text in Acts 15, some of the early Community, anxious to maintain their first fervor, set off for the desert where they practiced community of goods and celibacy. "This was the only kind of monk and the oldest: first not only in time but also in grace, and which preserved itself inviolate to the time of the Abbas Paul and Anthony, and whose traces we can see today in fervent coenobia" (*Coll.* 18:5).

There is also in the *Collationes* (16) a conference by Abba Joseph on friendship. There, as we have noted above, Cassian, consciously or unconsciously, draws upon the Hellenistic ideals of friendship and then describes how this is fulfilled in Christian community:

> How can he who has set out on the way we have described ever break with his friend? For he has radically cut out the first cause of arguments, which usually arise because of small material things of no real value, by calling nothing his own. He is observing with all his might that which we read in the Acts of the Apostles about the unity of the believers: "The multitude of believers was of one heart and soul and no one called anything his own; but everything was held in common" (*Coll.* 16:6).

CONCLUSION

We have seen in the early Christian texts a use of the summary statements in Acts which runs the gamut from literal application within a similar historical context (*Didache*) to historical romance (Cassian). Midway between these we find a typological use of the text as in the Pachomian literature. Though Pachomius is described as being the founder of the *koinonia* "after the apostles" there is no attempt to make an historical link between him and them except in so far as Pachomius was baptized into the same faith and Church as that in which they were.

If we consider Cassian's use of Acts to be little more than an expedient legend, and if we consider the *Didache* and the *Letter of Barnabas* to be inspired by the same historical context as Acts, we see that we are left with the Pachomian (and perhaps Syrian), the Augustinian and the Basilian (also St Jerome—*De Viris Illus.* cc 8 and 11) uses of Acts. How could we characterize this use of the text which shares with Luke an attempt to give verbal consistency to a charismatic moment in the history of the Church by describing it in terms of its ultimate ideal?

Typology

Before returning to consider Luke's typologizing we could perhaps pause briefly and consider the typological function of Scripture itself, especially in its relationship to monastic life. Monasticism is a way of life; or better perhaps, it is a way of living. It is the expression of some deep intuition within the human spirit which seeks to concretize man's nostalgia for God and make of this yearning the mainspring of the way a man lives on this globe. It is often as baffling for the one who seeks to live this way as it is for those who behold him, and yet to both there is an inner truth being said which requires for its saying not only the mouth of a man, but the whole of his being. In its mature state, this way of life, as is the case with any mature thing, harmonizes and resolves the conflicts that are inherent in it. But such maturity is rare, and so there are studies such as this present one in which we attempt with our minds to chart out a course for our lives that will lead to that knowledge of God which gives substance to the things we hope for. We should remember that God's revelation of himself to man, and God's revelation of man to himself, specifies and gives consistency to the vague intuitions and longings that all men carry in the center of their being as a certain fringe of conscious participation in their reality as the image of God.

It was the essential vocation of the Hebrew people, forced on

them by the initiative and the insistence of God, that they should
formulate and suffer the true meaning of man's experience of
incompleteness. "God" is not the culminating experience of an
intricate balance between self-abnegation and self-acceptance,
between understanding of this world and willingness to go beyond
it. God, the living God, is the incomprehensible Master and Lover
who enters into the details of human life with a meticulous jealousy,
only to subvert by revelation what he has expressly commanded;
who barges into life uninvited, forcing his people on by promises
already believed because of his trustworthiness. He saves his people
from the effects of their own evil even while punishing them. He
speaks, thundering and whispering, things which make the heart of
man reel with their secret and yet cry out in a new awareness of
being lonely. He is a God of mystery, beyond holiness yet present,
always the same yet always unexpected. "Yes, you are a hidden
God, the God of Israel, the Savior" (Is 45:15).

Every act of God, by the greatness of the potential it announces,
and by the disillusionment of man's small capacity to realize it, is an
act which points to the future. God stirred up such a vision of what
could be, that he tore off the protective and cautious covering over
man's heart and forced him to look into the abyss of what he truly
longs for. Because God chose to act this way with this people, the
salt of the haunting knowledge of God has stopped the world from
settling into corruption. Man is challenged out of a resentful caution
which seeks to wrest from a god of his own making a security that
even man suspects it cannot give. The price paid for this salt is high.
In the moving words of Gerhard von Rad: " . . . this people had not
been destined to find rest in a single revelation of its God."[46]

Radically, it is this awareness of incompleteness that has made
man, not only dissatisfied with himself, but dissatisfied with the acts
of God which have yet to yield all their promise. Thus, in the Bible,
the beauty and incompleteness of God's acts (including the creation
of man) form the basis of that continual process by which successive
events are called by the name of a previous event. Accompanying

46. *Old Testament Theology*, vol 2 (New York, 1965) p. 362.

this there is a transposition of name and function whose new realization partially fulfills the expectation aroused before while at the same time opening up new vistas of possibility. So we see, nearly four centuries after David, Ezechiel still presenting God as nostalgic for what never was: "Yahweh says this: I am going to call the shepherds to account. I am going to take my flock back from them and I shall not allow them to feed my flock . . . I mean to raise up one shepherd, my servant David, and to put him in charge of them and he will pasture them; he will pasture them and be their shepherd. I, Yahweh, will be their God, and my servant David shall be their ruler. I, Yahweh, have spoken" (Ez 34:10, 23). In the same vein, the sufferings of Jeremiah through which the anguish of God was incarnate for his people, is promised a redemptive meaning in the suffering of the Servant who "justifies many" (Is 53:11). For as we see the Servant, "like a lamb that is led to the slaughter-house, like a sheep that is dumb before its shearers never opening its mouth," we recall the prayer of Jeremiah: "Yet I was like a trusting lamb being led to the slaughter-house not knowing the schemes they were plotting against me" (Is 53:7 and Jer 11:19).

This transposition of themes, events and symbols from one level of history to another, has much in common with that activity by which the human mind strives to make sense of the welter of experience by relating it to some one concrete thing. It is the basis of much poetic imagery, and it is the dynamic underlying what we call the "analogical function." Yet the transposition or *Aufhebung*[47] effected in the Bible has this one unique characteristic: it is always the application to a new or expected concrete act of God of expressions already symbolizing (making present) a previous concrete act of God. This function is called Typology. It is based on the two most constant aspects of God's ways with men, namely the essential future-orientation of God's personal initiative, and his consistency. Because God is always the same, always thinking "thoughts of

47. Though this term has hegelian resonances, it is really quite apt for what I am trying to say here. See B. Lonergan, *The Subject,* The Aquinas Lectures, 1968 (Marquette U. Press, 1968): "a lower being retained, preserved, yet transcended and completed by a higher" (p. 21).

peace" (Jer 29:11), there is a continuity to the way he acts despite the baffling inconsistency he seems to evince. This continuity is discerned amidst the pain of incompleteness and incomprehension and it is asserted on the basis of common "structure-factors" whose biblical name is "the memory of God."[48] There are many studies made of this facet of revelation which concentrate on the successive layers of editing in the Biblical texts,[49] or on the dynamics of this function itself either within the Old Testament or in relating the Old and New Testaments.[50] There are also some studies which highlight the typological function of the Liturgy,[51] and others still which note the way that, within the New Testament itself, words and phrases now uniquely applicable to Christ are used of the vocation of the disciples and of the history of the Church.[52] Then of course there is the abundant wealth of patristic typology.[53]

This rather long discussion has been necessary in order to supply a "metaphysics of monastic typology," or at least the beginnings of

48. See, Childs, B. S., *Memory and Tradition in Israel,* Studies in Biblical Theology, 37 (London, 1962), esp. c 3: "God Remembers."

49. This process is often called "re-reading" (*relecture*). For an interesting example of the analytical use of this concept see: Sorg R., *Ecumenic Psalm 87* (Fifield, Wisc., 1969), and the references he gives there. Perhaps the word of caution expressed in my review of the work (*Cath Bib Quart* 32 [1970] 637) should be repeated here.

50. The most basic and helpful studies are: 1) von Rad, *op. cit.* Part 3, Section "C"; 2) Westermann, C. (ed.), *Essays on Old Testament Hermeneutics* (Richmond, Va., 1964) esp. the articles by von Rad, Eichrodt, and Pannenberg; 3) Anderson, B. W. (ed.), *The Old Testament and Christian Faith* (New York, 1963).

51. Daniélou, J., *From Shadows to Reality* (Westminster, Maryland, 1960); *idem, The Bible and the Liturgy* (Notre Dame, 1956).

52. Fr D. M. Stanley has a beautiful article on, "The Theme of the Servant of Yahweh in Primitive Christian Soteriology and its Transposition by St Paul," *Cath Bib Quart* 16 (1954) 385–425; and, though the word "typology" is not used, there is the study by T. W. Manson showing the application to the Church of the terminology and events proper to the Son of Man: *The Servant Messiah* (Cambridge U. Press, 1961), c 5: "The Messianic Ministry: The Passion of the Son of Man."

53. For a modest beginning in this vast subject, see: 1) Lampe, G., Woollcombe, K., *Essays on Typology,* Studies in Biblical Theology, 22 (London, 1957); 2) de Lubac, H., *Exégèse Médiévale,* 4 vols (Paris, 1959, 1961).

one, so that we can situate and understand what the early fathers are telling us about themselves and about their communities. First of all, their way of life finds a precedent and an echo in the hearts and ways of life of many men of the most varied views about God, existence, and the cosmos. Secondly, as they are conscious of themselves, they are simply responding to the Word of God as they have heard it preached in the Church. Thirdly, the Biblical images they use show that they are aware of having inherited an acute sense of the incompleteness still present in God's plan even as this has been brought to perfection in Christ. They know too, that this vocation which was always within the life of God's people, is now distilled in the life of Jesus and continued in the Church.

With regard to the first of these affirmations concerning the common human substratum of the monastic way of life, we should bear in mind that, as Father Hausherr has put it: "Nothing strictly spiritual is proper to the monk as such."[54] We are discussing *a way of life* whose inspiration lies deep in the human heart, and it is not surprising that the *anima naturaliter christiana* of humankind should express itself this way. The radicalizing and purifying of this drive began with God's call of Abraham (itself a theme dear to monasticism—Cassian, *Conf* 3). This distilling purification continued throughout that process described above, by which God's people were forced to go beyond their hopes by the renewed acts of God. The positing of causal dependence on the basis of material similarity is a hazardous undertaking,[55] and the various causal assignments made by scholars[56] serve rather to prove the universality

54. Cited this way in the *Bull Mon Spir,* 1968, n 126; Cist S 3 (1968) 73.

55. Cf *The History of Religions, Essays in Methodology,* ed. M. Eliade and J. Kitagawa (Chicago, 1961), esp. the articles by J. Daniélou and M. Eliade. I have touched on some aspects of this problem of comparing constellations of life-factors in, "Cistercian Monasticism and Modern Adaptations" Cist S 3 (1968), 287–290.

56. See the early part of the article by C. Piefer, "The Biblical Foundation of Monasticism" Cist S 1 (1966), 7–31; also the critique of A. Voöbus, *History of Asceticism in the Syrian Orient* (Louvain, 1958, 1960) by J. Gribomont, in his article "Le Monachisme au Sein de l'Eglise en Syrie et en Cappadoce," SM 7 (1965), 7–24.

of this human aspiration rather than reduce all expressions of it to one clearly isolated phenomenon.[57]

In the light of this, what can we say that Luke is doing in the way he describes the early community at Jerusalem? How did the early fathers understand him? These questions require a re-understanding of the faith-sophistication of the early Church. Our differentiated consciousness makes it necessary for us to take apart the various dimensions of Luke's reporting. We must separate history and myth and must attempt to understand myth in a new way if we are to join them again for the healing of our minds and an intuitive grasp of what is being said to us regarding early community life. Differentiation is an advance of the human mind but it is only a complete process when what was distinguished is placed back in a simpler more intuitive context. This process it seems to me is the hermeneutical problem confronting our modern "return to the sources." There are two ways of approaching this: 1) we may by scholarly effort recreate the thought-context which gave rise to our documents and then attempt to transpose that into our modern mindset; 2) we may by a living experience of community understand what is being described and thus arrive at an intuitive sympathy with the charismatic moment embodied in the Word of God. Actually, of course, we need both approaches if we are to understand and express ourselves in terms of revelation. Let us restrict ourselves here to a few lines about the use Luke is making of his summary statements in the early chapters of Acts.

The Summary Statements

Luke, in reworking the material he uses in his summaries, is purposely distilling out of the situation a certain ideal which was realized in a more diffused fashion within the historical life of the early community. This distillation or abstraction to a pure state never existed as such, neither in the early Jerusalem community nor in any subsequent attempt. The disciples of "one heart and one

57. The same defect can be seen, for instance, in most early paleontology. Cf. P. Teilhard de Chardin, *The Appearance of Man* (London, 1965).

soul" of Chapter Four are those who in Chapter Six are having a dispute over precisely that sharing of goods for which they are praised.

I have called Luke's procedure an artificial distillation of a reality which never exists in its pure state but only in combination with other factors which, while they may be considered "dross," are the human fabric without which the ideal could never be given historic consistency. The early texts which quote these summaries were instinctively aware of Luke's theological procedure and easily appealed to it for justification and explanation of their own attempts to embody that charismatic moment of the early Church in an alloy composed of their charism and their time.

We often speak of the summaries as an idealization, implying often that Luke is not describing the actual historical situation. Perhaps it would be better to call Luke's description a "type." This term has been applied to the relationship between the Old and New Testament beginning with the New Testament itself, but perhaps there was some wisdom in the way tradition continued to see in the life of the Church recurrent realizations of the types found in the Scriptures. The four senses of Scripture are well enough known, and de Lubac's study has made us conscious of them once again.[58] The little jingle cited by Nicholas of Lyre about 1330 contains a reference to the "anagogic" sense of Scripture: *Littera gesta docet, quid credas allegoria, Moralis quid agas, quo tendas anagogia*. The Eucharist is the ever recurring type of the heavenly banquet letting us know *quo tendimus*. It is a lived "anagogic" sense of the Scriptural words of institution. A true experience of community is also a type of our goal. When Luke says that "no one was in need (*endeēs*)" (Acts 4:34) he is pointing to the early community as being the realization of what was in his day understood to be a promise of the eschatalogical era: the Septuagent version of Deut 15:4 promises "there will not be among you any one in need (*endeēs*) because the Lord your God will surely bless you in the land which the Lord your God is giving

58. H. de Lubac, *Exégèse Médiévale*, vol 1 (Paris, 1959) "Exégèse Monastique," pp. 571–586.

to you." We are living in the period of partially realized eschatology. Whenever the sacred space of true communion is created, we know that that reality described in Acts is being realized once again among us and that this Church-event is itself a type, a further realization of the anagogic sense of the summary statements in Acts. There is the past, present and future of true typology, and the blending of event and myth. In a true gathering in the Name of Christ there is experienced a foretaste of that presence promised us forever. When we seek to find words which mediate our experience of this moment which derives from that act by which the Church was created and which leads to that moment when Church will be completed, we find that the words of the sacred text sum up, preserve, and intensify that experience: "The assembly of the believers was of one heart and soul and no one called anything his own; rather, everything was shared among them."

Francis Martin

Madonna House,
Combermere, Ont.

THE *DE INSTITUTO CHRISTIANO*

REFLECTIONS ON CONTEMPLATIVE COMMUNITY

Sr Michael Connor OCSO*

SINCE THE PUBLICATION of the texts of the *De Instituto Christiano (DIC)* and the *Great Letter* of Macarius by Werner Jaeger a few years ago, considerable study has been made of these documents. Uncertainty still exists as to the authorship of *DIC* and as to the manner in which the two works are related to each other. The technical aspects of *DIC*, however, will not be approached in this paper. Rather, I shall simply try to single out some points which come to light during a reading of this treatise on the monastic life.

The document, which in Virginia Woods Callahan's translation (the text ordinarily referred to in this study) is entitled "On the Christian Mode of Life," is divided into two parts: first, the spiritual life of the individual monk; then, life in community. This order is significant in itself. There is a decided progression or sequence in the text, and we shall try to follow this order.

Whether the treatise was written by Gregory of Nyssa—as Jaeger believed—or not, it was composed at the request of a group of monks who felt they needed help in living their monastic life.[1] In

* Sr Michael Connor obtained a MA in Classics from Johns Hopkins University before entering the Cistercian community at St Romuald, near Quebec, where she is now Mistress of Novices. Sister was Secretary of the first General Chapter of the Cistercian nuns and has been working on their new constitutions, having done extensive study on their history and development.

1. St Gregory of Nyssa, *Ascetical Works,* Fathers of the Church Series, vol. 58, tr. V. W. Callahan (Washington DC: Catholic U.Press, 1967), p. 127. (Hereafter DIC).

simplicity of heart, they consult a senior, a man of wisdom and experience, and ask his advice. These monks, like monks everywhere, had been trying to realize in their daily living the ideal of the apostolic life, but times had undisputedly changed since the time of the primitive Church, and adaptations were needed in the manner of pursuing this ideal. Precisions were also needed regarding how it should be expressed in daily life. The experience of community of the disciples of Jesus after the coming of the Spirit had been one where all were of one heart and one mind. We know that it was not so idyllic, and that even the first Christian communities had problems, but this ideal of community life continued to be uppermost in the hearts of the faithful and became integrated into the monastic way of life.

The fact that this group of monks took their questions to a man of wisdom after having thought through their problems of adaptation indicates that they possessed the docility necessary for growth in discernment. In the true tradition of the desert, they were asking for a "word of life," for something they could live by.

How did the monks see their problems? The very nature of their questions tells us:

1) What is the goal of this life for those entering upon it?

2) What is the good and acceptable and perfect will of God?[2]

3) What kind of road leads to this end?

4) How should those travelling upon it treat one another?

5) How should those in authority direct their brothers?

6) What suffering should one expect to endure if one is to become worthy to receive the Spirit?[3]

By way of introducing his reply, the author of *DIC* wrote: "I am writing to you some small seeds of instruction, selecting them from the writings previously given me by the Spirit, but also making use in many passages of the very words of the Scriptures as proof of

2. Rom 12:2   3. DIC, p. 128.

what I say, and for the clarification of my own views."[4] The treatise, then, follows the tradition common to all early monasticism, that of the Scriptures, but interpreted in a way so as to meet the specific needs of monks. By far the greater part of the text is concerned with the first question about the goal of the monastic life and the means by which the individual monk may attain it. Each member of the monastic community has received a call from God, and has consecrated his life to responding to this call. It is by the monk's response to this call (and every time we use the word "monk" in this paper we of course mean "nun" too), by his personal experience of God, that true community life begins. We find this affirmed also by contemporary personalist philosophers. Louis Lavelle expressed in his writings the belief that the monastic society would betray the interior personal exigencies of the monk, if in the common life where men find mutual assistance and are incited to progress, the sacred intimacy of their conscience was not guaranteed.[5]

Goal

How did the author envisage the goal of the monastic life? We are told that, from within this experience, the monk should be continually "moving toward God" in accordance with the law of reverence, in faith and a blameless life.[6] Further, the path of reverence passes through the narrow gate; its rule is fixed by "the right dogma of the faith."[7] And to arrive at a blameless life, one must pursue a course of virtue by means of ascesis, for "where there is faith, reverence, and a blameless life, there is present the power of Christ."[8] We notice the various terms signifying motion—so characteristic of Gregory of Nyssa—bringing home the point that grace is not given once and for all, but that the monk must cultivate

---

4. W. Jaeger, *Two Rediscovered Works of Ancient Christian Literature: Gregory of Nyssa and Macarius* (Leiden: Brill, 1965), p. 116.

5. M. H. Delepaut ocso, "Louis Lavelle et la vie monastique," C Cist 14 (1952), pp. 241–258.

6. DIC, p. 128.   7. *Ibid.*   8. *Ibid.,* p. 129.

D

his land continually, so that it will never cease to bring forth the hundred-fold. For this, perseverance is needed, for only he who perseveres until the end shall be saved,[9] perseverance even in trials and suffering, as "running with patience to the fight set before oneself."[10] As always there is the inter-action of personal effort and grace from above, permitting the Spirit to enter the soul and purify it so that it may arrive at true purity of heart (*puritas cordis*), so essential in the monastic and contemplative tradition and so in keeping with the Savior's words: "Blessed are the pure of heart, for they shall see God."[11] As a matter of fact, Werner Jaeger has called DIC the work in which the theology of the Eastern Church reached the culminating point of its tendency to bring grace and human effort into perfect balance.[12]

This striving forward coincides with the "perfect will of God" for the monk. That is, God wills that he should become a new creature, one that is no longer conformed to the world, but who is profoundly transformed by the blameless life of reverence and faith which he is leading. "The soul is brought to the full flower of its beauty by the grace of the Spirit which attends upon the sufferings of the person who undergoes the change."[13]

The preparation for reception of the Spirit was not simply a matter of ascesis; it was especially a matter of love. The monk denied himself so that he might follow the Lord more closely in love. And we are told, "it is necessary for anyone desiring to be closely united with another, to take on the ways of that person through imitation. Therefore, it is necessary for the one longing to be the bride of Christ to be like Christ in beauty through virtue as far as possible. For nothing can be united with light unless the light is shining upon it."[14] This light reaches the monk especially in prayer, and so he prays at all time—continually—in the Spirit.[15]

So much for the goal of the monastic life. One might think that this initial blueprint for the spiritual life is overly long in proportion

---

9. Mt 10:22.   10. Heb 21:19.   11 Mt 5:8.
12. Jaeger, *op. cit.,* p. 111.   13. DIC, p. 131.
14. DIC, p. 133-34.   15. Eph 6:18.

to the part of the text given to answering the queries on community life in the strict sense. Actually, this is not so, for without the goal fixed before one's eyes in faith, there is danger of stumbling. The author of *DIC* saw that man needs to possess in hope that which will permit him to run forward in joy and "excellence of heart."[16] Likewise, before there can be fruitful discussion of how the members of a monastic community are to live together, there needs to be understanding as to the common goal and the fundamental means of attaining it. These means are what the members "live by." They give consistency to the relationships which they experience in community.

Balthasar, in his writings on ecclesiology, has brought out the necessity of interpreting community relationships in terms of the individual man, unique before God. In doing so, he uses the image of the Trinity, more frequently spoken of today as being relational:

> The Christological solitude is the active source of all Christian community. The Church community is the true product of the solitude of Christ, his solitude on the cross, his solitude as the incomparable God-man, which is, in turn, the manifestation of his Trinitarian solitude, and ultimately of the primordial solitude of the Father in the generation of the Son.[17]

The Christian, the monk, in profound community with Christ, advances toward the community of the Church. But he does this in solitude.

Community Life

As we have seen, a need was felt among the fourth-century monks for adaptations in their way of living out the mystery of the *koinonia*. The author of *DIC* recognized that "a new code of conduct"[18] was needed, and in outlining it for the monks he drew not only from the Scriptures but from the sources of Hellenic

16. DIC, p. 145.
17. H. U. von Balthasar, *Church and World* (Montreal: Palm, 1967), p. 30.
18. Jaeger, *op. cit.*, p. 111.

culture. Throughout the treatise, as a matter of fact, are found allusions to various Greek concepts which are used more or less as handmaids for the acquisition of Christian goals. In the discussions on community, for example, there are a number of points of reference to the concept of the ancient *polis*. No matter where human beings decide to dwell together, or at what epoch, certain basic problems will always have to be faced. The questions being confronted in the monastic world resembled those mentioned in early Greek poetry, with reference to social issues and crises in the *polis*.[19] These issues and crises had provoked thought and led to the development of social wisdom. The Greek was to be, according to Simonides, "truly noble, in hands and feet and mind."[20] He owed it to himself to do his best and succeed, but it was also an obligation for him to do so. He was expected to keep the city's laws, to do nothing to disgrace it, to maintain a certain sobriety of behavior among his follow-citizens, and be worthy of his ancestry and his upbringing.[21] The individual man was essentially a member of society, but the good life of the state existed only in the good lives of the citizens.

The treatise speaks of analogous qualities which are necessary for community members: obedience with joy,[22] providing for the common needs of the brothers,[23] humility and simplicity,[24] doing nothing by reason of vanity.[25] They can also be easily translated into Benedictine terms:

—respect for the seniors, insisted upon by St Benedict, is a way of saying respect for the heritage they are passing on, respect for one's "ancestry" in the monastic tradition.

—sobriety—not coldness or aloofness—implying an atmosphere of respect and self-mastery, so that all the members may grow

19. *Ibid.*

20. C. Bowra, *Classical Greece,* Great Ages of Man Series (New York: Time, 1965), p. 50.

21. *Ibid.*   22. DIC, p. 147.

23. *Ibid.,* p. 145.

24. *Ibid.,* p. 147.   25. *Ibid.*

peacefully, according to the working of the Spirit within each one.

—The Greek "keeping the city's laws" may be correlated to respect for a certain community protocol, which is a necessity for the maintenance of a climate of human dignity. As Helene Lubienska de Lenval stated in one of her articles (in speaking of gestures in liturgy, and rite in general), every family worthy of the name has certain distinctive "rites" and ways of doing things which distinguish it from other families and bestow identity. This identity is an absolute necessity for community living, and is often transmitted by very humble and common-place media.

Charity

DIC, of course, does not stop at Greek concepts, but goes directly to the corner-stone of Christian community: Divine Charity. The Hymn to Charity (1 Cor) is quoted at length, for Charity is revealer of the Spirit,[26] and in a true Christian community concord such as Paul had recommended to the Collossians must reign: "Above all, put on love which binds everything together in perfect harmony."[27]

Therefore, just as in the case of the individual monk grace and human resources must work together if the mature measure of the fullness of Christ[28] is to be attained, so the Christian community of monks was to be a communion in the Spirit, as well as a group of men attentive to human wisdom.

This said, an answer could be sought for the questions posed by the monks as to "how they should live with each other, what kind of labors they should love, and how they should run the course together until they come to the city above."[29]

What they must expect to endure

Like all great spiritual masters, the author of DIC set a difficult, and exacting, program before his disciples. A monk must deny

26. *Ibid.,* p. 140.　　　　　27. Col 3:14.
28. Eph 4:13–15.　　　　　29. DIC, p. 145.

himself, he must "disdain the things that are revered in this life[30] and adjust himself spiritually to his brothers in God."[31] Heed the Word of God, it will guide the brotherhood harmoniously to the shore of the will of God.[32] In order to arrive at this state of openness to the Word, it is necessary also to practice effective poverty, for it is thus that the monk will seek the common good and not his own if in fact he possesses nothing.[33] This poverty constitutes true surrender to Christ.

Service

But most of all—and here we rejoin an aspect of religious life stressed so strongly today—the monastic life must be a life of service, in imitation of the Lord who said: "Whoever wishes to be first and great among you shall be last of all, and the slave of all."[34] Since Vatican II there has been a growing consciousness that office implies, primarily, a function of service, and that man brings himself to fulfillment as a person through service to his fellow-man. *Gaudium et Spes* stated: " . . . through his dealings with others, through reciprocal duties . . . (man) develops all his gifts and is able to rise to his destiny."[35] Man can find himself only in disinterested gift of self, but great self-denial is necessary so that he may have something to give. Thus it is that this subject is approached only late in the text, after faith and ascesis and reverence have been insisted upon at length. The monk's capacity for presence to his brother in service will be in proportion to his union with the Spirit. It is at one and the same time a way and a victory that is won by the accomplishment of hidden tasks as well as apparent ones, by "duties toward oneself"[36] as well as duties toward one's neighbor; a way, because it must be reinforced continually by charitable acts, and a victory because it is the manifestation of God's love in the world.

30. RB 4:20: ". . . to avoid worldly conduct. . . ."
31. DIC, p. 145.　　　　　　　　32. *Ibid.*
33. *Ibid.*　　　　　　　　　　34. *Ibid.*, Mk 10:43.
35. No. 25:1.
36. H. de Lubac SJ, *Catholicism* (London: Burns & Oates, 1950), p. 190.

In *DIC* it is noted that this service should be gratuitous and universal. Here, just as in RB, we find that the monk should be at the service of everyone, and this leads to two subjects of importance: the role of the superior, and the relationship of the brothers to each other, or to express it differently, the relationship of the individual members of the community to the group as a whole.

How should those in authority direct their brothers?

The very name fraternity (*fraternitas*) which had become current usage for describing the monastic community indicates the ideal of mutual service, but the author of *DIC* required more of the one to whom the spiritual welfare of the community had been entrusted than he did of the other monks. Greater authority means greater responsibility, and the monks were told that "those in charge in matters of supervision (must) work harder than the rest, think humbler thoughts than those under them, and furnish their own life as an example of service to the brothers, looking upon those entrusted to them as a deposit of God."[37] This is a close parallel of what we find in *Perfectae Caritatis*, where it is stated that superiors, through their service, should express the Lord's love for their communities.[38] Nor, according to our treatise, are superiors to "destroy thought with authority," but they should rather "exercise worthily the arts of supervision."[39] This implies that they will deal with each monk in the way that his particular nature requires "if he is to be successful in this life,"[40] They should praise, encourage, rebuke, or even punish, and should teach each one to act and serve in accordance with his place and office in the community.

The superior as described in *DIC* was truly a superior, meriting the joyful obedience of his monks, and having an obligation to instruct them so that "having educated well the souls of his disciples who look to him for guidance, he might bring their shining virtue to the Father,"[41] and present each monk to him as an heir worthy of his gift. Once again, we find a striking similarity to *Perfectae*

37. DIC, p. 146.   38. No. 14.
39. DIC, p. 146.   40. *Ibid.*   41. DIC, p. 147.

Caritatis: "Governing his subjects as God's own sons, and with regard for their human personality, a superior will make it easier for them to obey gladly . . . (He) should listen willingly to his subjects . . . Not to be weakened, however, is the superior's authority to decide what must be done and to require the doing of it."[42]

The Body and its Members

When we speak of community, it is good to remember that there are different types of community, and therefore different modalities of "being in community." But in no case is it a question of persons living together first of all as individuals, and then having the dimension of "being in relation" added. Rather, the relationships are woven into the mental and affective fiber of the persons. Being in community does imply, however, a becoming aware of this togetherness, on the part of each member. Fr Chenu calls this a "shock which interiorizes the meeting, takes hold of each of the participants body and soul, and leads them to a fusion of sensitivity and behavior."[43] This fusion, which permits mutual love and assistance to come to full flower in community life, is best expressed by the theme of the Body of Christ and its members, and it is this theme which is used in *DIC*.

From earliest times the Body of Christ, in its Eucharistic meaning, and *koinonia* were intimately bound together.[44] The unity of the Christians was explicitly associated with the celebration of the Eucharist,[45] and Paul made this unity among the brothers one of the requirements for the celebration of the Sacred Mysteries.[46] This was fundamental, and the starting-point for other interpretations of the expression "Body of Christ."

42. No. 14.

43. M. D. Chenu OP, *Le Peuple de Dieu dans le monde* (Paris: Cerf, 1966), p. 137.

44. Acts 2:42. *The Didache* 9:4, tr. J. A. Kleist SJ, Ancient Christian Writers, no. 6 (Westminster, Md.: Newman Press, 1948), p. 20.

45. I Cor 10:14–22.

46. I Cor 11:17–34.

The teaching found in *DIC* is based directly on the twelfth chapter of 1 Cor, and there the Apostle had joined to the basic meaning of Body of Christ a Greek concept of body as principle of unity and solidarity for members of a social group.[47] As Jaeger pointed out:

> It is highly significant that (this theme) recurs here (in DIC), when another social organism comparable to the ancient *polis* had arisen in the early Christian monasteries. The basis on which this new ideal community was established was different from that of the old city-structure, of course, but even so, the essential problem of its social structure and of the mutual cooperation of its members was the same. . . . The great issue at stake is that of the individual and the whole.[48]

Saint Paul had recognized that since each man is a member, none is sufficient to himself, but nevertheless each has a particular usefulness. The members, who derive their growth from Christ, should be knit together in love and encourage one another, for the members cannot live by their own life alone. They draw their life from the whole Body. Each member needs to be united not only with the Head, but with every other member if he is not to die. And when this inter-communication has become a reality, then there is true interpenetration of the Holy Spirit who enlivens the members and binds them together with the very life of God.[49]

The fact that there is diversity among the members of an organism is what produces its beauty. This diversity is also an essential condition of life, and it arises in the case of Christians, from the diversity of the gifts of the Holy Spirit granted to the members.[50]

In *DIC* this same path is followed. First of all, perfect balance between the whole and the members is insisted upon. The very foundation of life in community is mutual love and assistance, and

47. A. Feuillet and A. Robert, *Introduction à la Bible* (Paris: Desclée, 1959), vol. 2, 434.

48. Jaeger, *op. cit.,* p. 196.

49. F. Prat sj, *Theology of St Paul* (Milwaukee: Bruce, 1952), 2:286.

50. *Ibid.*

for the growth of these simplicity and humility are required, as well as the other virtues and qualities which have been pointed out during the course of this study. The author of *DIC* was a man of deep experience, and he knew that "simplicity gives way to obedience, obedience to faith, faith to hope, hope to justice, justice to service, and service to humility."[51] It is when the monastic community arrives at this point that it will be strong, for from these things come grace, and love, and prayer.[52]

CONCLUSIONS

A reading of *DIC* shows that the counsels given by the senior were founded upon two firm foundations: understanding concerning the action of the Spirit, and appreciation of human wisdom. Never once has it been forgotten that true Wisdom comes from God, who has given to each member of the monastic community his own particular way of reflecting the beauty of the Spirit.

The abundance of the gifts of the Spirit finds entry into the life of man by a long process of maturation, both humanly speaking, and in the life of grace. The more unified he is in his search for God, the more active the gifts of the Spirit will normally be in his life.

This search for God is the work of the whole man, and thus there was no reluctance to recommend the wisdom of secular culture to the monks when monastic life presented situations analogous to those found in society in general. Yet the wisdom of secular culture takes one just so far; one cannot arrive at the goal with simply natural means. Today there is perhaps a tendency to go to the other extreme, and in this new springtime in the Church, to have an over-simplified idea of the action of the Holy Spirit. Thus the necessity for discernment in the matter of charisms.[53]

Today we should hold fast to the truth that the monastic community, as an organic whole, is the "Body of Christ." The Head is

51. DIC, p. 151
52. *Ibid.*, p. 152.
53. *Ibid.*, p. 148: "... it is not for us to assess what is ours, through our own judgment."

Christ. The members are related to one another by virtue of their relationship with the Head from which they receive life. Therefore, the vertical dimension must always take precedence, the relationship of the individual man with God. Only then can his relationships with others have meaning, for only then will he be alive.

We might conclude this paper with a quote from Fr Henri de Lubac. What he says comes very close to the thought found in *DIC:*

> Catholic spirituality has not to choose between an "interior" and a "social" tendency, but all its authentic forms in their extraordinary variety will share in both. . . . Is not all spiritual life made up of contrasts, alternating rhythms, or rather experienced coincidences? Nothing would be more fatal than to believe that a true Catholicity is easily realized. No one can attain it save by the narrow way. Its first requisite is to be found in detachment and solitude, and the most charitable of men, the saint, is primarily, according to the ancient etymology, a being apart.[54]

The monk, the nun, sharing the solitude of Christ and of the Trinity, becomes able to enter in communion with others. In proportion to the authenticity of the response of each individual member to the Lord's call, the monastic community will come to the unity which Charity alone effects.

Sr Michael Connor ocso

St-Romuald
Quebec

54. De Lubac, *op. cit.,* p. 189.

SAINT BERNARD OF CLAIRVAUX AND THE CONTEMPLATIVE COMMUNITY

JEAN LECLERCQ OSB*

TODAY WE ARE ASKING ourselves many questions about the contemplative type of monastic life—questions to which, we like to believe, past experience may bring us the answers. And this hope is legitimate. Nevertheless, only to a certain extent, because men of preceeding generations were very different from us, and also the circumstances in which they lived. The interpersonal relations which existed among them presumed a very different sort of psychological character—on the whole, less delicate—than the ones which are found in a period where refinement, and even the refinement of feelings, is constantly developing. Besides, theology today accentuates the social aspect of the Christian and religious realities in a more intense and also more explicit manner than was done at a time when there was no need to react against an anterior period during which piety was marked by a rather excessive individualism, as was the case during the nineteenth and first third of the twentieth centuries.

However, the essence of the realities in question is identical in this second half of the twentieth century with what it was in the first half of the twelfth. And this can be verified not only by considering the Cistercians, but also the monks of other orders. A monk of

*Dom Jean Leclercq is a prodigious worker with over 600 titles in his bibliography. He has lectured in over 60 nations through all the continents and at the same time he has carried the work on the critical edition of the works of St Bernard toward completion. He presently holds a chair at the Pontifical University of the Gregoriana, Rome.

Clairvaux, Gerard of Péronne, could, at that time, write to an abbot of black monks—those we call Benedictines today—Peter of Cells: "Although the division of our orders separates us, charity unites us, for it is not the color of our habits, but the love of our hearts which is the foundation of our unity, much more: our unanimity."[1] To study what was a contemplative community in the Clairvaux of St Bernard will help us to discover what it was in other Cistercian monasteries and elsewhere.

The theme is vast, only a few avenues of research will be found here. Among the writings of St Bernard and others on the subject the texts are innumerable which treat, more or less explicitly, on the one hand, of contemplation, and on the other, of living in community. Neither of these will be examined here in itself; it will be question only of the relationship which exists between contemplation and community living.

This is a very real question. Do we have the right to associate these two words? Is not contemplative life, at least according to some, reserved for hermits, the cenobites only being allowed to carry on together a sort of ascetic research? Whatever may be the answer to this question for such or such anterior epoch, has Bernard left us a teaching on this point? Did he envisage the monk as a man who, standing alone, tried to live with God, even when he joined other recluses like himself, or, on the contrary, as a being-with-relations, able to sanctify himself only with and through others?

The research, here, will be limited to Clairvaux and to the time when St Bernard was abbot. Nothing will be said of what concerns other places and times. But the case of Clairvaux will illustrate, by a well-known example, what could be verified about other monasteries if we had as many documentary sources as we do have for Clairvaux. Nothing will be said of Bernard's political, ecclesiastical or even his doctrinal role. In fact, his interventions in these areas were personal and, consequently, the exception and not the rule of his milieu. Let us try to grasp the concrete conditions, the real and daily circumstances in the midst of which he elaborated his

1. Ep 49, PL 202:74.

monastic teaching. This will be revealed not only by his writings, but by facts which have been related by others. Such an inquiry presents difficulties, for the monks of the twelfth century hardly ever spoke of themselves; it is worth the effort to make an attempt though, even if we must admit, before beginning, that the results, will be limited.

CONTEMPLATIVE COMMUNITY AND THE CHURCH

In communion with the universal Church

1. *Solidarity*

We possess two sorts of data on the position of the contemplative community in the life of the universal Church: ideas or principles and actual facts. These enlighten each other reciprocally.

On the level of principles, Bernard stated very clearly the essentials concerning the existence and role of the contemplative community. It is rare that he speaks at length on this subject, which fact is revealing when we know to what degree he was "a man of the Church"[1]—not only did he deploy an intense activity in the service of the Church, but he set forth a vast and coherent doctrine on its essence and its members and ministers.[2] If he did not feel the need to specify often and at length how monasticism was situated in the Church's make-up, it is because at this period the traditional ideas were taken for granted.[3] At least the allusions he makes to this problem can be understood from this perspective. For him, as for the monks of his time and throughout the Middle

1. Such was the title of a collective work published in 1953: *S. Bernard, homme d'Eglise* (Bruges-Paris: Desclée de Brouwer).

2. This doctrine was studied at length by Y. Congar, "L'ecclésiologie de St Bernard," *St Bernard théologien* (Rome: *ASOC* 9, 1953), pp. 136–190, and I consecrated an article to it entitled "St Bernard on the Church, *Downside Review 85* (1967), pp. 274–294.

3. On the role of intercession which was traditionally recognized as belonging to monks, I cited texts in *Vie religieuse et vie contemplative* (Paris: Gembloux, 1969), pp. 114–135 and *Le défi de la vie contemplative* (Paris: Gembloux, 1970), pp. 57–59.

Ages, what constitutes the contemplative community as such is
that there God is sought by prayer and asceticism: it is "the order
of those who occupy themselves with God alone, living in penance
and continence."[4] And it is thus that it is differentiated from other
groups of men or *ordines*, in the one unique Church.[5]

Now if they unite themselves to God in the Church, it is not
exclusively for their own good, but also for the good of all the
members of this Church; they are one with all, called on to watch
over all, consequently responsible for all. More than once Bernard
reminded his monks of this, with a certain humor, during his
homey talks in which he used parables and comparisons (whose
signification he explained clearly). For example, when enumerating
the various properties of the teeth, one of which is "to masticate
for the benefit of the whole body," he makes an application to
monks: "They masticate for the benefit of the whole body since
they have been established in order to pray for the entire body of
the Church, that is, all its members, living and dead."[6] On another
occasion, developing with humor and imagination the symbolism
of the organs of the human body in order to show the bond, the
concatenatio, which unites all the members of the Church, he comes
to the stomach. It is a part not highly honored, and yet, it is this
organ that collects the food that nourishes the body, assimilates the
nourishment, sends out the juices necessary for life to the other parts,

4. *Soli Deo vacans, paenitentium et continentium ordo, Div* 35:1 =Abb 1,
S. Bernardi opera (Rome: Editiones Cistercienses, 1957) [Hereafter OB]
5:289, CF 34. On the expressions *soli Deo* and *vacare Deo* as definitions of the
contemplative life, I collected texts in "Etudes sur le vocabulaire monastique
du moyen âge" in *Studia Anselmiana* 48 (1961), pp. 29–31 and "Otia monastica: Etudes sur le vocabulaire de la contemplation au moyen âge," *Studia
Anselmiana* 51 (1963) in the index, p. 183, at the words *vacare* and *vacatio.*

5. *Div* 35 =Abb, OB 5:288ff, CF 34 and Y. Congar, "Les laics et
l'ecclésiologie des ordines chez les théologiens des XIe et XIIe siècles," *I laici
nella società "christiana" dei secoli XI e XII* (Milan: Vita e Pensiero, 1968),
pp. 83–117.

6. Div 93:2, OB 6:349, CF 49. In "Etudes sur S. Bernard et le texte de ses
écrits," *ASOC* 9 (1953), p. 65, I edited this text and indicated the different
editions which exist; cf. also H. Rochais, "Enqutê sur les sermons divers et
les sentences de S. Bernard," *ASOC* 18 (1962), pp. 130–132.

superior and inferior. Such are monks and hermits: "They are the ones who sustain the Church; they were prefigured by Moses praying on the mountain, by Samuel spending the night in the Temple and by Elijah sojourning in the desert. They send forth spiritual juices to all, to prelates and to their subjects. We can apply this saying to them: 'The human race subsists on account of a few; if they did not exist, the world would perish by lightning or by an earthquake'."[7]

Speaking of Palm Sunday, Bernard gives an allegorical signification to all who take part in the entry of Jesus into Jerusalem and to all who, since that time, continue to realize this mystery: those who acclaim the Lord, those who spread their clothing on the ground, those who cut branches from the trees. And to give the monks "not pride but consolation," *ut elationem caveatis . . . ut habeatis consolationem,* he tells them that they are the Lord's little ass. To all appearances their role is hardly glorious, no one pays much attention to them; but they are the ones who carry the Savior by their hidden, austere life.[8] Employing the traditional definition of the contemplative life: *soli Deo vivere,* he adds: "They are the ones who have chosen an excellent part: living for God alone, in the cloister; they are always united to him and they only think of what will please him. . . . Those who are thus united to him are the contemplatives."[9]

2. *Intercession*

The same Biblical expression used to designate union with God: *adhaerere Deo,* "to adhere to God," is applied by Bernard to the man who, united to all by the bond of charity, "carries all the

7. Text edited by H. Rochais–I. Binont, "La collection de textes divers du ms. Lincoln 201 et S. Bernard," *Sacris erudiri* 15 (1964), pp. 86–88 and which I analyzed in *Recueil d'études sur S. Bernard* (Rome: 1962), 3:169–171. The end recalls this text of Pseudo-Rufinus *Vitae patrum,* 3, Prol., PL 73:739: *Vere mundum quis dubitet meritis stare sanctorum, horum scilicet quorum in hoc volumine vita praefulget, qui omnem luxuriae notam tota mente fugerunt, mundoque relicto, eremi vasta secreta rimantur. . . .*

8. Palm 1:3, OB 5:44, CF 22.

9. Palm 2:5–7, OB 5:49f, CF 22.

E

others and is a burden to no one, *portat omnes et neminem onerat.*
This is the one who truly loves his brothers and the people of
Israel, the one who prays much for the people and the holy city of
Jerusalem."[10] What Bernard says of pastors, responsible for watching
over the entire flock, is verified also by these specialists of vigils,
these kind of professional watchmen that are contemplatives. This
passage, full of expressions drawn from the Bible and the Rule of
St Benedict, merits to be cited here. It is a commentary on the
words of the fiancee in the Canticle: "They found me, the watchmen who guard the city":[11]

> Who, then, are these watchmen? Those whom the Savior, in the
> Gospel, declared blessed if, when he comes, he finds watching.
> What good watchmen, those who, while we are sleeping, watch
> because they will render an account for our souls.[12]
> What good guardians, those who, watching with zeal, and
> spending the night in prayer, discover the ambushes of enemies,
> anticipate the wiles of the wicked, seize the snares, remove the
> traps, destroy the stratagems, reduce to dust the weapons.
> They are the ones who love their brothers and the Christian
> people, who pray much for others and all the holy city. They
> are the ones who, full of solicitude for the sheep of the Lord
> confided to them, give their heart to prayer, to watch until
> dawn before the Lord who created them and pray in the presence
> of the Most High. And they watch and pray, because they know
> that it is not enough to guard the city, and that if the Lord does
> not guard the city, it is in vain that he who watches guard it.[13]

The duty of intercession does not complete the monk's responsibility: he is also obliged to a living charity toward his brothers
and that in virtue of the engagement he made on entering the
Church:

10. *Div* 4:3, OB 6:96, CF 46. To speak of what is here translated by
"bond" of charity, Bernard, in this text and others which will be cited further
on, uses the words *gluten* or, as in Is 41:7 according to the Vulgate, *glutinum*,
which means glue or paste and which had often been used by the Fathers of
the Church to symbolize the union between Christians.

11. Song 3:3.

12. RB 2, 34, 37, 38; 3, 11, etc. . . .

13. SC 76:7, OB 2:258 where the biblical allusions are indicated.

All of us, in fact, are bound by oath, to our brothers, to all with whom we entered the unity of the Church. That is what is meant by professing the Christian faith: to live no longer for self, but for him who died for all. . . . The good you do to your brother is not optional; you are not free to do it or not to do it. You owe it to him in virtue of the promise that binds you; you are obliged to it by the profession you yourself pronounced. That is why it is said: "There is the race that seeks the Lord,"[14] the race and not a single individual. The Head and the body make one: Christ. And it means the entire race, because we run together toward the perfect realization of the fullness of Christ.[15]

In these texts, Bernard simply applies to monks what St Paul had said to all Christians: they are not only united, they are one. And if they are especially given over to prayer and asceticism, it can only be in union with all, for the good of all.[16]

In communication with the surrounding society

1. *The environment*

Because the mystery of universal salvation is realized in persons, communion is made concrete by communications, interpersonal relations, and that, not only in the interior of the community, among its members, but on the exterior, between them and the members of the Body of Christ who live around them. Whence the problem which must now be considered: how to reconcile solitude with God and separation from the world with these relationships that everyone maintains, more or less, with society? In theory, in the intentions of the Founders of the Order of Cîteaux and according to the principles of St Bernard and other masters of the spiritual life, these relations with the exterior were reduced to a

14. Ps 23:3.

15. *Div* 33:5–6, OB 6:225f, CF 46.

16. In the *Sentences*, 3: 101, OB 6 this text can also be read, which will be made clearer by what will be said later on donations. It is a question of these *pauperes Christi* which the monks are: *Hi tanguntur ab his quibus eleemosynis sustentuntur vel honorentur, et a quibus intercessores petuntur.*

minimum, and if we judge from the texts where this doctrine is exposed, we might get the impression that these relations were even non-existent; little or nothing is said about them.[1] But, on the other hand, if we examine the facts, if we consider the documents which reveal actual practice, particularly charters and chronicles, we remark that these relations were frequent. In fact, for a group of men to be actually inserted into an economic, social, political and religious context, contacts and conversations with men from different walks of life—ecclesiastics and especially, perhaps, laymen—were necessary. There is much that could be said on this subject. In a general way, we can indicate some "constants" in this area which are present throughout monastic history.[2] Let us try to suggest, without going into details, how they were verified in the case of Clairvaux during St Bernard's time. Again, we must limit our research to what concerns, not Bernard's activity in the religious politics of his time—for this was extraordinary, the correspondence and travel it entailed are the exception—but what concerns his community. Certainly, Clairvaux was, because of the personality and influence of its abbot, engaged in more contacts than others; but they were exactly of the same type as those found in other monasteries and they are, from this point of view, very revealing. They will enlighten us also about the real milieu for which and in which Bernard elaborated and exposed his monastic doctrine.[3]

Before characterizing these relations, it would be well to describe briefly the men with whom they were carried on. Clairvaux was located in the region between Champagne and Bourgogne. The society here, as everywhere else in this first half of the twelfth

1. Under the title "The Intentions of the Founders of the Cistercian Order," *The Cistercian Spirit,* Cistercian Studies Series, no. 3 (Spencer, Mass.: Cistercian Publications, 1970), pp. 96ff I recalled the texts stating the principles.

2. In *Contemplative Life,* CS19 (Spencer, Mass.: Cistercian Publications, 1972): "Separation from the World and Relations with the World," I collected the facts and ideas.

3. On economic life at Clairvaux at the time of St Bernard, we have an excellent study, which will be often cited here, of R. Fossier, in *Bernard de Clairvaux* (Paris, 1953), pp. 67–114.

century, was a violent society. In difficult economic conditions which left a feeling of continual dependence on the forces of nature, temperaments already rude became even more exasperated. Rivalries, quarrels, looting, threats, invasions, revenges, cheating and stealing of every kind gave occasion to local conflicts, often bloody, which involved much plundering and kept men—especially the poor and weak—in an almost constant state of fear. Thus they were all the more ready to seek refuge in the protection from on high. The result was a mixture of violence, often hatred and piety whose quality can be understood in the psychology of peoples or social groups who have maintained a primitive form of religion. The monks, who came from that society, bore its faults and its good qualities. But, by means of ascetiusm, they attained a certain domination over their instinctive impulses. Their example and influence contributed to the pacification of a society so spontaneously violent.[4]

This situation was aggravated further by the fact that Clairvaux was situated in the infertile region of the plateau of Langres with its rude climate and poor soil. The monks had to deal with a population which was marked with both rudeness and generosity. The little world of their nearest neighbors lived in small feudal groups each of which had to defend its own interests against the encroachments of the others and the tyranny of the powerful. One could not avoid taking sides in local politics, which in turn were bound up, through the intermediary of the great, to the national and international scene. Disputes over property limits and the relations with the rival lords or landowners of the neighboring district—whether they be laymen or ecclesiastics—intensified life in this entire area. If we look at a map showing the properties which surround Clairvaux, each with the name of the controlling family, we can understand that the group of men who lived in the monastery could not ignore these castles, villages and families, who made of this region something quite the contrary to an

---

4. Under the title "Violence and the Devotion to St Benedict in the Middle Ages," *The Downside Review* 88 (1970), pp. 344–360, I illustrated this by examples which are suggested here.

uninhabited desert.[5] And all these people had their own personalities, problems and difficulties. They were men, and so were the monks. Neither could go to God by ignoring, mutually, the presence of the others.

To illustrate these ideas, it will be enough to cite a page from an historian who has characterized the region of Clairvaux, its inhabitants and the rivalry which existed between two families, those of the Lords of Châtillon and Vignory:

Lying in an area of direct contact between Vignory and Châtillon, where their possessions interpenetrate, it is a place of passage and also a valley of military interest. It is alongside the lands of the bishopric of Langres which the Count of Champagne uses to expand his influence. There is no one dominating family. If the Châtillon maintain there the theoretic center of their power, La Ferté, they have their fiefs elsewhere. We find there only parcels of land which are under bitter dispute by innumerable rival competitors—nobles, priors like those of Cluny or Clémentpré-Morin, and especially commoners, either those little lords hard to situate in the nobility, the Félonie, the Molinier, the Chevalchiat, but also the simple laborers: the Coquille, the Couillards, and others. This region belongs to men from all parts, to lords from the north or east, to men like the viscounts of La Ferté, and these are rightly the masters. The creation of Clairvaux in the center of this area of small property owners responds, perhaps, to the aims of the Châtillon to unify all these separated parcels to their own profit. This situation will greatly assist the extension of the abbey.... A bit to the north is a region of large properties in the hands of the families allied to the Vignory or the lords of Vallage. But it differs by the uncontested predominance of the Vignory themselves. It is thus impossible to think of expanding in these parts without their consent. The history of their fight with Clairvaux illustrates this historical conjecture, and by its victory, the abbey will obtain immediate domination of the entire west bank of the Marne in this region. Such was, rapidly drawn, the situation in Champagne and Bourgogne when a few monks came to establish themselves in the middle of the most complex feodal region of the entire

5. Such a map, drawn very carefully by R. Fossier, is reproduced in *Bernard de Clairvaux*, p. 89.

province. Caught in between the violent battles of two great barons, the intrigues of lesser scale on the part of their allies, and the property entanglements, could the abbey impose itself? Or would it even be allowed to exist where all the land was claimed? Would it be able to employ to advantage the bonds that united it to the Châtillon, and to build a solid temporal domain in an area where there was constant division and many small holdings? It is after the death of its first abbot that this will be worked out.[6]

During his lifetime, Bernard and his monks had to enter into contact with this little world: communications were inevitable. In what did they consist? We can divide them into three categories, as they were determined by the principal elements of the life of a contemplative community: prayer, asceticism and charity.

2. *Prayer life and communication*

Traditionally, the first and the most common occasion in which monks had to deal with seculars came precisely from the purpose for which they had separated themselves from them: their prayer life. Because men believed in intercession and merit, they offered lands to those who gave themselves to this. Many charters of foundation mention this motive. The desire to be prayed for after death inspired the generosity of many giving an importance to all that is related with this: offices and masses for the dead, obituaries and necrologies, commemorations of all sorts. Every monastery established "societies" or "friendships" with benefactors who were concerned about their salvation or were preparing themselves for death.[7] The Cistercians wished to keep this form of relationship with the world at a minimum. They diminished the number of offices for the dead by grouping commemorations of friends and benefactors;[8] but they continued to accept the gifts made to them

6. Fossier, *op. cit.*, p. 75.

7. In *Aux sources de la spiritualité occidentale* (Paris: Cerf, 1963), pp. 255–267: "Monachisme et société," I gave indications on this point.

8. Lists of communities and persons with whom they formed associations of prayer and of whom they made a commemoration in case of death can be found in several Cistercian manuscripts; I have published some in *ASOC* 5 (1949), p. 110; 6 (1950), pp. 132–135; 15 (1959), p. 88.

for this intention. This involved three occasions of contact: the original foundation, the donation of lands and actual construction.

First of all the *foundation* of the abbey. We have already seen that sometimes the motives which provoked this were selfish: prestige or the possession of an abbey to consolidate the power of a local lord.[9] But normally, even if the intention was not entirely pure, the founders were intent upon obtaining the prayers of the monks who, they knew and could see, lived their vocation conscientiously. This is the explanation of the foundation of Clairvaux itself, and then of its daughters; two or three times a year, on the average, during the abbacy of Bernard, requests for foundations were received—or provoked. Each time—that is to say, at this rhythm, almost constantly—it was necessary to carry on relations with the founders. They went to see the proposed location, explore the area, look for the best site, *quaerere locum*, among the unoccupied lands.[10] They inquired about water, a road, a healthy climate, sources of wood and other construction materials, all that an agricultural exploitation required: pasturage for cattle, good land to cultivate food for men and animals, forest land and fisheries. They had to see the bishop in whose diocese the monastery would be located.[11] At the various stages in these excursions, they came into contact with other abbeys and with clerics and laymen. Then began a whole series of juridical negotiations to settle the affair and to assure its future. A contract was the result, agreed upon either in writing or orally, when a suitable arrangement had been found. It was not always necessary to draw up a charter.[12] All these preparations and then the beginnings of the foundation itself took time. It is often very difficult to determine the precise date of a foundation, even the exact year.[13] In a word, each one of

9. Fossier, *op. cit.*, p. 79.

10. *Ibid.*, p. 80.

11. *Ibid.*, p. 81.

12. *Ibid.*, pp. 86–87.

13. This explains the criticisms that are sometimes made of the dates proposed in the monumental and excellent work of L. Janauschek, *Origines Cistercienses*, I (Vienna, 1877).

the seventy foundations made by Clairvaux in the time of St Bernard was the occasion for meetings, interviews, discussions, exchanges of messages confided to carriers. There is here an aspect of the real activity of a monastery about which the documents say nothing or very little. When speaking of the influence of an abbey, one does not always think of reading the records of the cellarer; they are, however, voluminous. And yet, in the Middle Ages, as people wrote with less facility, and thus less frequently than today, oral communications had a very large part to play; usually it was necessary to speak to the men with whom one had to do business.

Once it was founded, the monastery received *donations*. Some were made in ready money: sums of cash or commodities in case of urgent necessity.[14] The most frequent consisted of lands. These sometimes led to disputes with the owners of neighboring lands, rectification of borders, changes of landmarks, sometimes lawsuits.[15] Then, on these lands, they had to establish granges, build them, organize the exploitation, assign the brothers their tasks, establish relations with the neighbors. The vicissitudes themselves of the gifts, the conflicts, even the quarrels they provoked, their number more or less frequent according to periods, the suits for restitution brought by certain lords, especially after the failure of the second crusade had marred Bernard's prestige,[16] all these were the source of many contacts.

Lastly, or more exactly, at the same time that the abbey was founded and enriched, it was necessary to *build* the monastery as well as barns and outbuildings. At Clairvaux—and this is not the only place where it was the case—it was even necessary to build twice. In 1133, that is, eighteen years after the installation, the prior, Geoffrey, convinced Bernard of the need of transferring the abbey to a healthier and more fertile site. Such a change was not made without consultations: Geoffrey "asked the advice of the cellarers, two former architects who had become monks, Geoffrey of Aignay and Achard, the novice master".[17] He encountered

14. Fossier, p. 91.   15. *Ibid.,* pp. 101–103.   16. *Ibid.,* pp. 103–107.
17. *Ibid.,* p. 101.

opposition from Bernard, but he persisted and in the end he gained his point.[18] Then it was again necessary to seek information and opinions, give orders and see that they were carried out. For this construction of Clairvaux II, "Geoffrey employed paid workers, which was against the rule of the Order, but he thus gave proof of an extraordinary sense of economic affairs."[19]

3. *Asceticism and communications*

The monks of Clairvaux, like those of all the other Cistercian monasteries, worked for reasons of asceticism and poverty, in the spirit of the Founders of the Order. It is above all in the domain of the economic life that one should study the incidences of contact between the community and its environment. Let it suffice here to indicate the areas of production and commercial exchanges. O'Sullivan has shown that certain of St Bernard's allusions in his sermons reveal a thorough knowledge of the resources that a drained, healthy, well-fertilized soil represent.[20] The same observation could be made about other texts. Here is an example where a scene of cultivation is presented in very precise detail: "When a forest is cleared, the trees are cut down, but they are not thrown far away; instead, they are burned, which makes this worn-out soil fertile and renews it . . ."[21] The hard work of the harvest season seems to have been considered as exceptional, as it was in the Rule of St Benedict.[22] During the busy period, not only the

18. *Ibid.*, p. 102.

19. R. Fossier, "La fondation de Clairvaux et la famille de S. Bernard," *Mélanges S. Bernard* (Dijon: 1954), p. 26, n. 6.

20. Review of D. H. Williams, *The Welsh Cistercians. Aspects of their Economic History* (Pontypool, Wales, 1967) in *Speculum* 46 (1970), p. 336.

21. Text and context in H. Rochais, "Enquête sur les sermons divers et les sentences de S. Bernard," *ASOC* 18 (1962), p. 82.

22. In his *Liturgical Sermons*, Bernard inserted for the period which preceeds August 15, three sermons for the harvest season, *In labore messis, OB* 5:217–227. He speaks of work in 2:1, pp. 220–221. On the interpretation of the passage of RB where it treats of harvesting, cf. O. du Roy, " 'Tunc vere monachi sunt.' A propos du Chapitre XLVIII de la Regula Benedicti," *Rev. bénéd.* 80 (1970), pp. 300–304.

master of the lay brothers, but also the community, was dispensed from the Eucharist: "How many times, in order to care for the properties—*pro administrandis terrenis*— we omit, and very rightly, the celebration of the Mass itself!"[23]

It was necessary constantly to coordinate the work in the granges, assign tasks to the lay brothers, for whom there existed, near the abbey, "a regional center,"[24] to take care of the fields, the cattle, the woods and the vineyards, the poultry-houses, the fishing ponds, the mill.[25] When, after a poor harvest and a long winter, famine appeared menacing, the monks and brothers became discouraged.[26] All this did not only affect the monastery but the prosperity of the entire area, and Bernard was very personally interested in it:

> He was often seen, going through the fields, encouraging his monks at work, helping with the tasks, supervising carefully, by frequent inspections, the functioning of the granges; the concern he showed for the vineyard of Brother Christian is indicative of a good abbot, as were the efforts he undertook to change the course of the Aube when he was convinced by the arguments of Geoffrey in 1135. The role he was brought to play in Christian politics, led him to become interested in the activity of the region where Clairvaux had been founded. The affair of the election of Langres is the most evident proof of this. He was present at the composition of the charters which would effect Clairvaux's future, such as that of Champigny on the borders of the Bourgogne.[27]

When the fruit of their labors had been harvested, the monks had to find a market for it. Thus the necessities of commerce, too, put them into contact with society, especially with village society where the fairs and markets were held. To go to procure salt and other commodities at the fair of Reynel, they used a donkey,

23. *SC* 50:5, OB 2:81, CF 31.
24. R. Fossier, *Bernard de Clairvaux,* p. 99.
25. *Ibid.,* pp. 111–112.
26. *Ibid.,* pp. 127–128.
27. *Ibid.,* p. 108.

which they had to buy;[28] a little problem for the community which perhaps explains the pleasure Bernard had in developing, in his sermons for Palm Sunday, the symbol of the donkey.[29] The symbolism of the market is also a theme he likes. More than once in his parables—those little stories he invented to exhort his monks without boring them—he compared the cloister to a market, where the monk discusses the prices and obtains good bargains from a salesman.[30] These were vibrant realities and images which were meaningful for all.

The historian of *l'Essor économique de Clairvaux* could write:

The question of commerce and communications is clearer. If the Cistercian regulations invited the monks to have the least possible dealings with the world, to stay not more than three days in a fair village, to abstain from all merchandising, it could not prohibit the abbeys from buying the necessary tools and produce. Bernard, when he sent someone to buy salt at Reynel, knew well that his monastery could not avoid frequenting these markets, which were the only source for these necessities. A primary point was to assure easy travel between the granges. Evidently, the Roman roads were badly kept. They had to go along the beaten paths which wound along the sides of the hills. The monks had to make their way along with their carts just as the peasants, but they often went horseback, and not in vehicles, when they journeyed to a town.

Very soon, the transportation of necessary merchandise to the abbey was favored by the kindnesses of laymen. From 1142 till the death of St Bernard, the count of Champagne and the count of Meulan granted an exemption from the tolls for going and coming from the markets. . . .[31] Besides, the Rule [sic] imposed serious restrictions to that activity; it prescribed, in fact, that monks could not go to a market situated at more than a three-day walk from their monastery. However, the fact that in 1157 this distance was changed to four days establishes the existence of a desire to be more indulgent toward these commercial necessities.[32]

---

28. *Ibid.,* p. 91.   29. See above, p. 11, n. 8–9.

30. The texts are in my "Etudes sur S. Bernard et ses écrits," *ASOC* 9 (1953), pp. 143–147; H. Rochais, "Enquête," *loc. cit.,* pp. 49–50 and *Div* 42:3, OB 6:257f, CF 46.

31. R. Fossier, *Bernard de Clairvaux,* pp. 112–113.   32. *Ibid.,* p. 98.

4. *The life of charity and communications*

Other contacts with society arose out of charitable activity. First of all, and perhaps especially, on the material level; for the spiritual needs of the majority were very limited. It is only because of spiritual progress that our epoch has witnessed that people come to make retreats at monasteries. What was expected of the monks could be reduced to intercession, for which the people paid, in a way, by making donations, and help of an economic nature in case of penury. We know that the monks did not refuse to assist in this way the people of the surrounding area. Of the cellarer, Geoffrey, one has been able to say that he:

> was helped by a series of good harvests in 1126 and 1127, which permitted him to keep some reserves. They had been able, not only to survive the famine of 1125, but to distribute portions of food to the starving poor who flocked in from all sides. This gained for the monastery the eternal sympathy of those bodies whose souls had been conquered by Bernard; a humbler task, less striking than the miracles that the holy abbot performed on his route, but "propaganda," as we would say today, just as fruitful, and disinterested.[33]

To know their neighbor's needs and to help them, they certainly had to be in communication with them.

One of the privileged forms that communications inspired by charity took was hospitality. We are especially well informed on this point by some monks who were at Clairvaux only in passing and by others who stayed there: the Englishman Raoul, journeying to Italy,[34] a young German, fifteen years old, en route to Paris accompanied by his teacher,[35] a duke of Lincoln on his way to Jerusalem.[36] The famous miracle of the beer is well known:

> One day a small troup of young knights, going to a tournament, passed not far from Clairvaux. Out of curiosity they made a

33. A. Seguin, "S. Bernard et la seconde croisade," *Bernard de Clairvaux* p. 396.

34. Cf. A. Dimier, *S. Bernard "pêcheur de Dieu"* (Paris: 1953), p. 37.

35. *Ibid.*, p. 40.   36. *Ibid.*, p. 41.

detour to see the famous monastery and visit its abbot, whose
reputation of sanctity was already well established. Lent was
approaching, and it was the custom that during those days of
penance all abstained from these contests and jousts. Actually the
Church, because of the danger of death to which they exposed
the participants, forbade them at all times with serious penalties.
St Bernard tried to persuade these young people not to go to the
tournaments, even for the few days which preceded Lent. But
that was asking too much; they refused to make such a promise.
So the Saint said to them: "I am sure that God will grant me the
truce you refuse." Then he had some beer, which he had blessed,
served, telling them to drink to their souls' health. They obeyed,
but rather apprehensively; at least some of them feared the effects
of divine grace. After they had left, they could not help telling
one another what they felt; all had been suddenly touched by
grace. They turned around immediately and joined, without
delay, the spiritual militia of Clairvaux. After a year of novitiate,
they all pronounced their vows.[37]

The heavy recruitment of Clairvaux supposes that some of the
candidates to the monastic life, like those mentioned above, felt the
attraction, then came to see for themselves. Did the monks also go
out to them? The accounts of Bernard's biographers mention,
when speaking of the miracles of the holy abbot, many "fruitful"
jousts among the peasants in the regions close to Clairvaux.[38]

Finally, we know that one of the treasures Clairvaux shared
with others was the collection of texts which Bernard had acquired
or had had copied from so many manuscripts. When the abbot of
Liessies asked to borrow several treaties of St Augustine, the prior,
Phillip, answered that they had the texts, but that they were inserted
in such large volumes that they could not be sent. And he added:
"If you cannot procure these texts elsewhere and if you wish really
to have them, we would advise sending a copyist with parchment,
so that you can obtain copies. As for me, I am at your disposition,
as I shall be all my life, in the heart of Jesus Christ."[39] The hospitality

37. *Ibid.*, p. 39.

38. R. Fossier, *Bernard de Clairvaux*, p. 93.

39. I edited and commented on this text in a study on "Les manuscrits
de Liessies," *Scriptorium* 6 (1952), pp. 51–53.

offered by the prior of Clairvaux to a copyist of Liessies was accepted.

Thus, opportunities to communicate with the exterior were not lacking. They were offered not only to the abbot, but to others. In fact in the case of Clairvaux, because the abbot had so many affairs elsewhere apart from those of the monastery, a large part of the initiative and contacts were taken by the prior,[40] cellarer, doorkeeper,[41] other officials and lay brothers.[42] During the first decades, the two cellarers were Gerard, then Guy,

> Bernard's brothers, older than he and more attached to worldy projects. The former took a long time to decide on his conversion, but this old soldier performed his tasks with authority and leadership. Meticulous, he was interested in the work of the fields and in the assignment of duties. The other was calmer, seemed to be more conscious of money matters, and was somewhat tenacious. Bernard would become impatient and irked to see that Guy seemed to prefer horses to his brothers. These two men did more for the monastery during this difficult period than all the encouragements of the great. It was they who laid the foundations for the first granges of Clairvaux.[43]

After Guy, whom we no longer hear of after 1142, less energetic types appear—a certain Renaud as cellarer with William as his assistant, mediocre and little known officials.[44]

We know how much Vatican II emphasized the "local" or "particular" Church. The insertion into its life does not only consist in juridical relations with the hierarchy. It means, for a contemplative community, that it really shares, in its own way, in the cares of Christians—bishop, clergy, laymen—of the region where it is established.[45] The case of Clairvaux at the time of St

40. Fossier, p. 97.

41. *Ibid.,* p. 110, n. 7.

42. See below, p. 95.

43. Fossier, p. 95.

44. *Ibid./* p. 104.

45. I considered this problem in *Moines et moniales ont-ils un avenir?* (Bruxelles-Paris, 1971), pp. 70–78, "Au service de l'Eglise particulière."

Bernard shows us how this was realized in a rather undeveloped area, during the twelfth century.[46] The point is not to try to imitate his example in the twentieth century and all over the world; but everywhere and always, we can be inspired by it.

THE CONSTITUTIVE ELEMENTS OF THE CONTEMPLATIVE COMMUNITY

"To live for God alone in penance and continence": this fundamental notion which permitted us to situate the contemplative community in relation to universal communion which is the Church, should now be explained. In what does it consist? What makes such a group of Christians exist? What builds, so to speak, such a community? The elements can be reduced to three principal factors: what unites its members is a common way of seeking God; what distinguishes them is the diversity that God has established among them; and since they are united and different, they must have exchanges, sharing, communications among themselves.

46. In order to better understand the insertion of a contemplative community in its environment, we might compare it with another kind of community, as a parish church and its clergy with their goods in a village. Warren O. Ault, "The Village Church and the Village Community in Mediaeval England," in *Speculum* 45 (1970), pp. 197–215, has studied these sorts of relations—often conflicting—created by problems of economy and work, but he did it especially for the 13th and following centuries. Let us not forget that probably, because of Bernard's sanctity, the case of Clairvaux is not to be compared with all the others. We know the Cistercians, Carthusians, and others, in order to create solitude, "chased" everything around them by means of dispossessions for which they have been severely criticized by some historians: "Occasionally as at Revesby which was founded from Rievaulx at the very time when the *Mirror of Charity* was being written, a physical solitude was actually created even at the expense of destroying three small villages almost without trace."—A. Squire, *Aelred of Rievaulx, A Study* (London: SPCK, 1969) cited by B. Smalley, who adds: "There is more than occasional evidence for the Cistercian policy of depopulation both in England and in Burgundy," in *The Journal of Theological Studies* 21 (1970), p. 511. J. Dubois OSB has studied closely this kind of problem, for example, under the title "Le domaine de la chartreuse de Meyriat," *Le moyen âge* 74 (1968), pp. 459–493 and "Quelques problèmes de l'histoire de l'ordre des chartreux à propos de livres récents," *Rev. d'hist. ecclés.* 63 (1968), pp. 39–44.

Unity

1. *In God: one truth to contemplate*

The perfect model of any contemplative community is God himself, one in three Persons, who each communicate to the other two. In him, absolute simplicity coincides with such a great diversity that the very differences—consisting, according to the language of theologians, of relations of opposition—constitute each of the Persons of the Trinity.[1] This is not the place to recall the entire teaching of St Bernard on this mystery. He explained it in several places, but especially towards the end of the *Treatise on Consideration* and in the *Seventy-first Sermon on the Song of Songs*. What he had to say about it in the former[2] is resumed, in a context of charity-in-community, in a sermon whose theme is the psalm verse: "Behold, how good and pleasant it is when brethren dwell in unity."[3] There are many kinds of unity: that of stones placed together, which makes of them a "collection"; that of the members of the body, which constitutes the human being or any other being formed of several parts; that of the body and the soul, which is a "natural" unity, coming from birth; that of husband and wife, which is "conjugal" or "carnal" unity—in the sense that "they are two in one flesh"—; that of a man with his neighbor, which is "moral" unity, one based on consent; that of the man who, being self-possessed, seeks God in all his actions, the unity of "virtue" or of "self-control"; that of the will attached to God alone and making one spirit with him, "spiritual" or "consecrated" unity; that which exists among the angels who will but one thing, a "social" unity; that of the Word with human nature in Christ, unity which is "personal" and "freely chosen." But beyond—or more exactly, at the source of all these unities of which at least one element is of

---

1. Cf. H. de Lubac, *Catholicisme* (Paris: Cerf, 1938), pp. 254–256 and what I have written under the title "The Catholic Church: a mystery of Fellowship," *Worship* 35 (1961), pp. 470–485 (in French in "La communion des Saints,") *Cahiers de la Vie spirituelle* (Paris: 1946), pp. 37–53.

2. *Csi* 5:18–19, OB 3:482f, CF 19; CS 71:9–10, OB 2:220f, CF 40.

3. *Div* 80 cites Ps 132:1, OB 6:32, CF 49.

F

the created order, there is the unity which exists in God himself, the "consubstantial" unity of the three Persons, their "unity of essence." It is rightly called "principal" because it is a principle, that is to say, at the origin and beginning of all the others.[4] And it is also the end; the others are destined to prepare for it, to participate in it. It is also the model of all, being the most perfect of all: "In affirming the Three, we do not refuse to profess their unity: in this Trinity, we do not admit any multiplicity, but neither any solitude in their unity."[5]

This teaching is repeated, with some subtle developments, in the *Seventy-first Sermon on the Song of Songs,* with a view to explaining conciliation in man and between men, as well as in God, but in the way of "plurality with unity," by means of a "consensus of wills" which respects "the natures without mingling them."[6] "Because of that unity, the hearts of many men have declared themselves to be one and many souls, a single one, as it is written: There was one heart and soul in all the company of believers."[7] In God, then, plurality coincides with unity, with "pure simplicity. . . . It is in the measure that God is one that he is simple."[8] "To live for God alone," stated in other terms, to lead the contemplative life, is to try to participate in the simplicity of God, and that in two manners: first, within one's self, then in relation to others, avoiding all duplicity and that kind of multiplicity which disperses.[9] "Be simple, not only by refraining from fraud or pretense, but also from multiplication of occupations, so as to be always in conversation with him whose voice is agreeable and whose countenance is beautiful."[10]

---

4. Cf. *Etudes sur le vocabulaire,* pp. 68–70: *"Princes"* or *"principles"*?

5. *Csi* 5:19, OB 3:483, CF 19.

6. *SC* 71:7–9, OB 2:218, CF 40.

7. *Ibid.,* 71:7, citing Acts 4:32.

8. *Csi* 5:17, OB 3:418, CF 19.

9. Cf. *Etudes sur le vocabulaire,* pp. 31–33: "Monachisme et simplicité" and the texts I collected under the title "La simplicité," *Chances de la spiritualité occidentale* (Paris: 1966), pp. 339–354.

10. *Asspt* 3:7, OB 5:243, CF 25.

This complete simplification of contemplative attention symbolized by abiding together, listening and looking, is already perfectly realized by those—angels and saints—who are in that celestial Jerusalem of which the Church here below is the beginning, and even the anticipation. Bernard says it, using a theme inspired by the Bible and the Fathers which is familiar to him. The third verse of Psalm 121, which is a praise of the holy City, object of the pilgrimage of the people of God, speaks of it in this formula: *cuius participatio eius in idipsum.* "Jerusalem, built as a city which is bound firmly together,"[11] is today's translation. Bernard gave a meaning to each word of the Latin text which, doubtlessly, is not in the original, but which does not lack value. It would be good to explain this here once and for all, because it will come up several times later on. It meant, for him, to participate in the being itself of God, in his *idipsum.* This last word appears twenty times in the Vulgate, and it was often commented on, especially in the third verse of Psalm 121, but also on other occasions. These texts merit a special study. Let it suffice to indicate two commentaries. One is from St Hilary, who compared this verse to the one in the Acts where it is said that the community of Jerusalem had one heart and one soul,[12] and to the one of 1 Cor where St Paul begged the brothers to have the same sentiments: *ut idipsum sapiatis.*[13] And the bishop of Poitiers had opposed the formula *in idipsum* to one saying the contrary: *In diverso.* Those who are unanimous in the perfect city can only participate in the same reality.[14]

Another admirable text is the one in which St Augustine spoke at length on the *idipsum* of Psalm 121, seeing in it the being itself of him who remains unchanged because he is eternal and immutable. He remains thus in Christ. In him the eternal Word participates in our flesh so that it, in him and because of him, can participate in his eternity. It is that mystery which Moses had already contemplated,

11. This is the translation of the Revised Standard Version.
12. Acts 4:32.
13. 1 Cor 1:10.
14. *In Ps.* 121:5, *CSEL* 22:573.

when he heard God say: "I am being itself." True stability is in God, our stabilities can only be a participation of his.[15] Such is the object —and the end—of contemplation.

We can now read one of Bernard's texts on the subject:

Do they (the angels) not take supreme delight in those things which represent a certain likeness to their city in us, as they admire the new Jerusalem on earth? However I say this: just as the unity of that city is in the sharing in the being of God (*in idipsum*), so we also ought to be unanimous in thought and word (*idipsum sentiamus, idipsum dicamus*), with no division among us, but rather all one single body.[16]

Elsewhere, Bernard describes the goods which are given us already in anticipation of future glory—"Joy, life, glory, peace, pleasure, charm, happiness, gaiety and exaltation, and all that it combines, being a participation in God's being, in him of whom St Paul says he will be all in all."[17]

From where does this beatifying and all-sufficient unity come? Of what does this participation consist? To know him with a unifying knowledge, because this knowledge is at the same time a fulfilled love—for us, by desire; for the saints, by vision: "They are present at the divine counsel, they know the mysteries of the Trinity, they hear words that cannot be repeated to men. 'How blessed, Lord, those who dwell in your house! They will be ever praising you.'[18] In fact, the more they see, understand, discover, the more they love and break forth in praise and admiration."[19] But for us, this participation in God's unity and being supposes, also, our being at peace with men: "Let us first be solicitous that the Lord dwell in each one of us, and then in all of us together. He will never

---

15. *Enarr. in Ps. 121*, 5–7, CCL 40: 1805–1807. Other texts of the Fathers are given in *Thesaurus Linguae Latinae*, vol 7, 2, fasc 3 (Leipzig: 1962), col 353.

16. Mich 1:5, OB 5:297, CF 25.

17. *Div* 1:8, OB 6:79, CF 46.

18. Ps 83:5.

19. Ded 1:6: OB 5:374, CF 34.

refuse himself to individuals, nor to men as a whole. Let each one, then, try first to be at peace with himself . . . ." And Bernard shows here what this interior pacification means.[20] Then he insists on the charity which must "connect" us, and make us "cohere," "glue" us, so to speak, to one another. "In this life, we cannot have a perfect knowledge; and it is better, doubtlessly, that it is so. In the heavenly dwelling, knowledge is the nourishment of love." Here below, we must prepare ourselves by "purity of heart," symbol of our entire ascetic effort. On this point, Bernard, in accordance with a theme which was dear to him and others, evokes the contrast between the beyond and the here-below, the *ibi,* or *illic,* and the *hic*: what unites, them, is the *interim,* the "already" and the "not yet," the presence which is already given, but which we must conserve by continual efforts.[21]

The idea of interior unification as a condition of union with others, and as a preparation for union with God, which has already commenced in us, is repeated in a Sermon for the Ascension: "As long as our hearts are still divided and we are *interim,* there are still many complications in us—these *sinus,* that is to say, these "creases" which suppress "simplicity." We do not possess perfect cohesion; thus it is one after another, and in some manner, member after member, that we must lift ourselves up until the union is perfect in that heavenly Jerusalem whose solidity comes from the fact that all participate in the being of God. There, not only each one, but all together begin to live in unity; there is no more division in themselves nor among them." And Bernard describes in realistic terms the suffering of the person who was tortured on the rack, which at that time was called the wooden horse. The man, stretched out, was attached to pieces of wood which pulled his members as far as possible in all directions. He was not cut in pieces, a thin layer of

20. Ded 2:3, OB 5:377, CF 34.

21. Ded 2:4, OB 5:378, CF 34. The vocabulary *hic-ibi-interim* is frequently used by St Bernard: SC 72:2, OB 2:226; Apo 8, OB 3:88, CF 1:43f, etc. . . . In presenting a *Nouveau sermon d'Isaac de Stella,* in *Rev. d'ascét et de myst.* 40 (1964), p. 281, I cited other texts. Several texts of St Bernard will be cited further on in this paper.

skin continued to cover his body. But inside, what a painful tension, what distortion and rupture![22]

How would it be possible for men to share in this perfect unity which is in God and those who are already with him? There is someone who realized perfectly, here below, all the "unities" man needs to succeed. Christ possessed "substantial" unity with the Father, "personal" unity with the Word, "spiritual" unity between his soul and body, "sacramental" unity with the Church, his Spouse. And because of that he was at the origin and he remains the source of every "charism," of every grace which enables men to unite themselves to God. Henceforth, we can seek God, sure of finding him, provided we do it in that charity which was first realized in the perfect unity of Christ.[23]

2. In man: one search for God

In what does this common search consist? In two sorts of efforts which correspond to the very nature of a contemplative community: in prayer and asceticism. The first guarantee of unity will be the acceptance of a "discipline," or obedience: it is in this way that man learns to live in peace, in good social relations—*socialiter*— as much as possible with all his companions—*cum universis naturae suae sociis*—and with all men. He then learns by experience the truth of this phrase: "Gracious the sight, and full of comfort, when brethren dwell in unity."[24] This unity, though, is fragile and menaced continually: "Three virtues help to guard it: patience, humility, charity."[25] This unanimity is the source of peace when it is possessed. We must not only persevere in it, but make it grow. Dwell in fraternal love, in mutual charity.[26] "Let us search together!"

We can discover by a simple grammatical form to what extent St Bernard is convinced of the communal character of contemplative prayer and asceticism: he likes to speak of these efforts in saying not

22. Asc 6:5, OB 5:153, CF 25.
23. Div 33:8, OB 6:227, CF 46.
24. SC 23:6, OB 1:142, CF 7.
25. Sent 1:32, PL 183:754.
26. Mich 2:1, OB 5:300, CF 25.

"I," but "we," using what might be called the "coenobitic plural." This way of expressing himself appears even in the passages where he describes the condition, the misery of every man, his "me" which, for the Christian, is at the same time an "us": a collective "me" or rather a universal one.[27] Likewise, the famous definition he gives of the Cistercian observance is stated in the plural: *Stemus in ordine nostro, quicumque elegimus* . . .[28] Here are a few other examples: "Let us fill the office of the angels whose destiny we share . . . let us tell them . . . and let us hear them . . ."[29] "Let us run after the Lord: we will be drawn along in the sweetness of his perfumes . . ."[30] And concerning the Spirit who will lighten the difficulties of asceticism, as he helped St Andrew during his martyrdom: "Let us seek the Spirit, my brothers, above all, let us try to merit the possession of this Spirit, or rather to possess more abundantly him whom we already possess. For he who does not possess Christ's Spirit does not belong to him. As for us, we have not received the spirit of this world, but the Spirit of God, in order to know the gifts God has made to us. The witness of his presence are the works of salvation and life, which we could never accomplish if the Spirit of the Savior was not present in us, he who vivifies our souls. So let us try to obtain that God multiply his gifts in us and make his Spirit grow in us, for he has already given us the first fruits."[31]

Then, seeking together, by means of aid, encouragement, the stimulation which comes from being together, sharing the same weakness, but also participating in the same Spirit of God, each one can have, in his own being, the experience of meeting the Lord, receive his visit: "Happy union, if you experience it! . . . Listen to the voice of this experience: For me, to adhere to God is good!"[32]

27. Adv 7, OB 4:195 F, CF 10. Under the title "Essais sur l'esthétique de S Bernard," *Studi medievali* 9 (1958), pp. 698–700, I analyzed this text.

28. Ep 42:1, LSB, Ep 151:1, p. 220. Under the title "St Bernard and the Rule of St Benedict," *Rule and Life*, CS 12 (Spencer, Mass.) Cistercian Publications, 1971), I analyzed this text, pp. 156–160.

29. SC 7:4–5, OB 1:33f, CF 4:40ff.

30. Ep 385:1–2.

31. And 2:4, OB 5:436f, CF 34.

32. SC 71:10, citing the Ps 72:18, OB 2: 221, CF 40.

And this personal union, this experience of the Word—*experimentum de Verbo*— described in such a ravishing manner in the *Seventy-fourth Sermon on the Song of Songs* is obtained in a community, in this case in the community of Clairvaux, if the interpretation made by a philologist is accepted.[33] Be that as it may, this formula of St Paul which, let us remark is always in the plural, is verified in the community: "In him we live, move and exist."[34]

This is a contemplative community, a community seeking. This is what makes it exist: the Being of God communicating himself to each one who is united to all, all making the same effort to receive him, each one in his own way, but all together. For, unanimity does not mean uniformity. We must now examine the question of that diversity that unity admits and even favors, the legitimacy of contrast in the midst of concord.

Diversity

1. *Differences that come from God*

The unifying object of the contemplative's search is the unity of God, one in three Persons. But those who seek God use different means, each according to their own personal call. God is so infinitely wise, generous and powerful that he never repeats himself. There are then necessarily, because of the positive will of the Creator, profound differences among men, even among those who have received the same vocation to seek him together in the same place and in the same community. One might apply to the members of a community that wonderful passage that Bernard wrote concerning the diversity of monastic orders in the Church: the Church is like a tunic without seams, in virtue of its unity, its indissoluble charity, and many-colored, because of the different charisms given by the one same Spirit. Just as there is a single direction but several roads leading to the city of God and a single house of the Father with many dwellings in it, so the Church is a pluralistic unity or a unified

---

33. J. P. Th. Deroy, *Bernardus en Origenes* (Haarlem: 1963), pp. 149–154. I summed up this interpretation in *Recueil d'études sur S. Bernard*, 3:206–208.

34. Acts 17:18.

plurality: *pluralis unitas unaque pluralitas.* In heaven, too, the "glory" of each will be different because the "graces" which prepared it and contained it in germ were different. And there as here below, *tam hic quam ibi,* charity will assure that order will reign among a varied multitude of "good works" on earth and "merits" in heaven; here and there, each star shines with its own particular beauty.[1]

The texts where St Bernard speaks of pluralism in the Church or the contemplative community are as numerous as those that speak of unity, for both have the same origin—the Holy Spirit—and the same end—the beatific vision. In saving and glorifying men, God respects and restores the differences he created among them. But here below, which will not be the case in heaven, this diversity may lead to division: *illic unitas, hic divisio.* And it is a duty for each to be sufficiently united in himself so as to remain united to others. What unites is what is eternal and absolute: charity; what can lead to separation is diversity, something secondary, contingent and relative, but certainly legitimate because it comes from God, but also something that our egoism tends to exaggerate, thus making it an occasion of sin. "What is necessary is unity, that excellent part which will never be taken away. Division will cease when the fullness of time will come. Then the entire holy city of God will participate in the being of God: *et erit totius sanctae civitatis Jerusalem participatio in idipsum.* In the meanwhile, *interim,* the Spirit of Wisdom is not only unique, he is multiple: he founds interiority on unity, but he maintains a distinction in the exterior manifestation of his presence. It was thus in the primitive Church, "where there was one heart and soul in all the company of believers; none of them called any of his possessions his own, everything was shared in common. May there be such unity of soul in us: may our hearts be united by loving unity, seeking it, attaching ourselves to it, agreeing about the essential, the *idipsum.* Then diversity remains superficial: it is no longer a danger or cause of possible scandal. In each of us there may exist a different capacity for tolerance—*propria cuique tolerantia* varying opinions on temporal matters—*propria quoque nonnumquam*

1. Apol 6–9, OB 3:86–89, CF 1:70–75.

in terrenis agendis sententia, and even sometimes different gifts of grace. Not all the members have the same role to play. But interior unity, unanimity, binds the multiplicity into a tight sheaf by the bond of charity and peace."[2]

2. *Differences which come from men*

This unity in pluralism is a fragile unity. Like everything else, we can abuse pluralism, and what was a good can become an occasion for evil. We can also exaggerate the importance of unity, or more exactly, not be content with it as a profound, interior reality but want it to be present in the exterior actions which give witness to it, and thus not sufficiently respect the vocation of each individual. Bernard defended those whom some wanted to take from their life of contemplation so that they might be, apparently at least, more useful. Not all are capable of doing everything; no one has the right to ask a man to do something for which he is not fitted: "It is not equally easy to remain quietly at prayer and to be fruitfully occupied, to obey humbly and command usefully, to let oneself be governed without complaining and to govern without fault, to obey with zeal and to give orders with discretion . . . ." Bernard counsels that we should imitate Jesus, who in his perfect knowledge of all, defended the woman who was accused of wasting money: "Why are you blaming that woman?"[3]

There are many ways of differing from each other. There are good ways and bad ways; there are some that come from institutions and others from persons. Bernard has often spoken of them.

2. Sept 2:3, OB4:352, CF 22. At the end of this text, Bernard speaks again of this matter which can be "glued" or "cemented," which unites dissimilar elements. This is again treated in Mich 2:2, OB 5:301. It is clear that Bernard used spontaneously in the first edition the form *gluten,* employed, doubtlessly, in the spoken language of the time, as it is in French today, to which he later preferred *glutinum,* judged to be more "Latin." Another symbol of unity is used there: that of stones of an edifice, between which there is a cohesion (*cohaerere*) differing from the "dust which the wind makes rise"; and the first edition ends, OB 5:302, with an allusion to "monastic peace" which reigns between "*fratres quietos et simplices.*"

3. Div 90:3, OB 6:339, CF 46, citing Mt 26:13.

In the *Forty-second Occasional Sermon*, which is certainly his,[4] he evoked with reality and optimism the life of a cloister surrounded by a valley, really Clairvaux, as he liked to see it. "It is wonderful for men to live together in accord in the same house, to live together like brothers. We see one who grieves for his sins, one who exults in praising God, one who serves all, one who teaches others, one who prays, one who reads, one who is merciful and one who punishes sins; one who distinguishes himself by charity, another by humility; this one remains humble in success, and that one is courageous in difficulties; this one is very active, and that one rests in contemplation." Is it not like an army, an entrenchment which the enemy fears because each one is busy with his own task? Today we would compare this monastery with an army of specialized technicians.[5]

In another version of the same Sermon, Bernard says that in this *paradisus claustralis*—this paradise of the cloister—one leads the *vita socialis*. God's gifts, the *charismata virtutum,* are diverse, like the flowers in a garden. And Bernard brings in again the theme of the merchant monk. That which each one does not have of such or such a virtue that makes up the riches of his brothers—*fratrum divitias*—he should observe and admire, even envy and try to imitate; briefly, he should acquire it—let him buy it—paying the price of a "sincere charity." Then, he will be able to say with the Psalmist that it is "gracious and full of comfort, when brethren dwell in unity." It is interesting to note that Bernard started to speak of this employing two words that he considered synonomous: "the cloister or the desert," *claustrum vel eremus,* thus indicating that the common life is at the same time a solitary life of the contemplative type.[6]

---

4. Cf H. Rochais, "S. Bernard est-il l'auteur des sermons 40, 41 et 42 De diversis?" *Rev. Bénéd.* 72 (1962), pp. 324–345.

5. Div 42:4, OB 6:258, CF 46. The comparison of Clairvaux with an army is developed by Nicholas of Clairvaux, Ep 7, PL 196:1602 and Ep 45, 1645–1646.

6. Sent 3:91, OB 6. On the application of the word *"eremus"* to the coenobitic life, I collected evidence in *Chances de la spiritualité occidentale* (Paris:1966) pp. 247–277.

Bernard often used symbols to describe the variety of graces and temperaments in his community. Thus, in the Palm Sunday procession, there are all kinds of gaits: quick and slow, ardent and weak, delicate and resistant—*duros corde*. These latter, like the donkey, do not know how to sing; they bray disagreeably. They always need to be urged forward and spurred along. But they advance, they carry the Lord![7] In the home that the Lord visits are Mary, Martha and Lazarus: specialists of contemplation, service, penance.[8] Or again, as Nicolas of Clairvaux says, Martha represents the lay brothers, Mary the monks and Lazarus the novices.[9] In the same group, some are standing and others are seated, some push forward, some remain at the same place.[10] In every cloister, there are the four kinds of monks described by St Benedict. Two are good and two bad. Among the good are those who realize the importance of solitude and those who insist on community life.[11] In the dwelling of the Lord, there are four classes of individuals. Some kneel at the feet of Jesus, like the Magi come from Ethiopia, like the repentant Mary, confessing her sins. Others are seated at his feet, like that same Mary while she listened to his words. Others rest on his heart. And others are seated at his side. Those of the first two categories live for themselves; those of the third, for themselves and their neighbor, like John the Evangelist drawing peace from the Lord's breast to give it, afterwards, to the world.[12] Bernard took pleasure in these texts and others in showing that the diversity that he had admitted in principle was really lived in his community.

It is not only a question of differences of temperament, as between introverts and extroverts. It is often a question of degree of fervor, which differs greatly. No more than St Benedict in his Rule,

7. Palm 2: 5–6, OB 5:48–50, CF 22.
8. Asspt 3:4–6, OB 5: 241–243, CF 25.
9. Ep 36, PL 196:1632.
10. QH 2:1–2, OB 4:389–391, CF 43.
11. "Inédits bernardins dans un manuscrit d'Orval," in *Analecta monastica* I (*Studia Anselmiana* 20) (Rome: 1948), p. 151 (Translated into English in *The Love of Learning and the Desire for God* [New York: Fordham, 1962], pp. 171–172).
12. Sent 1:35, OB 6.

St Bernard has no illusions about the average virtue in monks. More than once, he has forcefully denounced mediocrity, lukewarmness, lack of love, and even of fidelity to their vocation, which he had observed in monks. Even if we make allowance for literary exaggeration in these diatribes, we should recognize that he testified to the existence of monks with hard hearts and monks without joy, who, "if they share our labors, have yet no part in our consolations."[13] There are some who, at first had given all, and then, little by little, took back what they had given: "We are ashamed to say it, but the depth of our pain prevents silence. How many can we not find, my brothers, who wear the religious habit and have made a vow of perfection, to whom this terrible sentence of the prophet seems to apply: Jerusalem, if I forget you, may my right hand perish!"[14] And further, we find the portrait of those who have left all, being absorbed by worldly affairs: "We see them running eagerly after temporal advantages, rejoicing in a mundane way about passing profits, worrying with so much pusillanimity about losses, even very insignificant ones, of earthly goods; we see them scrambling around for all that in such a sensual way, talk about it with such impudence, mix in worldly affairs with so little religious spirit, that we might believe that that is their choice and that that is all that counts for them."[15]

Elsewhere again, St Bernard speaks of those monks who love themselves and not God, seeking themselves and not the things of God;[16] of those who compromise with death, weaken discipline, diminish fervor, disturb the peace and injure charity.[17] One day, he went so far as to exclaim, in a sermon: "How many bad fish I must drag along! How many fish, who cause me worry and grief, have I not gathered into my net, when my soul attached itself to you!"[18]

Such was the real Clairvaux at the time of its greatest abbot. And

13. Asc 3:6, OB 5:135, CF 25.
14. Ps 136:5.
15. QH 7:14, OB 4:422f, CF 43.
16. SC 34:4, OB 2:305, CF 40.
17. Ded 3:3, OB 5:381, CF 34.
18. Div 34:6, OB 6:233, CF 46.

there is nothing here that should surprise us. These men were so different from one another by their origin, character, formation, age and condition of life. It would have been unthinkable that there would be no conflict among them. Every level of social life was represented by the almost two hundred monks who lived at Clairvaux: members of the nobility, some of whom were of royal blood (even a king's brother!), little feodal lords who came from the neighboring country, peasants from the rural population.[19] There were men who came from several different French provinces, speaking different dialects, as well as strangers from northern and southern countries, and it is a well-known fact that in Europe living together like this has always caused difficulty. The "conflict of generations," the "age gap" is not an invention of our times, either. Bernard knew how to warn young monks about the dangers to which their youth exposed them, and especially about excessive fervor; but he could speak favorably of them, too—and doubtlessly, it was necessary to do this in front of the older monks who were so easily tempted to forget that they had once been young.[20]

To these individual differences of character there were added those coming from the institutions. In the community there were three classes of members and in each class, two categories. The classes were: the monks cleric—including those who were not priests, which seems to be the case of the greatest number—, the lay monks, and the lay brothers.[21] The categories were: the "officials,"

---

19. Cf *Bernard de Clairvaux* (Paris: 1953), p. 93, n 63.

20. I collected these texts under the title "St Bernard's Idea of the Role of the Young," *Contemplative Life*, CS 19 (Spencer, Mass.: Cistercian Publications, 1973).

21. Cf J. Dubois, "L'institution des convers au XIIe siècle, forme de vie monastique propre aux laïcs," *I laici nella "societas christiana," loc. cit.*, pp. 183–261; "Quelques problèmes de l'histoire de l'ordre des Chartreux à propos de livres récents," *Rev. d'hist. ecclés.* 63 (1968), p. 37 and the document I presented under the title "Le texte complet de la Vie de Christian de l'Aumône," *Analecta Bollandiana* 71 (1953), pp. 21–52, texts on "lay monks," p. 27. The fact that there were lay monks does not necessarily signify that the others were all priests or ordained in the sacred orders, but it would seem that they were assimilated with the clergy. This question merits to be treated at length elsewhere.

those who had the responsibilities, and because of that, often had to attend to affairs outside, and the "cloistered," those who remained habitually in the monastery.[22] The latter sometimes envied those who, at least occasionally, could shake off the yoke of the daily routine. "It is rare that peace reigns between these two categories: *raro pax inter istos est.* The abbot, prior and the brothers responsible for the spiritual welfare—*et alii fratres spirituales*—try to reconcile them."[23] The cause of the deepest division was in the fact that the lay brothers lived totally apart from the others, juridically and materially, they were separated; there were really two monasteries in one. These very distinct communities in the cloister were a practically inevitable reflection of the profound differences which existed in the feudal society between the *nobles* and the *ecclesiastics,* on one hand, and on the other, between the *peasants* and the *serfs.*[24] All would have had to have been very advanced in virtue to prevent such inequalities from degenerating into petty jealousies and rivalries so that a spiritual union could triumph over all the psychological causes of division. Everything in the establishment reminded the lay brothers of their state of inferiority in comparison with the monks, who were likened to the ecclesiastics. Their food was more modest. Gerard, the cellarer of Clairvaux, was praised for the fact that during his visits to granges, he ate with the lay brothers who lived there, being satisfied with what they ate, drinking water with them and not wishing to be served anything special besides the usual dishes. This inequality in diet—*dispar observantiae victus*—was more than once the cause of dissension and scandal, and it became necessary to prescribe that the same nourishment be given to monks and lay brothers alike.[25]

We must never lose sight of this institutional complexity in the contemplative community of Clairvaux if we wish to judge the

22. I cited the texts under the title et *"Claustrales Officiales," Otia monastica* (Rome:*Studia Anselmiana* 51, 1963), pp. 164–174.

23. Sent 1:26, OB 6.

24. I cited texts and facts under the title "Comment vivaient les frères convers," ASOC 21 (1965), pp. 239–258.

25. Cf *ibid.*, p. 245.

importance of the insistent recommendations of St Bernard, as well
as other Cistercian authors, in favor of unity, which in practice was
menaced in so many ways. As Bernard clearly recognized, unity
admitted different opinions about material questions and problems
of organization. It was not diversity that was decidely excluded, but
the very particular vice called "singularity." This vice did not
consist essentially in affecting singularity in some exterior detail,
some fad—there have always been the odd fellows—but in forming
a separate group, in establishing an autonomy in regard to common
observance, and in this sense, separating oneself from the community even while one continued to live in its midst. Singularity is a
form of self-sufficiency with pride as its foundation.[26] It is the enemy
of charity.[27] It consists, for the monk, in seeking his own interests,
in deviating from the "common will" by preferring his "own
will."[28] It leads to parties, cliques, clandestine conversations in
corners: *ubi singularitas, ibi angulus:*[29] charity avoids the corners:
caritas non quaerit angulos.[30]

Elsewhere, Bernard develops this text again, in a very beautiful
context: *Non amat Veritas angulos.*[31] Let us not think that this grave
abuse was absent from Clairvaux at the time of St Bernard. He
took the trouble to leave public testimony on this point: "I am very
surprised at the impudence of several of us who, as they trouble us
all by their singularity, irritate us by their impatience, slight us by
their stubbornness and rebellion, yet dare, by the urgency of their

---

26. Hum 41–42, OB 3:47–49, CF 13.

27. Cf *Etudes sur le vocabulaire*, p. 23: texts by Geoffrey of Auxerre and
others. On the original meaning of *singularitas*, see P. Antin, "A la source
de *singularitas* dans la vie monastique," *Archivum Latinitatis Medii Aevi*
(Bulletin du Lange) 36 (1967–68), pp. 111–112.

28. Cf *Etudes sur S. Bernard*, p. 58, n 1; P. Delfgaauw, "La nature et les
degrès de l'amour selon S. Bernard," *S. Bernard théologien* (Rome: ASOC 9,
1953), pp. 245–250.

29. Ep 11:3, LSB, Ep 12:3, p 44.

30. The formula is found in the text of John of Fécamp that I published
in *Un maître de la vie spirituelle au XIème siècle* (Paris: 1946), pp. 219, 27. It can
be located in the "Vita B. Davidis monachi Hemmerodensis," ed A. Schneider,
ASOC 11 (1955), p. 39: *Non enim angulos et diverticula quaerebat.*

31. Asc 6:13, OB 5:158, CF 25.

prayers, to invite the God of all purity into their sullied conscience."[32]

Elsewhere again, in the same published work, he denounced a very subtle form of singularity, that which consists in "not being satisfied with common life," presuming to add fasts, watching, self-chosen exercises of prayer and penance, preferring private practices to communal ones. This was a frequent temptation among the "newcomers"—the "novices," as certain manuscripts translate it—[33] an indiscrete zeal or rather that incredibly obstinate intemperance which we have repeatedly attempted to restrain."[34] Bernard, in this text, uses the expression "common life" in a sense which must be well understood. We sometimes say of it: *Vita communia maxima paenitentia,* which is interpreted as though the fact of living in community constituted the greatest source of suffering. Nothing could be farther from his thought: on the contrary, for him, community life is an aid and stimulant, an occasion of joy. Where the mortification comes in is in the resisting of the temptation to separate oneself from the community by consenting to what opposes it the most: singularity. In every monk this tendency may appear at one time or an other; and asceticism, penance, alone can conquer it. At Clairvaux, as in every contemplative community, some have yielded to it, and St Bernard was not afraid to recognize the fact and express his indignation against it. But this was less common than his felicitations to his monks for their heart felt understanding, for that was what dominated and set the tone. The group carries the individual, the procession advances, it draws along the loiterers. His experience of the life of a contemplative community profoundly marked the theology of St Bernard. As Fr Congar has written, the Church, for Bernard, "is like a choir of monks composed of the fervent and the distracted, but who, in the singing of the divine praises, blend into a single voice and represent an unique worshipper."[35]

32. SC 46:6, OB 2:59, CF 31.
33. Cited in OB 1:112.
34. SC 19:7, OB 1:112, CF 4:145.
35. "L'ecclésiologie de S. Bernard," *S. Bernard théologien,* p. 145.

G

Communication

1. *Relations with superiors*

How can we effect the synthesis between the unity, which comes from God and the efforts of men, and the diversity, which also comes from God and which is found in the differences he has created in men, differences which the grace of salvation respects and develops? It can only be through a sharing of what we hold in common, but what each participates in in his own way. In this regard a question, which is not new, arises immediately—one which St Bernard has already asked: how to reconcile interior solitude, in which each one meets God, with the communication necessary for sharing? Before giving some of the practical answers which were given to it let us cite a rather long, but very instructive text in which Bernard formulated some principles on this point; it is taken from the *Third Sermon for Advent*. We will see that the response differs depending on whether one is a superior or a member of the community, but all have something to receive from one another by way of counsel and mutual aid: the terms *consilium* and *auxilium* used here are borrowed from feudal society.[1]

> We owe our brothers with whom we live, under the double title of confrere and man, *aid* and *counsel*, for we too, expect counsels from them to instruct our ignorance and aid to help our weakness. But perhaps there are some among you who say to me in their heart: What counsels can we give to our brother? We do not even have permission to speak to him. What assistance can we give him? We cannot do the slightest thing outside of obedience. To that I answer: You will always find something to do for your brother if you have fraternal charity in your heart. As for counsels, can you give him better ones than to teach him by your example what he should do and avoid, than to attract him to what is better by counsels, not of the tongue, but of works and truth? Is there any more useful and efficacious aid than to pray devoutly for him, not to neglect to tell him his faults, to be determined, not only never to give him an occasion for

---

1. The two texts are associated in the texts cited by O. Prinz, *Mistellatanisches Worterbuch* 7, (Munich: 1967) col 1292.

falling, but, as much as possible, to remove all such occasions from him, like the angel of peace who takes scandals from God's kingdom? If you give your brother these counsels and this aid, you will fulfill your debt toward him and he will have no complaint against you.

But are you placed above others? You owe them, undoubtedly, the service of a greater solicitude. Your inferiors have the right to a vigilance and discipline on your part that does not let faults go unpunished. But, if no one else depends on you, you have, at least, yourself, and you owe yourself, likewise, vigilance and discipline. Thus, you have a body whose conduct evidently belongs to your soul. You should, then, watch over it so that sin does not reign there and that its members are not an occasion of iniquity. But you should also discipline it, so that it produces worthy fruits of penance; you should chastise it and put it in yoke. But the debt of those who will have to answer for several souls is certainly heavier and more dangerous. Alas! Unhappy man that I am, where could I go, if I was negligent in the protection of such great riches, a treasure so precious that Jesus Christ valued it more than his blood? If I had gathered the blood of the Lord which flowed from his wounds at the foot of the cross and carried it often in a fragile vase, what would not have been my fears in thinking of the risks I was taking? Now, it is certain that the treasure which I must keep is so precious that the wisest merchant, or rather Wisdom himself, gave all his blood to buy it. And moreover, it is in fragile vases, more likely to break than clay ones. Let us add, to complete the causes for anxiety and fear, that responsible for my own conscience as well as my neighbor's, I do not know either of them well. Both are as unfathomable as an abyss, obscure like the darkness of the night. Nevertheless, I am the keeper and I hear a voice that calls: "Sentinel, what have you seen tonight? Sentinel, what have you seen tonight?"[2] Not only must I not answer like Cain: "Am I my brother's keeper?"[3] but I must, with the Prophet, exclaim aloud that "Vainly the guard keeps watch, if the city has not the Lord for its guardian."[4] I can justify myself only by the care with which I do my duty, watching with vigilance and discipline, as I said above. If these four things— the respect and obedience due to my superiors and the assistance

2. Is 21:11.
3. Gen 4:9.
4. Ps 126:11.

and counsel asked by my brothers— are not lacking, Wisdom
will not find his dwelling lacking in the things which concern
justice.[5]

Here now is a text which was especially meant for superiors. It
was written for abbots on the occasion of a general chapter, to
which some had come from long distances—often by sea or river—
which explains the type of comparison employed:

As for prelates, they go to sea in ships and they labor in the midst
of waters. They are not restrained by the narrow passage of a
bridge, nor by the shortness of a ford. They can sail in any
direction they please, and go wherever it is necessary, to the
crossing of the bridge or the ford, to watch over those who
advance, discover and eliminate the dangers, animate the lukewarm and encourage the weak. They climb to heaven and descend
to hell; sometimes they occupy themselves with sublime and
spiritual things, and sometimes with terrible and infernal ones.
But where can the ship be found that is able to withstand the
shock of such terrible waves, and sail with certitude in such great
dangers. I will answer: "Death itself is not so strong as love, and
the ardor of love is as inflexible as hell." Also, as it is said elsewhere: "Love is a fire no waters avail to quench." That is the
ship needed by prelates; it should have three sides, like all ships,
and be conformed to the doctrine of St Paul, when he states that
"charity is born of a pure heart, a good conscience and sincere
faith."[7] Purity of intention for a prelate consists in trying to be
useful without letting it be felt that he is superior. He should
seek in his role as superior not his own personal interests nor
worldly honors or similar things, but God's good pleasure and
the salvation of souls. But to purity of intention, he must still join
an irreproachable conduct, be a model for the others, living the
Rule himself before teaching it to others, as is taught in the Rule
of our Master.[8] He must not teach his disciples by his conduct
to do what he has taught them was contrary to their interests, if
he does not wish the religious to murmur when he corrects them

5. Adv 3:6, PB 4:179f, CF 10.
6. Song 8:6–7.
7. 1 Tim 1:5.
8. RB 2:13.

and say: "Physician, heal thyself."[9] Where that condition exists, the result is the complete condemnation of the superior and the loss of many subjects. If I speak in that way, it is not because I have succeeded in avoiding such an evil, but Truth itself has cried to me, as it cries to every superior: "He who is over others must be irreproachable."[10] With the Lord, the superior should be able to answer with a clear conscience to those who blame him: "Who can convict me of sin?"[11] I do not mean that we can live in this world utterly free from sin, but I say that a superior must especially avoid falling into the faults that he reproaches in his subjects.[12]

2. *"Confession"*

Let us try now to see how the sharing of experience took place in the contemplative community in practice. We have seen that it included both a meeting with God and a realization of the weaknesses to which all men are subject. In regard to these, it first took the form of what was then called "confession." This word did not usually signify at that time, as it does today, the private administration of the sacrament of penance—with avowal, exhortation, absolution—but that "revealing of thoughts," which was later called "disclosure of conscience," the "spiritual colloquy" with a counsellor. The fact that confession could be in the form of a conversation is clearly stated in a sentence of St Bernard: *accusatio devota in ore, quae fit confitendo vel ad invicem colloquendo.*[13] Let us not forget that there was no organized novitiate, with classes or conferences in common, which are periods of collective and some-

9. Lk 4:23.

10. 1 Tim 3:2.

11. Jo 8:46.

12. Div 35:6 = Abb 6, OB 5:292f, CF 34.

13. Sent 3:97, OB 6. An example of long monastic "confession" is found in the treatise *De interiori domo*, 25–27, PL 184:520–532. We can find the vocabulary of "confession" applied to a conversation between friends in St Albert the Great, *Ethica*, 8, 3, 6, ed Borgnet, *Alberti Magni opera* 7 (1890), p. 546: *eo quod talis videntur esse secundum quamdam confessionem quae fit inter amicos (confessionem vocamus, quod pacti quamdam habet virtutem): propter quod politicus judicat de eis. . . ."*

times systematic spiritual direction. As it was and still is the case in the tradition of Oriental monasticism, as it is the case today for many laymen, all the formation received was given during these "confessions," these private conversations held during periods of personal difficulty—darknesses, doubts, temptations, faults—but also in times of consolation. In St Bernard, as in the Bible and the Fathers, confession does not concern only, not even chiefly, sin, but rather graces received. The "confession" of praise is more important than the avowal, the greatness of God more than the wretchedness of man.[14] Every time we read, in St Bernard or some other text of his time, the word *confessio*, we should determine by the context if it means sacramental confession made to a priest or a disclosure of conscience between monks or nuns, and if the accent is on the avowal of sins or gratitude for pardon.

The *confessio*, understood as a spiritual colloquy, was not only practiced with the abbot and prior, but also, according to a formula of St Bernard already cited, with "spiritual brothers," who were not "officials" or "obedientiaries." These latter were especially busy with the administration of goods and the material organization of the monastery. Somewhat as in the houses of Jesuits, there was a "minister of temporal affairs" and a "minister of spiritual affairs."[15]

Can we get a notion of the character of these intimate dialogues? Bernard has left us two descriptions of them which are as suggestive as they are brief. In the first, he speaks of confidences he has received:

Many of you too, as I recall, are accustomed to complain to me in your private conversations (*privatis confessionibus*) about a similar languor and dryness of soul, an ineptitude and dullness of mind devoid of the power to penetrate the profound and subtle truths of God; devoid too, entirely or for the most part, of the sweetness of the spirit. What do these, except that they yearn to

14. I have developed these ideas in "Confession and the Praise of God," *Contemplative Life*, CS 19, and "Confession et louange de Dieu chez S. Bernard," *La vie spirituelle* 120 (1969), pp. 588–605.

15. The expression recalls the *spirituales seniores* spoken of in RB 46:5.

be kissed? That they yearn is indeed evident, their very mouths are open to inhale the spirit of wisdom and insight: insight that they may attain to what they long for, wisdom to savor what the mind apprehends.[16]

So, in this text where we find the expression *privatis confessionibus,* the usual avowal of faults is not found, the monks do not accuse themselves of their sins. They complain, they lament; apparently they even accuse God: *conqueri solent.* But, in reality, they admit, by what they say, their lack of fervor and spiritual understanding. They make an act of humility and express their desire for God. And the spiritual man who, on God's side, witnesses this, is there to encourage them.

In another place, St Bernard spoke of the spiritual direction that he and others had received from the monk Humbert:

What a counsellor! How honest and discreet! I could appreciate it all the more since I had more often the opportunity of placing my head on his breast. But I am not the only one who knew him well; in this respect, you have been able to know him as well as I. Who is there, when struck down by the number and strength of his temptations, has not learned from his mouth of their source and their remedy? He knew so well how to penetrate into the corners of a sick conscience that the man confessing to him might believe that he had seen everything, assisted at everything.[17]

We can also believe that these spiritual relations existed among other monks of whom Bernard did not have the occasion to speak.

3. *Formation*

One question we cannot help asking is how they then formed young monks. Now, on this point, we must accept a disappointment: some of the things which interest us the most are things of which the monks of the Middle Ages speak the least. We are left with but a few allusions. "One monk forms others"—*illum alios erudientem,* these three words, already noticed in a description of the

16. SC 9:3, OB 1:43f, CF 4:55.
17. Humb 4, OB 5:444, CF 34.

community of Clairvaux, tell us that they formed, but not in what
manner. Elsewhere, the brief references to initiation to monastic life
are enveloped in Biblical poetry, borrowing the image of the
maternal womb. They leave us unsatisfied.[18] This absence of texts
on the subject of formation confirms a statement already made in
other places; in the monasteries, there was no organized teaching,
outside of the one which consisted in learning to read and which
was "pre-monastic," that is, given before the beginning of the
monastic life itself. What forms one is the contemplative community all together; the only pedagogy is example.[19]

In his published sermons, St Bernard has sometimes, although
rarely, spoken of novices; but, curiously, he did not always address
them directly, and what he wrote for others about them was
marked both with that vagueness and exaggeration which a stately
literature requires. In *Sermon Nineteen on the Song of Songs* he
warns them, as we have seen, against an excessive fervor which
would incite them to try to surpass the austerity commonly
practiced.[20] In the *Third Sermon on Psalm Ninety,* he alludes, by means
of poetic images, to these young plants—*novellae plantationes*—who
are subject to illusions.[21] Geoffrey of Auxerre has reported two
exhortations in which Bernard happily (*iucunde*) comforted his
monks and especially the young recruits—*tirones*. One of their
problems consisted in being "corrected harshly, even for the
slightest failings," *etiam super minimis negligentiis increpari*.[22] At any

---

18. Ep 2:2, LSB, p. 11; Ep 233, LSB, Ep 312, pp. 382–384.

19. This conclusion which I reached in a study entitled "Les études dans
les monastères du Xe ua XIIe siècle" in *Los monjes y los etudios* (Poblet: 1963),
105–117, was confirmed by A. de Vogüé, reviewing this work in *Rev.
d'ascét. et de myst.* 40 (1964), p. 501. It is also that conclusion which lead me
to make new investigations on "Pédagogie et vie spirituelle du VIe au IXe
siècle," which will appear with the acts of the congress held at Spoleto in
April 1971 on the *Schools of the Middle Ages*. "We do not know with exactitude anything about the studies preparatory to the priesthood in the Cistercian
abbeys."—P. Villaret, *Bernard de Clairvaux*, p. 43, n 14.

20. SC 19:7, cited above, p. 97, nn 33–34.

21. QH 3:1, OB 4:392, CF 43.

22. Text cited in *Etudes sur S. Bernard*, p. 69. Similar expression: *tirocinii
nostri tempore, ibid.* p. 153.

rate, Bernard encouraged them but he did not give instruction on how to become monks.

Fortunately the tradition of Clairvaux has conserved the memory of some of his doings—now legendary—in favor of those whom he had, like fish, caught for God and brought to the pond of Clairvaux.[23] Geoffrey of Auxerre in his great panegyric of Bernard writes: "At that time, many of them, like sheafs of first fruits from the harvest, were beaten and crushed. In the meantime, as it often happened, either for the interests of the monks or the entire Church, he had to absent himself for a few days; but he remained with them in spirit. When he returned, he went immediately to see the young recruits, around eighty in number. He greeted them, spoke a bit—*quibus salutatis, non multum locutus,* and called one of them. He said: 'Be sure that when you did not see me, I saw you, sad and very tired; I heartily desired peace for you; I cried with you.' Then, drawing him nearer, he embraced him and consoled him magnificently—*osculatus ac magnifice consolatus est eum.*"[24] There is no teaching here, only an understanding heart. Elsewhere, Conrad of Eberbach, describing the same scene with more details, mentions the "exhortations" of St Bernard to the novices. This second account contains supplementary information which is worth citing: "Having finished the business which had been the reason for his departure, as soon as possible after his return—*quam citius,* he went to the novitiate. The little ones, still young, whom he had nourished with his milk, were comforted by his consolations, all the more so because they had been deprived of the sweetness of his counsels for a long time . . . So he entered the novitiate, and with his calm and edifying conversation—*in lingua sua illa placabili et aedificatoria,* he made them joyful and smiling—*hilares*—and more fervent in the observance of the Rule." Here is noted the conversation that he had with the novice of whom he had thought during his absence: "I held you in my arms; I caressed you, but you turned your face away; you

23. On these comparisons, *Etudes sur S. Bernard,* p. 252 and A. Dimier, *S. Bernard ,,pêcheur de Dieu,"* p. 7.

24. *Sermo in anniversario obitus S. Bernardi* 3, PL 185:575.

cried, so that my cowl was all wet with your tears." And saying this, Bernard gave him some spiritual advice—*spiritualibus monitis,* freed him from his sadness and restored him to the liberty and joy of spirit."[25]

An allusion of the biographer Herbert tells us much, also, about the care he took of the novices: "One day, as was his custom (*solito more*) he entered to console the brother novices—*ad solatiandos novitios fratres,* who, at the time, were over a hundred. He started by inflaming them with the love of heavenly realities by his ardent words—*illo suo ardenti eloquio,* exhorting them in a very consoling way—*in exhortatione et consolatione multa.* In terminating, he promised them that if they persevered, they would all go to heaven."[26]

Lastly, here is a fact which takes the form of a parable. It reveals Bernard's goodness, which alone can explain the huge recruitment of Clairvaux. "Dom Henry, the first abbot of that Danish monastery which is called Vitskol, that is, School of Life, *Vitae Schola,* used to relate that, when he was a novice, along with ninety others, he was formed by the teaching of Blessed Bernard—*sub disciplina Beati Bernardi institueretur.* One day as they were lying down to rest, Bernard came to visit his sons in the dormitory. He was followed by a lay brother carrying a basket full of cheese. Approaching Henry, then master of the novices—*tunc prior novitiorum*—he offered him, with great kindness, a piece of cheese, saying: 'Eat, my brother, for you still have a long way to go.'[27] Then going among the novices, he gave each one this extra snack, repeating the same thing to each one. Thus, while he gave in an enjoyable way—*iucunde*—a little extra strength to their bodies, at the same time he stimulated their spirits in the hard and narrow path they had begun to follow."[28]

What should we conclude from these texts and facts? First of all,

---

25. *Exordium magnum,* D 2, c 12, ed B. Griesser (Rome: Editiones Cistercienses, 1961), pp. 105–06.

26. *De miraculis* 2:11, PL 185:1302–1303.

27. 1 Kings 19:7.

28. *Exordium magnum,* D 6, c 10, ed Griesser, p. 366.

that St Bernard himself took great personal care of the novices, many of whom he knew had entered Clairvaux under his influence or because of his presence, and this even though there was what we might call a "novice master." He was aware of the difficulties of their life, their trials, temptations and moments of sadness. And he moderated the requirements of his teaching by much understanding, indulgence, kindness and good humor. The word *iucunde* reappears several times. But did Bernard teach the novices in a special way? Nothing is said of it, and everything indicates that he taught them the same as the monks. Nothing gives us any basis for saying, for example, he offered some method for learning how to pray. Everything, on the contrary, confirms the impression that the only two means of formation were the example of the older monks and confession, in the sense that was given above.

4. *Conversations*

Lastly, the communications among the members of the contemplative community of Clairvaux assumed many other forms. The intimate conversations Bernard had with his monks, and which we know were so different from the sermons he had published—so much simpler in their expressions and contents[29]— provided for "vertical input," as we say today, instruction given by superiors to subjects. But we know that it was traditional, in the Cistercian Order as in traditional monasticism, to have colloquies either about religious subjects or as a means of relaxation, of *recreatio*—but this word does not signify "recreation" as it is understood in modern usage.[30] This custom must have been present at Clairvaux as elsewhere. Bernard himself has left us some proof of this. On one occasion when he returned from one of his trips, the brothers expressed to him their surprise that he would accept a present of some dogs from a monk. They persuaded him to send them back

---

29. Cf *Etudes sur S. Bernard*, pp. 76–80 and *Recueil d'études* 3:167–171.

30. I cited these texts under the title "La récréation et le colloque dans la tradition monastique," *Rev. d'ascét. et de myst.* 43 (1967), pp. 3–21. About the medieval Cistercian tradition, p. 16 especially.

and, let us remark—we will soon give another example of this—he took the advice of his monks.[31] How many conversations of this sort must have taken place!

The necessities of the various occupations also required a good bit of fraternal conversation. Did they not have to assign the lay brothers to the different granges, settle their relations with the community, fix the turn of those who returned periodically to the monastery, organize the work, etc.? Herbert related, incidentally, that one day Bernard "went to visit his brothers busy harvesting in a field."[32] Most probably he did not go there just to keep silence. Let us consider again the activity of that chancellery where his secretaries—those he called *scriptores nostri*[33]—received his instructions about letters to write, where the person in charge assigned each one his duties, revised the texts, sent out the mail-carriers.[34] Let us not forget the scriptorium where they made copies of Bernard's works, transcribed those books of which he desired such a large quantity, and decorated them in a style he had originated.[35] Let us recall those art shops which produced paintings, statues, stained glass windows, ceramic tiles, altars—briefly everything that was needed for the housing and life of a vast community.[36] Nothing of all this could have been accomplished without the exchange of ideas.

Let us analyze a characteristic text—that last passage of the Letter Seventy where, counselling an abbot to be indulgent with a fugitive monk, Bernard confesses what had happened to him. It is a page which the editors of Clairvaux thought best to eliminate from his papers when the cause of canonization was being prepared. Cer-

---

31. Text in *Etudes sur S. Bernard*, p. 137.

32. *De miraculis* 3:20, PL 185:1328.

33. Ep 387, LSB, Ep 308, p. 378.

34. I gave indications on these subjects in studies entitled "Recherches sur la collection des épîtres de S. Bernard," 14 (1971) pp. 205–219 *Cahier de civiliation mmédiévale* and "Lettres de S. Bernard: histoire ou littérature?" *Studi medievali*, 1971.

35. I reproduced and characterized some specimens in *St Bernard and the Cistercian Spirit*, CS 16 (Spencer, Mass.: Cistercian Pub., 1972).

36. Cf *Bernard de Clairvaux*. pp. 527–530.

tainly they had to speak to one another, if such an event was to have taken place. Here are the main lines:[37]

First conversation: a stormy one between Bernard and his brother Bartholomew. Bernard becomes angry and expels Bartholomew—*furore commotus, vultu et voce minaci, praecepti ut de claustro exiret.*

Second conversation, or more exactly, series of conversations: Bartholomew went immediately to one of the monastery granges. There is excitement in the community; everyone is speaking of the affair at the abbey and in the granges. Bernard learns where Bartholomew is and tells him to come back. But he refuses to return, unless it is not as a fugitive put in the last place, but like an innocent man who has been sent away without counsel being taken and without judgment.

Third conversation: Bernard asks all the brothers to debate on this affair and his own attitude, without assisting himself at the meeting.

Fourth conversation: the community deliberates, judges in Bartholomew's favor (which is tantamount to condemning the abbot): "the expulsion was not made according to the rules."

Fifth conversation, of which nothing is said, but which we can imagine: the welcome given to Bartholomew by the monks who, doubtlessly, were very moved by the whole affair, and by Bernard who had had the humility to doubt his decision, to refer it to the judgment of the community and who will confess this moment of anger in a published letter. There is no doubt about the fact that he offered excuses and asked pardon.

37. The text is in PL 182:183. n 204; in *Etudes sur S. Bernard*, p. 90; in *St Bernard and the Cistercian Spirit*. About the circumstances of its suppression in the manuscripts of Clairvaux: *Etudes*, pp. 90–91, 102 and about the manner in which Rancé persuaded Mabillon to suppress it in his edition: *Recueil* 2:319, 326. On the file of texts that were prepared at Clairvaux shortly after the death of St Bernard in order to obtain his canonization: A. M. Bredero, "Etudes sur la 'Vita prima' de S. Bernard," ASOC 18 (1962), pp. 33–46. We are surprised that A. Dimier, "S. Bernard et ses abbayes-filles," ASOC 25 (1969), p. 261, n 81, could still say that the passage *Rem similem* with which Ep 70 ends, "seems to be an interpolation."

Lastly, sixth conversation, when, at Clairvaux, they decided to suppress this text: certainly they had to talk about that more than once!

We can even imagine, without being too fanciful, a seventh or series of conversations, when those who knew of the incident because they had witnessed it or had read of it in the register of letters that Bernard himself had published, expressed their surprise on seeing that some were trying to suppress it. Doubtlessly, they would not have been convinced by the kinds of arguments that Rancé put forth against the historicity of this "scandalous fact," for they had the highest regard for this abbot who was holy enough to admit his weaknesses publicly and to submit to the decision of his monks who did not approve his conduct. It can be explained by the fact that it was a question of preparing the dossier for the canonization to be presented to Rome.

This example—for it is really an *exemplum,* in the strict meaning of the term in spiritual literature—that Bernard wished to include in his writings, falls into the same category as another kind of communication which was practiced at Clairvaux, as elsewhere, that of fraternal correction. It took a form that has been called the "chapter of faults."[38] We have two very precise accounts of this. One concerns a monk of Clairvaux who refused to wash the dishes when it was his turn: "One day when Blessed Bernard was in chapter at Clairvaux, someone complained—*facta est conquestio*—about a brother who neglected to wash the bowls at the kitchen, even though it was his week, according to the custom of the Order." Bernard reproached him with it. But he "confused, murmuring something foolish and childish in a low voice, said, to excuse himself, that the work in the kitchen was too dirty and common." Bernard then corrected him severely, humiliating him profoundly. He closed, though, with a smile: "My son, be as eager to wash the bowls as you are to eat what is in them!"[39] On another occasion,

38. On the origins of the history of this observance, *Le défi de la vie contemplative,* pp. 226–270.

39. John the Hermit, *S. Bernardi vita quarta* 16, PL 185:549–550.

Bernard was at Pontigny. The brothers asked him a question about one of the members of the community who was sinning by that "singularity" described above. Bernard began to dialogue with him and encouraged him in such a persuasive manner that the guilty one immediately became "like an ordinary sheep of the common flock."[40] One of the rites in which they expressed pardon was the washing of the feet. Should we think that that was never the occasion for a reconciliation?

Many questions remain and we have to resign ourselves to the fact of not being able to answer with certainty and exactitude. What interests us the most about the monks of former ages is precisely what we know the least about. They have scarcely informed us at all about the details of daily life. I remember Fr Louis Merton once wrote me about the criticisms that were being made of his *Sign of Jonas:* "What I wouldn't give to have a diary of a Cistercian of the twelfth century!" But at the time, parchment was expensive. Monks did not buy it to be used for insignificant matters, at least what they considered insignificant; it would be so valuable to us. At least, through the little facts which escaped from the pen of Bernard and his historians, we can catch a glimpse of the intense very human life, which was the object of the communications that the members of a community as contemplative as Clairvaux exchanged with their abbot and among themselves.

CONCLUSION: EVALUATION OF A COMMUNITY

Fr Anselm Dimier has given this title, "Evaluation of a Community," to a suggestive chapter where he characterized the monks of St Bernard—the lukewarm and the fervent, those who are forgotten and those who are remembered as saint or blessed, as ecclesiastical dignitaries or writers.[41] Also, his erudition has permitted him to draw up a list of some two hundred "religious of Clairvaux, who lived during the abbacy of St Bernard" and with whom we are

40. Text in *Etudes sur S. Bernard*, b. 200, n 3.
41. *S. Bernard ''pêcheur de Dieu*,'' pp. 160–170.

acquainted by the documents.[42] What a variety in their social and geographical origins! What an expansion, if we consider the countries where they went! All Christian Europe was represented at Clairvaux and was influenced by it. What diversity, also, in the occupations of all these men! Of each one named or mentioned— for some are anonymous—an indication is given of what he did or what he became. The alphabetical list runs something like this: abbot, apostate, archbishop, architect, bishop, cardinal, cellarer, companion of Bernard during his voyages, founder, hermit, instructor of monks in Cistercian usages, interpreter (for Bernard for German), master of lay brothers, messenger, novice master, pope, porter, priest, prior, secretary, sub-prior. And there are those of whom nothing is said in the documents.

Certainly, Clairvaux was a contemplative community, as exceptional as its abbot. This extraordinary man exercised an influence which is unique in the history of monasticism; he did it by his personality and his writings, but also by the intermediary of his monks, many of whom were very ordinary, but some of whom transmitted his message in their own writings or influential activities. He was at the source of a literature which treated of the contemplative community, composed by anonymous or known authors like Geoffrey of Auxerre, Aelred of Rievaulx, Hugh of Barzelle, Baldwin of Ford, Alain of Lille, Helinand of Froidmont, and others.[43]

Neither Bernard nor his disciples hid the difficulties and problems inherent in leading together an existence whose object is the contemplative search for God in prayer and asceticism. Within each one of these men, and among them, how many were the possible conflicts, and how many real ones! But by God's grace, how many the means to vanquish them! To conclude, let us recall again one of

42. *Ibid.,* pp. 173–195.

43. I indicated these texts in presenting a "Sermon sur l'unité dans un ms. des Dunes," *Cîteaux* 11 (1960), pp. 212–213; also in *Etudes sur S. Bernard*, pp. 199–200. One of the most insistent is the one published by J. Morson, "The De cohabitatione fratrum of Hugh of Barzelle," *Analecta monastica* 4 (Rome: Studia Anselmiana 4, 1957), pp. 119–140.

those passages in which the customary teaching of St Bernard at Clairvaux has been condensed:

> Peace is fourfold. Peace with God and with one's neighbor, peace in the flesh and in the spirit. But so that all these forms of peace may be solidly established, we must give them a foundation; peace in the flesh will be founded on temperance; peace of the spirit, on fortitude; peace with one's neighbor, on prudence; peace with God, on justice. "Glory to God in the highest heaven,"[44] that is peace with God. "And peace on earth to men of good will,"[45] that is peace with one's neighbor. "Peace be to you, see my hands and feet,"[46] that is the peace of the flesh. "Receive the Holy Spirit,"[47] that is the peace of the spirit.[48]

Jean Leclercq OSB

Clervaux Abbey
Luxembourg

44. Lk 2:14.
45. *Ibid.*
46. Lk 24:36–39.
47. Jo 20:22.
48. Sent 1:29, OB 6.

SEEKING GOD IN COMMUNITY ACCORDING TO SAINT AELRED

Charles Dumont ocso*

TO THE MODERN MIND, contemplation and community hardly seem to go hand in hand. Contemplation belongs to the domain of the private, the interior, the individual; community to the domain of the public, the exterior, the visible. Surely the problem of the relations between society and the individual is particularly acute here, since solitude, silence and withdrawal from the world are essential conditions for any contemplative life.

It would seem however that this conflict made itself felt only gradually. The English mystics of the fourteenth century,[1] the Flemish and Rhineland mystics of the fifteenth century and the Spanish mystics of the sixteenth century laid an ever increasing

*Fr Charles Dumont is a monk of the Abbey of Notre Dame de Scourmont in Belgium. He is editor of *Collectanea Cisterciensia* and has published a number of articles on Aelred of Rievaulx. He has also prepared the critical edition and translation of some of Aelred's Works.

1. ". . . the religious climate of the age was sympathetic to a personal and 'mystical' approach to the way of perfection; the older conception of the monastic life as the only secure way of salvation, the ark in the flood, had lost its wide appeal and its place had been taken, for earnest seekers, by the way of personal, if not solitary, endeavor. Similarly, with the breakdown of the vast theological synthesis, the way of truth might be shown in a more concrete form by the seer—a Catherine of Sweden, a Bridget of Sweden or a Julian of Norwich—or found for himself by the solitary contemplative." D. Knowles, *The English Mystical Tradition* (London: Burns & Oates, 1961), p. 43. In the same book, Prof. Knowles describes Hilton as "a strong, original, masterful and independent personality," Rolle as "individual in style and approach," and the author of *The Cloud* as "profoundly original.'

115

emphasis on the individual and psychological side of the contemplative life. Civilization played a decisive role in this evolution:

> The primitive is a condition of life wherein the instinctive, subjective and collective values tend to predominate; the civilized condition of life is when the rational, objective and individual take command.[2]

But any civilization that developed the individual absolutely, regardless or rather in spite of society, would produce only monsters. An equilibrium is necessary. It seems to us even more necessary today than in the twelfth century, since today, in a total society that threatens to engulf private life more and more, individualism has reached its paroxysm. This conflict is at the root of a good many of the problems of religious life today.

It is very interesting to study the life of a contemplative community of the twelfth century, because it was at this period that original thinking on conscience and freedom began to bring out the value of the person. I have no wish to minimize the decisive role of St Bernard, who took up these two themes outlined by St Anselm. But a knowledge of St Aelred seems to me very useful here, for, as all his writings bear witness, he was more exclusively intent than St Bernard on forming and leading a contemplative community.

Aelred was independent and even original, careful to speak the new language and to take part in the effervescent renaissance of the twelfth century with its daring speculations. But while Abelard became "the first modern man," Aelred, like St Bernard, remained attached to tradition—to St Gregory, and above all, to St Augustine. Faithful to tradition yet men of their times, the Cistercians, in a sense, saved the ancient discipline by adapting it to the spirit and language of the age. The idea of poverty, for example, which was to lead "evangelical" sects into heresy, found its realization in Cistercian austerity; and freedom was able to flourish within the Cistercian community by means of an admirable balance that one is tempted to call pluralism. The success of the Cisterican Order was

2. L. van der Post, *Journey into Russia*, as quoted in *The Tablet*, Feb. 6, 1971, p. 129.

due to the soundness of its spiritual doctrine—renewed though it was—quite as much as to its organization; and it was by the spiritual freedom it allowed to the communities that the Order's organization helped to bring it this success.

One of the things that strikes one most in reading our Cistercian authors is the breadth of the theological synthesis to which all being and all action are referred. In Aelred's spiritual world, and according to his anthropology, the expression "contemplative community" loses any suggestion of paradox and becomes perfectly straightforward.

Contemplation and charity

Contemplation, because it is essentially the restoration of charity, spontaneously creates a genuine community; and any community worthy of the name must be to some extent contemplative, because this contemplation–charity is the bond of its unity. Contemplation and community interact. Aelred's doctrine on this point is extremely precise, as I hope to show. But first it is necessary to retrace the main outlines of this theological synthesis, which he himself expounds at the beginning of his great treatises and in several sermons and to which he constantly refers back.

Like every true contemplative, like all the mystics, Aelred is homesick for unity. He feels a need to put everything into its proper order, not so much intellectually as affectively, and to gather everything together in the peace and tranquillity of a loving heart and a loving community. Before all multiplicity there is the unity of God, where every being has its origin and end.

All these things should bring you back to unity, because one thing alone is necessary. And this one thing can only be found in the One, near the One, with the One, in whom there is no change or shadow of alteration. He who cleaves to him is made one spirit with him. He is carried away into this One ever identical with himself, whose years do not pass away. This cleaving is charity.[3]

3. *De institutione inclusarum* [hereafter RR] 26 SC 76 (Paris: Cerf 1961), p. 106, tr M. P. Macpherson "A Rule of Life for a Recluse" *The Works of Aelred of Rievaulx* vol. 1, Cistercian Fathers Series no. 2 (Spencer, Mass.:

Contemplation is here clearly defined as a cleaving to God. To cleave to God to such an extent as to be one spirit with him *is* charity.[4] This deliberately voluntaristic, non-intellectual nature of contemplation is very marked in all Aelred's work.[5] It is within this general picture of the restoration of charity that one must situate monastic community if one wants to grasp the importance that it has in the blueprint of the spiritual or contemplative life. Indeed, it is so important and indispensable for the Cistercians that if one abstracts from it their spirituality becomes incomprehensible and their ascesis falls apart.

The image of God regained in community

At the beginning of *The Mirror of Charity* (*Speculum caritatis*), a youthful work whose breadth and finesse he was never later to equal, Aelred outlines a veritable system of Christian metaphysics. In the created world man has the capacity to be happy because he is

Cistercian Pub. 1971), p. 74. Cf *Speculum caritatis* [hereafter MC], 1:15 and 3:1 (CCM 1:18, 105) [CCM 1 = *Aelredi Rievallensis, Opera omnia*, 1, *Opera ascetica.* Ed. A. Hoste and C. Talbot. Corpus Christianorum, Continuatio Mediaevalis I. Turnhout, Brepols, 1961]. tr P. Fortin, "The Mirror of Charity," *The Works of Aelred of Rievaulx*, vol. 3, Cistercian Fathers Series, no. 17 (Spencer, Mass.: Cistercian Pub., 1972).

4. "Joseph" interpretatur "augmentum." Scire debeamus quod Dominus creavit rationalem creaturam ut esset particeps beatitudinis illius, ita ut nihil aliud illi posset sufficere ad beatitudinem, nisi solus Deus. Et haec est tota perfectio rationalis creaturae et omne bonum adhaerere illi. Et ideo recedens ab eo, tendit ad nihilum. Et hoc modo omne detrimentum hominis fuit, recedere a Deo. Idcirco, quando homo convertit se ad Deum, tunc incipit augmentum ejus. Et ideo si volumus ad ipsum ascendere, primum est ut convertamur ad eum et sic incipit augmentum nostrum. *In nativ. B.M.V.*, PL 195:329, tr T. Berkeley, *The Works of Aelred of Rievaulx*, vol. 4, CF 23.

5. Eia, fratres, hoc judicio videat unusquisque utrum sit discipulus Jesu, non interroget sapientiam suam, non sensum, non facultatum distributionem, non corporis consumptionem. *Si enim linguis hominum loquar, et angelorum,* ait Apostolus, *caritatem autem non habeam, nihil sum* (1 Cor 13). Non, inquam, exteriora haec interroget, sed cordis sui amorem exploret. Qui enim diligit Deum, diligit et fratrem suum. Si ita tamen diligat, ut idem Jesus praecepit: *Hoc est praeceptum meum, ut diligatis invicem, sicut dilexi vos.* (Jn 15) *In festo omnium sanctorum,* PL 195:349.

made in the image of his Creator and is able to cleave to him whose image he is: "My joy lies in being close to God" (Ps 72:28). This cleaving is not material, like that of a seal in wax, but belongs to the spiritual order.[6] The relation between the image and the model is dynamic and causal. Hence we understand, why, when the image no longer cleaves to its model, it becomes deformed. Following St Augustine, Aelred describes the soul as being the image of the Trinity by its three faculties, memory, intellect and will. But it is significant that all Aelred's attention is devoted to the last, the will or the faculty of loving. Our happiness depends on all three, but chiefly on the third, because love is beatitude itself. Where there is no love there cannot be joy. "Memory can give us much, the intellect can understand deep things, but there will only be joy if the will turns towards the things given or understood."[7]

Endowed with free will, man was able either to lead a perpetually happy life in unfaltering love of God, or to turn his love away from him. He chose the latter course; but when he turned away from God his love grew cold and he fell into destitution.[8] Blinded by

6. Huius beatitudinis sola rationalis creatura capax est. Ipsa quippe ad imaginem sui creatoris condita, idonea est illi adhaerere, cuius est imago, quod solum rationalis creaturae bonum est, ut ait sanctus David: *Mihi autem adhaerere Deo bonum est.* Adhaesio plane ista non carnis, sed mentis est. MC 1:9, CCM 1:16.

7. Verum licet in his tribus vel his tribus ipsa perficiatur beatitudo, in hoc tamen tertio proprie est ipsius beatitudinis gustus. . . . Pariat licet multa memoria, capiat licet profunda scientia, nulla tamen delectatio si non ad parta vel nota ipsius fiat voluntatis conversio. *Ibid.* p. 16–17.

8. Potuit et ipsum amorem suum ad aliquid minus reflectere, sicque ab eius amore recedendo frigescere, seseque miseriae addicere. MC 1:11, CCM 1:17. Cf *Sermones inediti*, ed C. H. Talbot, Series Scriptorum S O Cist. (Rome, 1952), p. 71–2: Ubi enim superabundat iniquitas et refrigescit caritas, ibi collocat sedem suam. . . . *Ponam,* inquit, *sedem meam ad aquilonem et ero similis altissimo* (Is 14:14). And there follows a striking description of the envious monk within whom Satan has taken up his abode: "in illa mente, quae a caritatis calore refriguit." This love is the vision of God, as we see from a passage in a sermon for the Feast of St Benedict: "Transiit namque cum Moyse, ut videret illam magnam visionem; non quomodo rubus arderet et non combureretur, sed quomodo beati angeli, et aequales angeli sancti Dei semper amore ardeant, et in eis numquam amor refrigescat." PL 195:247, tr M. B. Pennington, " St Aelred's Sermons for the Feast of

concupiscence, he turned his love towards what was less worthy of it. By loving wrongly he lost God and lost himself.[9] In trying clumsily to be like unto God by his "curiosity," that is, in seeking a model other than him whose image he was, he became more and more unlike him.[10] Because he no longer cleaved to God his memory sank into forgetfulness, his intellect sank into error and his love shrank.[11]

However, while the image of God has been deformed and corrupted by sin, it has not completely disappeared.[12]

How can the ruined image be restored? Once more, it is the will, now rectified by charity, that will lead the two other faculties.

> It seems to me obvious that just as it was . . . by an affection of the mind that man in his pride departed from the supreme Good and, growing cold, corrupted the image of God within him, so it is by an affection of the mind that he will draw nigh to God in humility and be renewed in the image of his Creator. Hence the

St Benedict", (hereafter ABen-Cist, S 4 (1969), p. 82. It was Origen who, following Greek philosophers, put the soul (*psyche*) into etymological relationship with *psychros*, growing cold. But Aelred probably found this theme in St Augustine, *Enarr. in Ps.* 147, 23:10 (CC 40:2159). See on this question: M. Aubineau sj, "Exégèse patristique de Mt 24:12: Quoniam abundavit iniquitas, refrigescet charitas multorum," *Studia Patristica* 4-2:3-19 (Oxford 1959), (Berlin: Akademie Verlag, 1961).

9. We quote the text in full, to show the verbs indicating the deviation of love: Libero ergo male usus arbitrio, amorem suum ab illo incommutabili bono deflexit, et ad id quod minus erat propria cupiditate caecatus reflexit, sicque a vero bono recedens, et ad id quod ex se bonum non erat deficiens, ubi aucupabatur profectum, invenit defectum; perverseque diligendo seipsum et se perdidit et Deum.—MC 1:12, CCM 1:17.

10. Sicque iustissime actum est, ut qui contra Deum Dei appetebat similitudinem, quo voluit fieri curiositate similior, eo cupiditate fieret dissimilior. *Ibid.* This view about *curiositas* is interesting; it is also curious to see curiosity conquered by fraternal charity. In a sermon for Pentecost, Aelred gives three characteristics of the dove: without spleen, moaning, and flying in flocks—*gregatim volat.* It is thus that the Holy Spirit makes us wrestle against the three concupiscences. By the unity of the community the pride of life is conquered and the curiosity of the eyes disappears: curiositas oculorum fraternae caritatis evanescit dulcedine. *Serm. ined., op. cit.,* p. 110.

11. "amorem cupiditas coangustat," MC 1:12, CCM 1:17.

12. "corrupta est itaque in homine Dei imago, non abolita penitus," *ibid.*

Apostle says: "Your mind must be renewed by a spiritual revolution, so that you can put on the new self that has been created in God's way."

How will this renewal be brought about, if not by the new commandment of charity, of which the Savior said: "I give you a new commandment"? If the mind perfectly puts on this charity, it will doubtless reform also the two other faculties which we said had equally been corrupted, the memory and the intellect. It is therefore most salutary for us to have, thus summarized in a single precept, the putting-off of the old man, the renewal of the mind and the restoration of the divine image.[13]

Aelred was to say later that the image remains in man's "nature." *Natura* here is not used in the scholastic sense but in one nearer to the etymological root: *nasci, nativitas*; it signifies a being's radical aptitude, what it was made for, what it was born for. And, precisely Aelred says: "Charity raises our soul toward what it was made for, whereas cupidity lowers it toward what it instinctively seeks since its fall."[14]

More than twenty years later, Aelred gives this theological synthesis again in his treatise on *Spiritual Friendship*. This time he takes some of his inspiration from the Stoic vision of the universe which he finds in Cicero. God, the *ratio aeterna*, wills his creatures to be united in society and thus bear the mark of him who is the supreme unity.[15] That is why there is no tree unique in its kind,

13. Ideo saluberrime nobis indicitur istius unius praecepti compendium, in quo et veteris hominis exspoliatio, et mentis renovatio, et divinae imaginis consistit reformatio. MC 1:24, CCM 1:22. The same reasoning, identifying love with the will and hence defining charity by union, the cleaving to the Will of God, can be found in MC 2:53, CCM 1:91. See also, in the definition of the religious life: Ergo qui ordine voluntario ad culmen perfectionis aspirat, primo caritatem, qua Deo maxime propinquamus, immo qua Deo inhaeremus, eique conformamur, in qua totius perfectionis plenitudo consistit, MC 3:96, CCM 1:151.

14. MC 1:26, CCM 1:23.

15. Voluit autem, nam et ita ratio eius aeterna prescripsit, ut omnes creaturas suas pax componeret, et uniret societas; et ita omnia ab ipso qui summe et pure unus est quoddam unitatis vestigium sortirentur, *De spiritali amicitia* [hereafter SF], 1:53, CCM 1:298, tr E. Laker, "Spiritual Friendship," *The Works of Aelred of Rievaulx,* vol. 2, CF5 (Spencer, Mass.: Cistercian Pub., 1972).

why the animals seem by their cries and play to enjoy the good of society, why the joy of the angels is increased by their fellowship in charity, and why man was not created alone. Woman was drawn from man's side so that nature itself might show us that all human beings are equal, with the equality that is proper to friendship.[16] From the beginning nature set in the human heart the sentiment (*affectus*) of friendship and charity; but by the fault of the first man charity grew cold, cupidity crept in, personal preoccupations were put before the common good, and envy and avarice tarnished the brightness of charity and friendship.[17]

In a very fine sermon for Pentecost Aelred develops this doctrine of the image again, adapting it this time to another Trinitarian theme of St Augustine, *natura, species* and *utilitas*. While "nature" remains, beauty and utility have been lost. Here again, it is the aspect of service (*utilitas*) that holds Aelred's attention. God shares his goodness with his creatures; and he has created many men, with the same nature, so that they may render each other service and thus resemble and show forth that aspect too of the divine goodness. But man has made himself useless to himself by sin; he cannot be of use to others until the charity poured forth into human hearts by the Holy Spirit has restored in him the image of the goodness of God.[18]

16. . . . sed ad expressius caritatis et amicitiae incentivum, de ipsius substantia masculi feminam procreavit. Pulchre autem de *latere* primi hominis secundus assumitur, ut natura doceret omnes aequales, quasi *collaterales.* SF 1:57, CCM 1:298. This equality of the sexes, proved by a play on words but based on their common "nature," is interesting for the period.—In his letter to Gilbert Foliot, Bishop of London, Aelred says: Tam enim tuae sublimitatis, quam meae humilitatis oblitus, legibus amoris innitor, cui nihil humile nihil sublime. And a little further on: Diligere enim Deo, angelis, hominibusque commune est. Amor igitur quidquid extra naturam est non attendens, copulat naturam naturae, ut sit illis cor unum et anima una. PL 195:361–2.

17. At post lapsum primi hominis, cum refrigescente caritate cupiditas subintrasset, fecitque *bono communi privata praeponi* amicitiae caritatisque splendorem avaritia invidiaque corrupit. SF 1:58, CCM 1:299.

18. Sed quia anima rationalis Dei nil conferre potuit, creati sunt eiusdem naturae plures, ut in hac etiam parte similitudo divinae bonitatis, quae refunderet in multos, mutuis beneficiis appareret. Si igitur hanc distinctionem inter naturam, speciem et usum perspexistis. . . . Descendit et Spiritus sanctus,

These three expositions with their differing formulations explain clearly enough the fundamental doctrine of the restoration of the image of God in us by charity. This restoration takes place both in the soul and in the community. Society, disrupted by selfishness, returns to its original unity in the ordered peace of monastic communities united in charity.

The Community

In his prayer as abbot Aelred writes:

> . . . is not this your family,
> your own peculiar people, that has been led by you
>   out of the second Egypt, and by you has been
>   created and redeemed?
> And lastly, you have gathered them together
>   out of all parts, and made them live together
> in a house where all men follow a common way of life.[19]

The history of the People of God is re-enacted in each community, as in the Church and in each soul. Jerusalem, the *visio pacis*, Aelred says, is the Holy Church, each community and each soul.[20] One can see that this allegorical equation effaces any oppositions between the monk and the community. The primary expression of the religious and contemplative life is this ideal of community.[21] Like the apostles in the cenacle, the true disciples of Christ are gathered together in the same place; and by the charity poured forth in their hearts by the Holy Spirit they are able to appreciate "how

---

per quem diffusa est caritas in cordibus vestris, ut per illam utilitas amissa reparetur, sine qua nec alteri quisquam utilis invenitur. *Serm. ined., op. cit.,* p. 108–9. See St Augustine, *De civitate Dei* 11:24–5.

19. "The Pastoral Prayer," [hereafter PP] tr R. P. Lawson, *The Works of Aelred of Rievaulx,* vol. 1, CF 2 (Spencer, Mass.: Cistercian Pub., 1971), p. 108.

20. *Serm. in Apparitione Domini,* PL 195:228.

21. Conventicula fidelium in una societate viventium, communis vitae societatem. *De oneribus* [hereafter SI] 18, PL 195:438, tr. A. Barrett, "The Burdens of Isaiah," *The Works of Aelred of Rievaulx,* vol. 5, CF 26. Migne by mistake counted an Advent sermon on Isaiah as the first of the sermons *De oneribus,* so that this one is 19th in the Patrology.

good, how delightful it is for all to live together like brothers." But to live together in the same place becomes impossible as soon as division and dissent arise.[22]

Aelred made several commentaries on the verse of the Canticle of Canticles: *nigra sum, sed formosa*. This, he says, describes the individual soul arrayed in virtues, but also the community:

> Each of you, my brethren, before coming here, had a soul that belonged to him alone. You have been converted to God, and behold, the Holy Spirit, the fire from heaven that Our Lord has cast upon the earth and would see kindled, has reached your souls and out of all your hearts has made one heart and one soul. This soul, our community, has all the virtues of the angels, and above all, that unity and concord thanks to which, although there are superiors and inferiors, what belongs to each individually belongs to all and what belongs to all belongs to each.[23]

This last formula, *singula omnium, omnia singulorum*, recurs frequently and expresses perfectly both the renunciation or detachment and the spiritual enrichment that result from this unity.[24]

This early community has its model in the early community of Jerusalem, but also in the Pauline doctrines of the Body and the Church. The monastic community is a miniature Mystical Body. The weak and the sick have no reason to be sad; the strong have no reason to be proud, because it is not for themselves that they are strong but for the others. Consciously to withhold one's services out of negligence or laziness is to defraud the community, for the virtues and capacities of each member belong to all. If the true unity of charity reigns among the brethren, what each does is for all and what belongs to all belongs to each, provided only that he does not

22. *Serm. ined., op. cit.*, p. 111.

23. *In fest. omnium sanctorum*, PL 195:347. Cf SI 5: Exaltate vocem (Is 6:2). . . . Potest in vocis exaltatione fervor ille exprimi, qui in turba fratrum valde necessarius est, ut per oris sonum interior ille ignis erumpat undique, et sic se erigant invicem et accendant, quatenus una flamma effecta de multis. PL 195:382.

24. Inter fratres tanta unitas, tantaque concordia, ut singula videantur omnium, et omnia singulorum. MC 2:43, CCM 1:87.

leave the community or separate himself from it by discord and envy.[25]

The same idea is developed in the *Third Sermon for the Feast of St Benedict*. It should be noted here how attentive the Abbot of Rievaulx is to the gifts and weaknesses, the different aptitudes and needs, of each of his monks:

"For each one has his proper gift from God; one this and indeed another that." One can offer more work; another, more vigils; another, more fasting; another, more prayer; and another, more *lectio* or meditation. From all these offerings one tabernacle is made, so that, as our legislator declares, no one says or presumes that anything is his own, but all things are common to all. This is to be understood, my brothers, not only of our cowls and robes, but much more of our virtues and spiritual gifts. Therefore no one should glory on his own over any grace given him by God as if it were his own. No one should be envious of his brother because of some grace, as if it were exclusively his brother's. Whatever each one has he should consider as belonging to all his brothers, and whatever his brother has, he should not doubt that it is also his own. Indeed, almighty God can immediately bring to perfection anyone he pleases, and give to each one all the virtues. But his loving provision for us is such that each one needs the other, and what anyone does not find in himself, he has in the other. Thus humility is preserved, love increased and unity realized.[26]

We see in this text that it is the community's perfection that is sought and that even spiritual graces are pooled.

It is in this sermon, too, that the well-known passage about the lay brothers occurs:

Let not our lay brothers bewail that they do not sing or watch as much as the monks. Nor the monks, that they do not work as much as the lay brothers. For in very truth I say: whatever one does, this belongs to all; and whatever all do, this belongs to each. For just as the members of one body have not all the same

25. *In fest. omn. Sanct.* PL 195:347.
26. PL 195:249. ABen. p. 85.

function, yet, as the Apostle says: "The many are one body, each one a member of the other." Therefore let the weak man say: I am strong; because, just as in him his brother has patience in infirmity, so he in his brother has strength in endurance.[27]

The Cistercian community was organized into three categories. It is not easy to tell how much importance this diversity had in practice, but it must be mentioned here. There were the *prelati,* the *obedientiales* and the *claustrales.* The last were freer than the others to give themselves to spiritual exercises (*lectio, oratio, meditatio*), and were also of course the most numerous. They do not seem always to have appreciated the privilege of regular observance, and Aelred puts them on their guard against the vices that threaten them: laziness and criticizing superiors and officers."[28] Needless to say, the beautiful ideal of the community of brethren, image of the Trinity, was humbly lived out in the midst of a good many difficulties and failings. Nor does Aelred hide them:

> Beware lest dying flies destroy the sweetness of the oil. The sweetness of the oil is the sweetness of fraternal love; the flies, cupidity, envy and suspicion, which destroy such love. For no one who sets his heart on anything of this world loves perfectly.[29]

The abbot

There are two ways of leading a flock. One can drive it before oneself by threats, so that the sheep walk in fear. Or, if they are well trained, one can walk ahead of them and they will follow spontaneously. Correspondingly, there are two ways of following a shepherd. The monk who, having experienced it several times, has acquired a taste for the sweetness of God, follows the shepherd willingly. He can say: "I run in the way of your commandments, for you have enlarged my heart."[30]

This distinction between fear and love (*minatio, secutio*) is classic.

27. *Ibid.*
28. *In fest. SS Petri et Pauli,* PL 195:295–7.
29. PL 195:249. A Ben, p. 86.
30. *Serm. in Adventu,* PL 195:217.

Every monastic life is marked by these two stages. But the distinction is perhaps rather eclipsed today by all the talk of "adult" and responsible behavior. The two are not unconnected, but the classic distinction belongs to the spiritual order rather than the psychological or sociological order; and it is of the highest importance still.

Moreover, it is not only bishops, abbots and priests who should feel pastoral concern. Every monk is a pastor, by the example of his life and virtues.[31]

The abbot's role in the good ordering of the community is obviously primordial. It is he above all who unites it.

All of us here in this community form one single body. Some perform the duties of the feet, others of the eyes, others of the hands. It seems to me, my brothers, that the superiors fulfill the function of the hands. It is with his hands that a man feeds himself, defends himself and organizes himself. The superior feeds the others with his doctrine, defends them by his prayers, gives them their tasks, and comes between them and outward cares.[32]

In particular, it is the abbot who is bound to each and all by an attentive and often painful affection.

"Who suffers, and I do not suffer with him?"—to care for all, to fear for each, to be saddened by their loss, is a heavy burden. If you are pained, my brothers, when a brother leaves us or lives badly—you who are his brothers—, think what pain I must suffer—I who am both his brother and his father, am responsible for him and shall have to give account of him.[33]

In the *Twenty-eighth Sermon on the Burdens of Isaiah*, Aelred draws up a sort of directory for those with pastoral duties. It is also one of the spiritual itineraries so frequent in Aelred's work.

"Flying backwards and forwards like bewildered nestlings" (Is 16:2). Speaking of these birds, Aelred distinguishes two nests in

---

31. *In fest. SS Petri et Pauli*, PL 195:300.
32. *In assumptione*, PL 195:360.
33. *In festo omn. Sanct.*, PL 195:342.

which the soul is fledged, fed by a spiritual father and by its mother, grace. They are the nest of regular discipline and the nest of wisdom. This distinction is highly traditional. In Clement of Alexandria it already corresponds to the two degrees of *Pedagogue* and *Didascalos*, and still more broadly, to *praktike* and *theoria*. The first nest is that of asceticism, discipline and obedience, "for one cannot command well if one has not first learned to obey." Next, formed for living (*informatus ad vitam*), the soul passes to the nest of widsom, that is, to

the investigation of the Scriptures, to be enlightened in knowledge. When it has learned to refer everything in Scripture that has life and savor (*in Scripturis omne quod vivit et sapit*) to the love of God and neighbor, then, borne aloft on these two wings of knowledge and charity, it will fly to the mountain of contemplation.

One should note the order of the six degrees (especially the last two) in which this whole itinerary is summed up: conversion, purification, virtue, knowledge, contemplation, charity.[34]

Paradise now . . .

This formation of a contemplative community ought really to be described a little, and perhaps its difficulty and gradualness stressed. It is an aspect of the monastic life that is perhaps rather neglected today. In the definitions given of the monastic life its different stages and its dynamism are rarely presented.[35] And of course, one must first know where one is going. For Aelred, the aim is to form, here on earth, a community united in charity. He gives several allegories of this community: the zither, each string of which gives a different sound but blends with the others to make a single harmonious

34. SI 28, PL 195:482–5. With this graceful remark on one who, from being a disciple, becomes a spiritual master: qui hactenus audisti, deinceps dicas: 'Veni.' Cf nidus disciplinae, MC 1:16, CCM 1:19.

35. On the active nature of charity in this present life: Nec praetereundum, quod in naturarum aut formatione aut reformatione, quasi *in motu* caritas esse memoratur . . . ubi vero ipsa creatura Dei contemplatione et dilectione perficitur, *stare* nimirum perhibetur. *Serm. ined., op. cit.*, p. 35.

sound;[36] the wolf living peaceably with the lamb;[37] and the society of the angels.[38] But he twice compares it to Paradise regained. Once in a moment of euphoria as he passes down the cloister where his brethren are seated:

> I found not one in all that multitude whom I did not love and by whom I was not confident that I was loved. I was filled with a joy so great that it surpassed all the delights of this world. For I felt as though my spirit was transfused into all of them and that the affection of all had passed over into me, so that I said with the prophet: "How good, how delightful it is for all to live together like brothers."[39]

The second text comes from a sermon on the Annunciation:

> The peace of the cloister is paradise. A paradise even more beautiful, it seems to me, than that in which Adam was placed.

And then comes the usual description of the brethren each shining with a particular quality or charism.

> I think this paradise is preferable, by its beauty and spiritual fecundity, to the paradise from which the first man was cast out.[40]

Anyone who knows the significance of the paradise theme in monastic spirituality cannot fail to perceive the weight of this comparison. The same can be said of Aelred's comparison of the monastic community to the society of the angels. By these two comparisons we see that the monastic community realizes the restoration of the divine image, the unity of persons in charity.

36. "In cithara quoque cum multa sint chordae, et unaquaeque proprium habeat sonum, ita tamen omnes certis proportionibus et numerorum rationibus disponuntur, ut in unam concordiam omnes conveniant et pulcherrimus sonus fiat unus de omnibus. SI 21, PL 195:496. Baldwin of Ford gives the same allegory in his sermon *De duplici resurrectione*, PL 195:433–4.

37. *Serm. in Adventu*, PL 195:215.

38. *In fest. omn. Sanct.*, PL 195:347.

39. SF 3:82, CCM 1:334.

40. *Serm. ined.*, *op. cit.*, p. 88.

I

The three Sabbaths, or the three loves

It should be emphasized that the perfectly united community is an end; it is the perfection of charity and the very goal of contemplation.

It is also a means, a degree of purification. After *The Degrees of Humility* of St Bernard, Aelred, his best disciple, and all our twelfth-century authors took up the triple distinction between the love of self, of others and of God. It is classic, but at the beginning of the third book of *The Mirror of Charity* Aelred presents it in an original manner by commenting allegorically on the three kinds of Sabbath: that of the seventh day, the seventh year, and the Jubilee. The three loves are distinct and yet astonishingly bound up with one another. "Each is in the others and all are in each. To have one is to have the others, and if one is missing the others also disappear."[41]

It is rather imprudent to compare these three degrees of charity with the corresponding degrees of St Bernard. Pedrick,[42] followed by Hallier,[43] has pointed out that on this point the theology of Aelred is clearer and more coherent than that of St Bernard. The contrast must not be pressed too far, however: St Bernard never said that cupidity leads to love, and Aelred is not to be ranked among the partisans of what has been called ecstatic love.

For St Bernard as for St Aelred, love is an *élan* of the soul that only needs to be straightened out in order to take its right orientation again; and St Aelred, like St Bernard, maintains an ontological love of self right up to the highest degree of the love of God. If this love of self is absent, he says plainly in the text mentioned above, the love of others and the love of God will also disappear.

What St Bernard expresses less clearly is that a certain (*quae dam portio*) love of God precedes the love of self and of others, just as grace precedes an act of charity. This love of God is as it were the

41. MC 3:3, CCM 1:106.

42. B. Pedrick OSB, "Saint Ailred on the Relationship between Love of God and Love of Self. His solution compared with that of St Bernard." *The Buckfast Abbey Chronicle* 15 (1945). p. 16–26.

43. A. Hallier OCSO, *The Monastic Theology of Aelred of Rievaulx.* CS 2 (Spencer, Mass.: Cistercian Pub., 1968) p. 42.

soul and life of the two other loves. With this reservation, however, it remains true that the love of self precedes the love of one's neighbor, and the love of one's neighbor is a stage on the way to the love of God.[44]

These three stages or Sabbaths are three degrees in which the soul rests in an ever-increasing peace. In the first Sabbath, freed from sin, it recollects itself (*colligitur ad se*) in the purity of its conscience; in the second Sabbath, freed from cupidity, it opens up and goes out of itself (*extenditur extra se*) in a most sweet union of many minds; and finally, in the third Sabbath, freed from all tension, it is ravished out of itself (*rapitur supra se*) up to the very contemplation of God.[45]

Aelred says that it is by the purification carried out by the two other loves that the soul enters into the contemplation of God. But it is chiefly the second love that concerns us here, since it takes place within the community. In terms almost identical with those of St Bernard, Aelred describes it as a widening, an opening out in which the monk feels his soul unite with all his brethren in charity, embrace them all, so as to form with them one heart and one soul. The tumult of the desires is stilled and the heart somehow dilates and its capacity increases. Fraternal community life is therefore indispensable to the development of charity. The Cistercian community is a school of charity (*scola caritatis*), and we see here the very definite meaning that this schooling has. One learns to love by loving, and the heart that has renounced its narrow selfishness must learn to widen itself and to share with others the peace it enjoys. It is thus that it will learn to love God. One day, all love of self and others will be engulfed by love of God like sparks engulfed by a fire, and man will love himself and others only in so far as he and they are engulfed by God.[46]

44. MC 3:4. CCM 1:107.

45. MC 3:7–19, CCM 1:108–14.

46. *Ibid.* In a sermon for All Saints Aelred comments on the Beatitudes and takes up, in his own manner, St Bernard's commentary *De gradibus humilitatis*. Blessed are the merciful, whose "own necessity" makes them understand that of others. Nam qui student benefacere profecto mererentur Deum intelligere. Thus they purify their hearts and will see God. PL 195:351–2.

Meanwhile—*interim*—these three loves are born of each other, feed on each other, enkindle each other, and tend toward their perfection together. But although these three loves are inseparable, just as a king chooses different spices in his storehouse, so we in our changing lives ceaselessly pass from one to another, now enjoying the peace of our consciences, now the joys of brotherly love, now, more fully, the contemplation of God.[47]

This last point is important, for the image of successive degrees might give the impression that the first two are to be passed once and for all. We change from one to another according to circumstances and our dispositions, just as we alternate between spiritual and ascetic activities (*spiritualia, corporalia*).[48] And as we shall see, it is the same with human friendship and the divine friendship to which it leads.

The Cistercian way of life is very balanced, owing to its suppleness in adapting to the realities of human existence (with its temporal necessities), the weakness of our minds (which cannot fix themselves on the same thing for long) and the variety of characters and temperaments that will be found in any community. Within the same general framework of life, and without any dispensations from the different elements of the regular discipline, each monk can give the preference to what best suits his aptitudes and tastes—even in the beginning of his monastic life, as a passage from the *Twenty-eighth Sermon on the Burdens of Isaiah* attests:

Behold, my brothers: arriving fresh from the world, some are poorly educated or ignorant, others subtle and learned; some are slaves of their passions, others have no problems; some have led an easy life, others a hard life; some are lazy, others hard-working;

See also this fine passage: Si, etiam, tu in virtutibus dives alium his egentem agnoveris, si non spernas in eo carnem tuam, antiquae scilicet tuae infirmitatis similitudinem, sed quibusdam compassionis brachiis in tuum eum inducas affectum, egeno domus tuae ostium aperuisti. *Serm. ined., op. cit.*, p. 62.

47. MC 3:5, CCM 1:107.

48. Cf. C. Dumont, "L'équilibre humain de la vie cistercienne d'après le Bienheureux Aelred de Rievaulx," C Cist. 18 (1956), pp. 177–89; "St Aelred: The Balanced Life of the Monk," MS 1 (1963), pp. 25–38.

some are violent, others naturally gentle. The nature and dispositions of each must therefore be carefully studied: what he finds difficult, by what spirit or passion he is led, his habits, the examples or persons who influence him—all this has to be examined for each one. Some are to be protected from outward occupations and dangerous company, others, taking refuge in the shade of silence, flee occasions of anger and irritation. For some, it will be poverty or work or vigils that will save them from their roving hearts and unstable minds. Others will defend their souls against temptation by psalmody, silent prayer and *lectio*.[49]

Do people still come to the monastery today to conquer their passions more surely? I do not know. It is almost bad form to speak of them in our polite society. I suspect we are living in the illusion of a certain naturalism. But by drawing a veil of silence over this ethical aspect of the Cistercian vocation one makes its methods impossible to understand, and destroys their cohesion and inner logic.

Eremitism in common

If the common life—the *amor socialis,* or the "grace of living in society," as St Bernard was to say—occupies so important a place in the monastic project as lived at Cîteaux, Clairvaux or Rievaulx, one will not be surprised to see our Cistercian authors mistrust or even condemn the eremitical life. Here in St Aelred is one of the most explicit of the many relevant texts. It is about the three days' journey that Moses required Pharaoh to allow the Israelites to make, so that they might sacrifice to God in the desert (Ex 8:23). Our modern Moses, St Benedict, also prescribes a journey of three stages. Many complete the first stage, leaving the world, and even the second, giving up their evil habits:

But because they go apart by themselves into some forest or some other place, and eat when they want, fast when they want, watch when they want, sleep when they want, labor and rest when they

49. SI 28, PL 195:485–6.

want, without doubt they have not completed the third day's journey.[50]

That is, they have not abandoned self-will.

And those who live in community and seem to have left doing their own will, if they still seek certain freedoms so that they can go out when they want, speak when they want, work when they want, read when they want, do whatever they want as much as possible according to their own likings, they have not completed the third day's journey either.[51]

The renunciation of self-will and the development of the life of charity are for the Cistercians the chief motives for living in common. But by their silence and their respect for and insistence on the spiritual activities of *lectio* and meditation it is clear enough that they lived the lives of solitaries. They managed to find times and places for solitude. "Remember, my son," Aelred writes to Ivo, "what you are wont to murmur in the corners when, like the turtle-dove, that most chaste, solitary and mournful bird, you seek hidden retreats and build for yourself, in spite of the surrounding crowd, a daily solitude."[52] All the early Cistercians stressed this quality of their life.[53]

50. A Ben, PL 195:241–3, tr p. 74.

51. *Ibid.*

52. *De puero Iesu duodenni* [hereafter JT] 3:21, ed A. Hoste OSB, SC 60 (Paris: Cerf, 1958), p. 98, tr T. Berkeley, "Jesus at the Age of Twelve," *The Works of Aelred of Rievaulx,* vol. 1, CF 2:28.

53. "By the wonderful favor of God's loving care, in this solitude of ours we have the peace of solitude and yet we do not lack the consolation and comfort of holy companionship. It is possible for each of us to sit alone and be silent, because we have no one to disturb us with interruptions, and yet it can be said of us: 'Woe to him who is alone'. . . . We are surrounded by companions, yet we are not in a crowd." Guerric of Igny, *Liturgical Sermons,* tr Monks of Mt St Bernard, CF 8 (Spencer, Mass.: Cistercian Pub., 1971), p. 23–24.

Nihil certe tam facit ad amoris negotium quam solitarium esse, id est monachum. Nam religiosa et quieta monachi conversatio ipsa est quam sanctus amor desiderat: solitudo. Nec tamen amoris huius pietas in tantae solitudinis otio constituitur ut piae sollicitudinis timore privetur. Sed timorata

The freedom of charity

If we should submit ourselves to a senior we should submit ourselves also to the monastic tradition, and especially to the Rule of St Benedict, our spiritual father—he who, as St Paul would say, begot us to the spiritual life. St Benedict, or rather the Holy Spirit in him, ordered the monk's life within a community whose chief end was charity. This has two consequences: the freedom of our commitment, and discretion. Our commitment to the monastic life is as free and voluntary as love (*libertate spiritus*). This point is brought out particularly well in Book Three of *The Mirror of Charity*, where Aelred contrasts this *ordo voluntarius* with the *ordo naturalis* and the *ordo necessarius*. Even if the commitment is irreversible it is free to the end, because it has been chosen spontaneously; one must be very careful, he insists, not to forget this fact. This very interesting passage on the meaning of the monastic life has unfortunately been cut in two by the insertion, made by the author himself, of a "Disputation on the Rule and Profession." After this long excursus, Aelred again insists on the freedom of the *ordo voluntarius* by which anyone who tends toward the height of perfection must consider unceasingly the charity by which we draw near to God, or rather, by which we cleave to God and become conformable to him (*immo qua Deo inhaeremus eique conformamus*). It is the fullness of perfection, our end, the mark toward which we run. But besides meditating on charity, we must walk with unflagging enthusiasm along the path traced out for us by our vows and our profession: that is, the path of abstinence, watching, *lectio* and work. But if it should happen that charity, their only *raison d'être*, is violated because of one of these exercises, then obviously steps

---

et timida est semper amans anima, ne in amoris sui periculum sit a bono opere per negligentiam otiosa. "Res est solliciti plena timoris amor" (Ovid). Adam of Perseigne, PL 211:596, CF 21.

Omnes quippe in multitudine solitarii ibi erant, vallem plenam hominibus, ordinis ratione caritas ordinata singulis solitariam faciebat; quia sicut unus homo inordinatus, etiam cum solus est, ipse sit turba; sic ubi unitate spiritus et regulari lege silentii, in multitudine hominum ordinata, solitudinem cordis sui singulis ordo ipse defendebat. William of St Thierry, *Vita Prima Bernardi*, PL 185:248.

must be taken, and the exercises modified according to the capacities and state of mind of the individual. Here Aelred quotes texts of the Rule prescribing discretion.[54]

Social relations at Rievaulx

No one has spoken better of Aelred than Professor Knowles. An expert in twelfth-century English monasticism and charmed by Aelred's personality, he says:

> Gentleness, radiance of affection and wide sympathy are not the qualities which most would associate with the early Cistercians, but they are assuredly the outstanding natural characteristics of Alred.[55]

Aelred lacks the triumphant and compelling force of St Bernard, but

> he has something altogether his own, a delicacy, an intuition which, from being a gift of mind alone gradually came to be a reflection of the whole spirit, and which makes of his later years of rule an episode *sui generis* in English monastic life.[56]

And Professor Knowles stresses a quality which will have been appreciated in the texts we have quoted:

> The limpid sincerity with which he laid bare, in his wish to help others, the growth and progress of his own mind and heart from the human to the divine.[57]

54. MC 3:80–1 and 96–7, CCM 1:144–5 and 151–2. The same idea can be found in Isaac of Stella: "Any way of life that enables one to practice more sincerely the love of God and the love of one's neighbor for God's sake is thereby more pleasing to God, whatever may be the observances and habit with which it is lived. It is for the sake of charity that everything must be done or not done, changed or not changed. Charity is the principle by which, and the end towards which, everything should be directed. Nothing is done wrongfully that is truly done for and according to charity. May we receive it from him whom without it we cannot please. . . ." PL 194:1793, tr A. Saword, Cist. S 4 (1969), p. 250.

55. D. Knowles, *The Monastic Order in England* (Cambridge Univ. Press, 1949), p. 242.

56. *Ibid.*, p. 241.

57. *Ibid.*, p. 265.

I should like in this section to pick out some traits, remarks or allusions in Aelred's life and works that would help us to picture to ourselves the nature and forms of the social relations in the community of Rievaulx and its filiation. But the task is not easy. The strict rule of Cîteaux forbade any originality in this domain, and if, as is manifest, Rievaulx was an exception to the rule, it is not surprising that the traces are scanty—when they have not been deliberately effaced.

There is also the historical distance and the personality of Aelred himself. Anyone who has some familiarity with him will agree with Dom Knowles that

It is not easy to think of another in that age—unless it is Abelard—who so arouses and baffles all our endeavours to comprehend what comes so near to us and yet remains so far away.[58]

It must be admitted that his biographer, though he was his secretary and infirmarian, gives us little help. His pompous and conventional style and useless chatter can be very irritating; he could have told us so many interesting things. Moreover, the *Vita Aelredi* was probably intended to further the cause for Aelred's canonization. It contains the different parts necessary in such a document, and the *Letter to Maurice,* an apology for an apology, certainly seems to confirm that the literary genre is hagiographical.

Still, Walter Daniel does give us some data, sometimes unconsciously. The most interesting passage for the question that concerns us here is the description of the colloquies that took place, during the last ten years of Aelred's life, in the cabin that he had had built for himself beside the infirmary:

The construction of this cabin was, indeed, a great source of consolation to the brethren, for every day they came to it and sat there, twenty or thirty at a time, to talk together of the spiritual delights of the Scriptures and of the observances of the Order.[59]

58. *Ibid.,* p. 241.

59. Walter Daniel, *The Life of Ailred of Rievaulx.* Tr and ed, F. M. Powicke (London: Nelson, 1950), p. 40.

Were these gatherings wholly exceptional or did our twelfth-century monasteries, or at least Rievaulx, hold regular and more or less organized colloquies? A few texts in Aelred's works do at any rate allow us to affirm, I think, that meetings and colloquies were held. To begin with, there is the scene set in the first book of *Spiritual Friendship*. The work was intended for a monastic public, and Aelred is not afraid to speak of the way the monks gather round him each time he visits the abbey of Wardon, a daughter-house of Rievaulx.

> Just now, I was sitting in the turbulant group of the brethren. What a hubbub! One was enquiring, another arguing; one was asking questions about the Scriptures, another about moral theology, another about the vices and yet another about the virtues.[60]

The subjects dealt with are serious; they are the usual subjects: Scripture, moral theology, the vices and the virtues. But the manner of discussing them does not please Aelred; already we see here disputations and "questions" with no real effect on the lives and spiritual progress of those who take part in them. In the treatise, "Jesus at the Age of Twelve," Aelred writes to Ivo about the theological problem of Jesus' growth in knowledge (a problem that can still cause trouble today): "But as for you, my son, do not seek 'questions' but devotion; not what makes a discourse subtle, but what arouses the soul (*unde affectus excitetur*)."[61]

The second and third dialogues in the *Spiritual Friendship* are between three persons, Aelred, Walter Daniel and Gratian; they argue quite freely and tease each other at times.

The colloquies are mentioned in some of Aelred's sermons. The actual word *colloquium* is used several times, as is also the formula *convenientibus nobis in unum*. In the very fine sermon for the Presentation of Jesus in the Temple, Aelred sets the aged Simeon before his hearers as an example of the soul in search of God. Using the words

60. SF 1:2. CCM 1:289.
61. JT 1:10–11. Hoste, p. 69–70. CF 2:13–14.

of the Song of Songs, where the bride asks the watchmen: "Have you seen him whom my heart loves?" Aelred gives a commentary which I shall abridge a little:

> We must seek God when we are at leisure and alone, we must seek him when we are gathered together. . . . I am ashamed of our lukewarmness. Do we really love? Do we really seek? Do we really care about seeking? [It is not for me to try to judge what others do when they are alone, and what occupies their hearts; but I can judge what I actually hear.] My dear brothers, when we are gathered together, what do we seek? Obviously, each one seeks what he loves. There can be no denying that. There is no one who does not speak more readily of what he loves: out of the fullness of the heart the mouth speaks. And some speak of nothing but food and drink, others of rumors, others of their charges or the livestock or the buildings. One speaks "idle words and such as move to laughter," while another roars with laughter. There is hardly one who seeks the Word, hardly one who says to his watchman: "Have you seen him whom my heart loves?" On the contrary, in many of these meetings there is nothing but detraction, criticism, anger, quarrels, arguments. . . .
>
> "Prompted by the Spirit he came to the Temple": and you, if you have sought in the bed of your repose, now by reading, now by praying, now by meditating—you must seek in the city also, among other people, by questioning, conferring, discussing in the streets and market places, profiting by the words and examples of others; and seek among the watchmen, that is, the perfect, by hearing whom you too will be prompted by the Spirit to come into the Temple.[62]

In *The Mirror of Charity* we find this passage:

> If a mutual exchange in words (*verborum collatio*) gives us pleasure, let our conversation be about morality or the Scriptures. . . . And if, as is sometimes helpful, we relax our minds by turning to less lofty, more amusing subjects, let our relaxation be befitting and free from frivolity.[63]

62. In Ypapanti Domini. *Serm. ined., op. cit.,* p. 50.

63. MC 3:112. CCM 1:160-1.

For the Feast of St Benedict, speaking of fasting, Aelred deplores the ravages the passion of gluttony (*gastrimargie spiritus*; *gulae passio*) is making:

It is this [gluttony] that has almost the monopoly of the conversation in almost all our meetings, so that as soon as we come together (*conveniamus*) there is scarcely a conversation in which it does not hold first place. Nor does the impious beast blush to interrupt even holy and edifying words and to mingle its filth with the Scriptures, if by chance these have held the floor.[64]

In another sermon, speaking of Adonias, which means *Dominus Dominator*, he applies this name to the proud monk who loves salutations and the first place in choir and the refectory, and insists on speaking before the others at the colloquies (*primam vocem sibi vendicat in colloquiis*).[65]

In the *Fifth Sermon on the Burdens of Isaiah*, speaking of Isaiah's injunction, *exaltare vocem*, which he interprets as meaning "raise the level of your conversation," Aelred comments:

This is a healthy and necessary precept, especially at present, when almost every tongue is wagging the whole day long about trifles and harmful matters and rare are they whose conversation rises to higher things. Ah, my dear brethren, I am ashamed to say how detraction is heard on all sides and judgments grow heated whenever we are together. I am not speaking of those who love the world and talk about nothing but money and scandal; but what shall I say of those who seem to have renounced the ways of the world? Almost all their discussions and conversations are about their stomachs—and not merely about pleasing them, but about stuffing them. They are now troubled by anger, now cast down by gloom . . . because their mood is always dependent on their stomachs. . . . These people do not raise the level of their conversation, but lower it shamefully. And so do those who speak all day about the affairs of others, boast about their own doings, detract from others and, forgetting serious and useful things, speak only of what is vain and ludicrous.

64. *Serm. ined., op. cit.*, p. 65.
65. *Serm. ined., op. cit.*, p. 166–7.

It is against all these things that the prophetic word orders us to *exaltare vocem,* raise the level of our conversation, so that our own words may be of heavenly matters which will either instill the fear or love of God, or increase our knowledge or improve our morals.[66]

There is another question we may ask about these colloquies. To what extent did the abbots and monks speak of their spiritual or mystical experiences? Gilbert of Hoyland, who knew Aelred, says of him, "He showed great prudence in his mystical discourses, which he held only with the perfect."[67] St Bernard himself said in the *Twenty-second Sermon on the Canticle:* "I speak in public, in community, of what I have myself received *in communi.*" Aelred says simply that one may have experiences which it is impossible to express.[68] In one sermon he makes a distinction between the graces meant to be communicated and those meant to be kept to oneself (*eroganda, servanda*). Knowledge, wisdom and the understanding of the Scriptures are to be communicated to others, without arrogance but without reserve. The hidden graces (*occulta*) of compunction, devotion, prayer and contemplation are to be kept to oneself.[69]

Should one seek the company of holy monks? This is praiseworthy; one profits from their example, and if one is equally advanced both sides find support in the mutual exchange (*mutua collatione*). But if it necessitates a long journey one must think the matter over and not just follow the movements of one's heart. *Noli esse nimium justus*—Paul and Barnabus were separated from their brethren at Antioch, and Paul from Timothy![70]

Faced with the manifest fact that colloquies were held at Rievaulx, one may wonder to what extent they were authorized by the

---

66. SI 5. PL 195:384–5.

67. Prudens erat eloquiis mysticis quos inter perfectos dispensabat. *In cant.* 41. PL 184:217.

68. Sunt et alia quaedam experimenta quae sentiri quidem possunt ac explicari minime. *Serm. ined., op. cit.,* p. 142. Cf St Bernard: Melius impressum quam expressum innotescit. SC 9:3, OB 1:44, CF 4:55.

69. PL 195:356–7.

70. MC 3:55–6, CCM 1:131–2.

Cistercian discipline. Rievaulx and its houses in Yorkshire and Scotland were far from Cîteaux, and it is almost certain that St Bernard never made a regular visitation there. There is a statute of the General Chapter of 1152 which certainly seems to be aimed at the Abbot of Rievaulx, both for the colloquies that took place when he visited other monasteries and for those he held in his own infirmary.[71] And the same prescription is repeated in 1154: "Monks are forbidden to hold conversations when abbots arrive."[72] Eighty years later two statutes deal equally rigorously with the same question.[73] Whether these colloquies were legitimate or not, the fact that the General Chapter took up a position with regard to

---

71. 1152:4: *Cum quot monachis liceat abbati hospiti simul loqui.* Constituimus ut nullus abbas ad aliam domum veniens, monachum de labore sine licentia retineat, nec cum pluribus simul quam duobus loquatur, praeter abbates visitatores. Quos ei in auditoria, vel in locum proximum auditorio monachorum evocare liceat. Ceterum per curiam vel in infirmitorium, aut extra terminos sine abbatis licentia vel prioris si abbas defuerit, monachum ducere, exceptis ut diximus visitatoribus nulli liceat. Dum autem abbas cum duobus loquitur, si tertius supervenerit, stando breviter si necesse sit loqui poterit, sed consedere etiam rogatus non praesumat. Infirmis vero de infirmitorio vel cum duobus loquitur tantum vel cum singulis loqui poterit sive sit sanus sive infirmus, exceptis servitoribus qui ei deputantur si in infirmitorio fuerit, sed nullus nisi jussus vel evocatus ab eo accedere ad eum praesumat. Similiter infirmis et servitoribus eorum in infirmitorio vel juxta, et hoc (cum) tantum duobus abbas hospes loquatur, exceptis his qui ei, si in infirmitorio fuerit, deputantur, nullus nisi jussus et evocatus ab eo ad eum praesumat accedere. *Statuta Capitulorum Generalium Ordinis Cisterciensis,* vol. 1, ed. J. Canivez (Louvain, 1933), p. 46.

72. 1154.28: Prohibantur multiloquia monachorum in adventu abbatum. *Ibid.* p. 58.

73. 1232.5: Propter collationes illicitas de medio tollendas, statuitur ut quando monachi causa solatii ad colloquium ab ordinis custode vocantur, illud colloquium sit de sanctorum miraculis, de verbis aedificatoriis, et de his quae pertinent ad salutem animarum, exclusis detractionibus, contentionibus et aliis varietatibus. Hoc ipsum conservent abbates, ubicumque convenerint nisi de suis necessitatibus loquantur, et adiicitur praesenti statuto ne servitores inter se coram infirmario colloquantur. *Ibid.* 2:101.

1233.6: Definitio anni praeteriti de colloquiis abbatum et monachorum taliter reformetur: studeant abbates monachi pariter et conversi, ut quando ad colloquium conveniunt, talia inter se habeant colloquia, quae gravitatem redoleant et salutem respiciant animarum, attendentes quod de omni verbo otioso redditturi sunt aequissimo iudici rationem. *Ibid.* 2:112.

them shows that they did exist. Moreover, they were authorized later on, and we know that under Abbot de Rancé they were held in honor at La Trappe.[74] At Tamié the room for colloquies is still shown to visitors today.

FRIENDSHIP IN THE CONTEMPLATIVE COMMUNITY

Dom Leclercq has pointed out that St Bernard's ascetical and mystical teaching must be understood as primarily intended for monks.[75] This is even more true of the whole of St Aelred's spiritual doctrine. His *Spiritual Friendship* cannot be understood unless it is studied in the setting of the monastic community and from the point of view of spiritual progress. I will only treat here of two points which seem to me important and particularly enlightening: friendship as a degree leading to love of Christ, and the distinction between friendship and charity.

Friendship leading to Christ

Five times in his treatise on *Spiritual Friendship* Aelred repeats in almost identical terms the idea that the experience of a human friendship can lead to entry into the divine friendship. The experience one has in human friendship of a perfect harmony of feeling, brought about by Christ, is thus close (*e vicino*) to the experience of

74. VI. Conférences.—On prendra de ses lectures le sujet ordinaire des Conférences, et ces lectures seront de l'Ecriture sainte, de Saint Jean Climaque, de Cassien, des Vies des Saints Pères des Déserts, des Traités Ascétiques de Saint Basile, de S. Ephrem, des ouvrages de Saint Bernard, et de quelques ouvrages qu'ils ont composé plus pour échauffer le coeur, que pour éclairer l'esprit.
VII. On en bannira toute matière de Théologie Scholastique, de disputes, et de toute autre chose capable de déssecher le coeur, et elles se passeront de telle sorte, qu'elles soient utiles et encourageantes. A. Rancé, *Les Règlements de l'Abbaye de N.–D. de la Trappe* (Paris, 1616), p. 104–105.
75. "On n'a pas toujours remarqué suffisamment que toute la théorie bernardine de la restauration de l'image de Dieu en l'homme est une doctrine monastique". *Essais sur l'esthétique de S. Bernard, Studi Medievali*, 3 series, 9 (1968), p. 697.

friendship with Christ. The soul will therefore enter into friendship with Christ as though moved by the desire to taste more fully a joy which it already knows. This is quite in line with Cistercian spirituality, in which as we have already seen, the second degree, the love of others, opens the heart to the love of God. Thus the one experience leads to the other:

> The ascent, therefore, from the Christ who inspires the love with which we love a friend to the Christ who offers himself to us as a friend to love, does not seem to me too hard or contrary to nature. It is one happiness following another happiness . . . one love following another love. The friend who cleaves to his friend in the spirit of Christ becomes one heart and one soul with him; and so, by degrees of love, he ascends to friendship with Christ and becomes one spirit with him in a single kiss.[76]

The text, as we see, insists on the fact that Christ is already present in the experience of human friendship. This principle is formal, and is well expressed in the very first phrase of the first dialogue: "Here we are, we two; and Christ, I hope, makes the third." In Book Three, answering Walter's remark that he would be content with the cheerful camaraderie spoken of by St Augustine in the *Confessions,* Aelred replies that that friendship may be tolerated, but,

> with a deepening of the religious spirit and of zeal for spiritual things, with the gravity of a riper age and the illumination of the spiritual senses, a youthful friendship may develop into something nobler and more sublime, just as we said yesterday that from friendship with man one may eventually pass over into friendship with God, because of the likeness between them.[77]

This last text expresses more clearly and without the precautions of the others the passage from human friendship to divine friendship. Moreover, the traffic is not one-way; there is an alternation:

76. SF 2:20–1, CCM 1:306.

77. . . . ab hominis ad Dei ipsius amicitiam, ob quamdam similitudinem diximus facilius transeundum. SF 3:88, CCM 1:336.

Was it not a foretaste of heaven . . . thus to soar aloft from the sweetness of brotherly charity to the more sublime splendor of divine love; and now to mount the ladder of charity right up to the embrace of Christ himself, now to descend it and repose pleasantly in the love of my neighbor?[78]

Friendship is therefore a school of the love of God. One grasps better how much trust Aelred puts in this doctrine if one examines the First Book. Aelred and Ivo are discussing the nature of friendship, and the whole conversation turns on the definitions given by Cicero and Sallust. For Cicero friendship is "agreement on things sacred and profane, accompanied by goodwill and love", and for Sallust it is "to will, and not will, the same things." It will be remembered that for Aelred the restoration of the image is effected by a total cleaving to the divine Will, with which a man finds himself in perfect conformity of will and feeling. One sees immediately that by its very definition friendship realizes this agreement of wills. But for the Christian there is an ambiguity lurking in the two pagan formulas, for one may agree in evil. Aelred therefore adds the following reservation: "spiritual friendship is only possible between good people who share the same sort of life and similar habits and aims."[79] They alone are capable of true friendship, and consequently, it is they who will be able to give us the idea and experience of the happiness that comes from a conformity of mind and heart.

Friendship and charity

It is the Fall of man that has made the above reservation necessary. Now that evil has entered the world, one must distinguish between charity and friendship. Friendship is the most sacred form of charity—*amicitia caritatis sacratissimum genus*[80]—but it is a limited form. Charity is due, by God's commandment, to our enemies and

78. SF 3:127, CCM 1:348. See also SF 3:132-4, CCM 1:349 and 2: 14 CCM 1:305.
79. SF 1:46, CCM 1:297.
80. MC 3:110, CCM 1:159.

K

to the evil,[81] whereas spiritual friendship, which would not naturally have made any distinction, has been obliged to limit itself to those with whom agreement is possible.[82] Certainly, Aelred will manage to fit into the Noah's ark of his heart both friends and enemies. But whom does he consider worthy of his friendship? Or, more precisely, does he discriminate between the members of his community? Throughout the whole treatise on *Spiritual Friendship* no decisive answer is given. If one compares the fewness of the famous friendships among the pagans, with the multitude of the believers who have but one heart and soul, or with the martyrs who died for those they loved because greater love has no man than this,[83] it would indeed seem that all Christians are friends, and *a fortiori* the members of a monastic community.

When, walking along the cloisters, the Abbot of Rievaulx exults to feel himself loved by all his brethren as much as he loves them, this certainly seems to be friendship and not merely a duty of charity.[84] But each time that Aelred recalls the friendship between Christians, the martyrs or monks, the monks with whom he is speaking at once ask him whether he considers all these brethren as friends. And Aelred replies, as though with regret, that only those with whom he shares his secrets are his friends. Are there two degrees of friendship, or is Aelred illogical? No, this ambiguity is the very ambiguity of our human condition. The solution is eschatological. The more friends one has, the happier one is:

81. In fact, to love one's enemies is the perfection of charity, as is clearly affirmed in MC 3:10, CCM 1:110: Inde ad illud transeundum est, in quo fraternae caritatis summa consistit, in quo homo Dei filius efficitur, in quo divinae bonitatis similitudo plenius reparatur, sicut ait Salvator in Evangelio: *Diligite inimicos vestros. . . .*

82. SF 2:59, CCM 1:299. Charity and friendship correspond to the motivations which Aelred studied with such finesse and subtlety, *ratio* and *affectus*.

83. SF 1:25–30, CCM 1:293–4. Aelred says that the first Christians fulfilled perfectly Cicero's definition of friendship; to be of one heart and one soul is the *summa consensio* of friendship. An Aelredian vocabulary would be very useful; terms which could be included in it to express the experience of voluntary consent, the foundation of love, are: *consensio, in unam convenire sententiam, eadem sententia, omnia sua esse sentiat, loquatur ex sententia.*

84. SF 3:82, CCM 1:334.

This is that great and wonderful happiness that look forward to . . . each one rejoices in the happiness of his neighbors just as he rejoices in his own happiness; and so the beatitude of each one belongs to all and the whole of the beatitude of all belongs to each.

This is a familiar formula with Aelred. He continues:

There, there is no hiding of thoughts, no concealing of affection. That is the true and eternal friendship, which begins here but reaches perfection there; which belongs to *a few* here, *because there are few who are good*, but belongs to all *there*, because there *all are good*. Here, where fools and wise men are mingled, it is necessary to test one's friends; there, no testing is needed, because all are blessed with an angelic and all but divine perfection.[85]

And the last lines of the treatise repeat this eschatological hope, toward which is directed all Aelred's doctrine on the monastic community and the friendship within it:

And then . . . this friendship, to which here we admit only a few, will be poured out on all, and by all will be poured back into God, for God will be all in all.[86]

Such is the ultimate aim of all the exercising of charity, all the asceticism and all the discipline of the monastic life: universal friendship.

Meanwhile (*interea*), what joy they will have in conversing together, confiding their aspirations to each other, examining everything together, so as to come to the same conclusions about everything.[87]

---

85. SF 3:79–80, CCM 1:333–4. On the eschatological nature of the monastic community, see the very fine article by O. Brooke, "The Human Person and Community Structure," MS 5 (1968), pp. 7–18.

86. SF 3:134, CCM 1:350.

87. Interea quam dulce habent conferre invicem, sua studia mutuo patefacere, simul examinare omnia, et de omnibus in unam convenire sententiam. SF 3:132, CCM 1:349.

Should not this text from *Spiritual Friendship* figure on the invitations and convocations to our meetings, and even our regional conferences and General Chapters?

This historical exposé calls for no particular immediate conclusions. The reader will have been able to discern in it elements that are still of value today and others that are obsolete. But it is perhaps worth stressing how much this spirituality, based on the experience of fraternal charity and centered around the social nature of the Christian life, is in accordance with the aspirations of our age. A sociability guaranteed by permanent attachment to a community whose joys and sorrows one shares is of a different quality, has quite a different sort of sincerity and authenticity, from the play of ephemeral encounters, social contacts and exchanges of information that are the boast of our modern society, in which more people than ever before suffer from loneliness. The dilemma facing fallen man: "either to annul himself by isolation or to debase himself by aggregation,"[88] is transcended in the Cistercian ideal of a community of loving and freely consenting persons. Both alternatives of the dilemma leave man solitary; and as Berdyaev has admirably written:

Love and friendship are man's only hope of triumphing over solitude. Love is, indeed, the best way of achieving this end, for it brings the Ego in contact with the Other Self, with another Ego in which it is truly reflected. This is the communion of one personality with another. An impersonal love, which is not concentrated on any individual image, does not deserve to be called love. Only love can effect that complete fusion with another being which transcends solitude.[89]

88. J. Rostand, *Pensées d'un biologiste* (Paris, 1954), p. 222. Cf G. Duhamel, *Chronique des Pasquier,* vol. 1 (Paris: Mercure de France, 1964), p. 791: *L'homme est incapable de vivre seul et il est incapable de vivre en société. Comment faire?* . . . *Au fond, l'idée d'une association humaine qui ne serait pas subie mais demandée, mais acceptée avec joie, ce n'est pas absurde. Nous sommes des intellectuels nous autres, c'est-à-dire de mauvaises têtes. Notre échec ne prouve rien pour la foule des autres hommes.* (The failure was that of a "lay community," the "Désert de Bièvres").

89. N. Berdyaev, *Solitude and Society* (Glasgow, 1938), p. 119–120.

The spiritual art of Cîteaux succeeded because it was an act of confidence in love, which outreaches knowledge, and because it recuperated it, straightened it out, reorientated it and developed it in fraternal life, bringing it back to God, its beginning and end.

A better knowledge of our Cistercian authors, and of Aelred in particular, could help us a good deal in our renewal. As long as twenty-five years ago, in 1946, Père de Lubac wrote:

> Works of popularization, however intelligent and well adapted they may be, cannot create Christian thought; and to the extent that Christian thought is lacking, the very work of adaptation cannot be done. . . .
>
> Before the way in which we present Christianity can be adapted to the present generation, it is absolutely necessary that, in essentials, Christianity should be itself. Once it is itself, it is quite ready for adaptation.
>
> . . . Habit and routine have an unbelievable power to waste and destroy.
>
> But how can we rediscover Christianity, otherwise than by returning to its sources, trying to grasp it in its periods of explosive vitality? . . . can we rediscover the meaning of so many doctrines and institutions which are always tending in us toward dead abstraction and formalism, otherwise than by trying to get back to the creative thought from which they have resulted?[90]

If we draw only from alien or more ancient wells, or wells dug by means of modern scientific techniques, we run the risk of letting our own well silt up. And its water has a flavor all its own.

Charles Dumont ocso

N.D. de Scourmont
6483 Forges, Belgium

---

90. *Paradoxes*, 2 ed (Paris: Seuil, 1958), p. 37–38. C 3: "Adaptations" p. 25–32 is well worth rereading.

TOGETHER UNTO GOD

CONTEMPLATIVE COMMUNITY IN THE SERMONS OF GUERRIC OF IGNY

M. Basil Pennington OCSO[*]

T HE COMMON MEANINGS constitutive of communities are not the work of isolated individuals nor even of single generations. Common meanings have histories; they originate in single minds; they become common only through successful and widespread communication; they are translated to successive generations only through training and education. Slowly and gradually they are clarified, expressed, formulated, defined, only to be enriched and deepened and transformed. . . .[1]

This is the task that lies before us today: to clarify, to express, to formulate the common meanings of the Cistercian contemplative community so that we may in our own living of these meanings enrich, deepen and transform them. In an effort to make some contribution in this direction I would like to turn to the writings of a significant early Cistercian, Guerric, second abbot of Igny.

Guerric of Igny is sufficiently well known. For those who would want a succinct account of his life I would refer them to the excellent

1. B. Lonergan, "Existenz and Aggiornamento," *Focus* 2 (1965), p. 9.

*Fr Basil Pennington is a member of the Cistercian community at St Joseph's Abbey, Spencer, where he teaches Cistercian Spirituality, Pastoral Theology and Canon Law. He holds degrees from the Pontifical University of Thomas Aquinas (Angelicum) and the Pontifical University of the Gregoriana, Rome. He presently serves as Managing Editor of Cistercian Publications. Father has published numerous articles in some 25 periodicals and edited the papers of the previous Cistercian Symposia.

Introduction in the recently published English translation of his Sermons.[2] Here I would like to note only a few significant facts.

First of all, Guerric was a mature man when he entered Clairvaux.[3] He arrived with a solid formation, both intellectual and spiritual.[4] Thus he was well prepared to absorb and profit by whatever additional formation he was to receive at Clairvaux. At the same time, this added formation would always be colored by his previous life experience. *Omne quod recipitur secundum modum recipientis recipitur.*[5] In this he was typical of the Cistercian Fathers. All of them were relatively mature men when they entered upon the Cistercian way of life.[6] This accounts in part for the rich variety to be found among them. It also makes us aware that what Guerric has to teach us about the contemplative community does not depend exclusively on Cistercian sources.

The second fact that I would like to note assures us that what he does teach is authentically Cistercian. Guerric benefited by more than ten years of tutelage under Abbot Bernard of Clairvaux.[7] And so well satisfied was the Master with his disciple's living knowledge of the Cistercian way of life that he did not hesitate to promote him

2. J. Morson and H. Costello, "Introduction" in Guerric of Igny *Liturgical Sermons,* vol. 1, CF 8 (Spencer, Mass.: Cistercian Publications, 1970), pp. vii–xviii.

3. It is difficult to assign dates for the birth of Guerric and his entrance into Clairvaux. Morson and Costello see reason for saying he was born between 1070 and 1080, though he could have been born some time in the following decade (*ibid.* ix). He probably entered the monastery in 1124 or 1125 (*ibid.* xiii). Thus he would have been in his forties or at least in his late thirties when he entered.

4. *Ibid.,* xi ff.

5. A principal frequently enunciated by Thomas Aquinas, e.g., *Summa Theologiae,* 1, q. 75, a. 5.

6. Bernard of Clairvaux's twenty-three years and Aelred of Rievaulx's twenty-four years at entrance might seem quite young to us, but for those times this was a relatively mature age. G. Raciti would hold that Isaac of Stella was around thirty-five when he entered ("Isaac de l'Etoile et son siècle," *Cîteaux* 12 [1961]. pp. 303 ff). William of St Thierry was at least fifty when he entered Signy.

7. Morson and Costello, p. xv.

as abbot of Clairvaux's thirteenth daughter house.[8] Bernard was confident that what Guerric would teach his monks would be true to the Cistercian charism, and so we, too, can be confident that this is the case.

Finally I would like to note that in the Sermons of Guerric we probably have the truest reflection of actual chapter talks of a Cistercian Father. Undoubtedly, his Sermons were edited for publication.[9] Nevertheless he wanted them presented as talks he gave to his monks and primarily for their benefit: "But what have we to do with outsiders. This sermon is really addressed to you. . . ."[10] In the course of his Sermons he often spoke of his own community[11] and shared insights that he had drawn from their experience.[12] Thus from a study of Guerric's Sermons we can extract perhaps the most actual and concrete image of the early Cistercian contemplative community.

COMMUNITY

Guerric's understanding of the communion that is to exist among members of a community was deeply theological. He spoke often of the Church, specifically of the Body of Christ, an organic cohesion that was to be intimately co-ordinated.[13] This Christian community can express itself in many various forms. The community Guerric was especially concerned with was the Church of

8. There is some controversy as to the extent of Bernard's influence in the election of Guerric as abbot of Igny. See *ibid.* xvii, also *Ser. for Rogation Days*, 36:1 (References to the *Sermons* of Guerric are according to the new English edition *The Liturgical Sermons of Guerric of Igny*, 2 vols., CF 8 and 32 [Spencer, Mass.: Cistercian Publications, 1970–71], from which the translations used here have been taken. The number after the colon refers to the paragraph.)

9. Morson and Costello, p. xix ff.

10. Pentecost, 38:2.

11. E.g., 3 Christmas, 8:5, 3 Ser. for St Benedict, 24:6.

12. E.g., 3 Annunciation, 28:5: "You have shared your experience with me and have told me how a quiet and disciplined spirit is strengthened, grows fat and flourishes in silence. . . ."

13. E.g., 1 Advent, 1:1;4 Advent,4:3; 2 Christmas, 7:1; 1 Epiphany, 11:4; 2 Benedict, 23:3ff; 2 Easter, 34:1; 1 Assumption, 47.

the Desert.[14] It was a Church, a community made up of chosen individuals[15] called to follow in a "holy way"[16]—a way of life patterned on the Apostles.[17]

This community lived a well-ordered life marked with various observances which were so many "exercises of wisdom": the divine office, private prayer, *lectio divina,* appointed daily labor, silence.[18] Manual labor played a very special role in its life.[19] Everything was shared;[20] the members were to be "poor with the poor Christ."[21]

Guerric had a well-developed theology of poverty.[22] Material poverty is a blessed thing.[23] But not absolutely essential.[24] Far more important is the spirit of poverty[25] which consists in humility of

14. 1 Advent, 4:1: "If then you have fled away to remain in the solitude continue to stay there. . . . The desert will feed you more abundantly . . . much more frequently and in an even more wonderful way will he satisfy the needs of all you who have followed him into the desert. . . ."

15. 1 Pentecost, 38:2.

16. 5 Advent, 5:4.

17. 1 Peter and Paul, 44:3: "But you, brethren, who share the same property and the same house, who share also the same heart and soul, you ought especially, I think, to glory in them (the Apostles), since like olive branches you have imbibed from their root not only the sap of faith but also a pattern of life and the model of our Order."

18. 1 Benedict, 22:5.

19. 3 Assumption, 49:1.

20. 1 Peter and Paul, 44:3; see n. 17 above.

21. *Super Exordium Cisterciensis Coenobii,* c. xv: "Instituta monachorum Cisterciensium de Molismo venientium" in *Nomasticon Cisterciense,* ed. H. Séjalon (Solesmes: S. Petri, 1892), p. 63.

22. See the study of A. Louf, "Une théologie de la pauvreté monastique chez le bienheureux Guerric d'Igny," C Cist 20 (1958), 207–222, 362–373.

23. 1 Pentecost, 38:3; All Saints, 53:5.

24. 4 John the Baptist, 43:4: "I know that many people have lived temperately and modestly in an abundance of worldly possessions and glory, while many too have behaved evilly whose garments were rougher and whose food more sparing."

25. All Saints, 53:5: ". . . I still want to impress upon you that truly blessed poverty of spirit is to be found more in humility of heart than in a mere privation of everyday possessions, and it consists more in the renunciation of pride than in a mere contempt for property."

heart and the renunciation of pride. Christ from his birth gave an example of this.[26] The poverty at Igny was very real.[27] Yet there was no Manichaean fear of possessions: "Sometimes it may be useful to own things."[28] Even when little is possessed, "The world is full of riches for the man of faith."[29] He uses them to help him to know and love God. Guerric even went so far as to equate material things with the Sacred Scriptures: "Creation points to the Creator in the same way as do the Scriptures."[30] Guerric's community would gratefully share in the goods of this world[31] but it would seek to use them wisely[32] and would be very conscious of the social obligations that flowed from such possessions: "Let us watch ourselves, brethren, lest we begin to be judged for the death of our impoverished brethren if we hold back unnecessarily or use for ourselves what could go to support their lives."[33]

Finally, the community which shares this same program of life, with its labors and its poverty, is to be a stable community. The members are to "take root."[34] While Guerric, explicitly following St Benedict, laid emphasis on stability, he was nonetheless not categoric:

> For myself, I would not think it a wise plan to suffer certain loss for a hope that is uncertain even if the progress of some individuals bids me refrain from too hasty a judgment. Most certainly there is a great difference between those who become discontented out

26. 5 Christmas, 10:4f.

27. 1 Epiphany, 11:6.

28. All Saints, 53:1.   29. *Ibid.*, 3.

30. *Ibid.*   31. *Ibid.*

32. 1 Lent, 20:2; "When bodily health or fine weather, or a plentiful supply of necessaries are to be had we should use them and distribute them with such moderation that they do not become an occasion of sin but rather a help to virtue."

33. 4 Purification, 18:6.

34. 1 Benedict, 22:2: "Just so, the good man, planted in the house of the Lord, cannot take root nor be founded in charity unless he abides there with stability of place. And if he does not become rooted, he will never flower nor bear lasting fruit."

of love of wisdom and those . . . made restless by some light and frivolous matter. . . .[35]

One must take great care to discern by what spirit he is moved; it is possible that a true love of wisdom, a desire of a deeper contemplative life could motivate a monk to change his stability.

Communal Discernment

Perhaps Guerric's most precious contribution in regard to community life was his teaching, brief but concise, on communal discernment. I would like to quote the passage at length. Here Guerric employed the biblical image of the two harlots who came before Solomon for judgment:

> Hence the disputes of the carnal with the spiritual, even in Chapter meetings where the true Solomon presides invisibly as judge. "My son," the carnal say, "is alive and yours is dead. I have the Spirit of God, you have not; the love of God is alive in me, it is dead in you." They strive to make their own the authority of religion, the true substance of which is possessed by the spiritual, so that by depriving them of authority they may introduce customs to suit their own wanton desires. And in fact the mother wishes the child to be given alive and whole to her rival: she does not begrudge glory to her as long as she possesses virtue. But the other says: "Let it be neither mine nor yours, but let it be divided," because she desires to keep for herself the honor of holiness and leave to others the toil. But the judge makes no mistake, although he sometimes pretends not to notice. Solomon's sword finds the mother and allots to her undivided both the affection of charity and the effect of power, both fervor in working and favor in commanding.[36]

Evidently at Igny as at early Cîteaux and even before, at Molesme, the monks of the community sought together to determine the way they were to go. In this communal discernment not all were motivated by the Holy Spirit. There were human spirits and contention. "But the judge makes no mistake." In the end those who are truly concerned with the welfare of the community, the true

---

35. *Ibid.*   36. 3 Christmas, 8:5.

mothers of the community's life, will prevail, not by contention, but by the witness of their love and the power of the Lord.[37]

Roles in Community

In Guerric's community there is a superior, there is no question about it. But his role is one of humble service. He is to be a man who evaluates himself humbly, or rather truthfully; he is to be subject to all even while his office requires him to rule.[38] Guerric's image of the abbot is undoubtedly influenced by Benedict's *Rule for Monasteries*.[39] He is to be skilled in the art of healing—of healing minds and hearts. He is to be a teacher. If he is not gifted with learning and eloquence, and Guerric prayed for these,[40] he should at least teach by the example of his life, living the common life in the midst of his brethren.[41]

It is a faith community, where the monks are to regard each other as brothers, sons of one Father. One with Christ, his Spirit animates them to say with him: "Whoever does the will of my Father who is in heaven, he is my brother."[42] A brother to be loved with affection.[43] Guerric's ideal was no mere exercise of "charity," but a real striving after a community of love. Each member is to seek as much to be loved as to love.[44]

37. For an excellent study on discernment see J. C. Futrell, "Ignatian Discernment," *Studies in the Spirituality of Jesuits* 2 (1970) 47–88, and a fuller study in *Making an Apostolic Community of Love* (St Louis: Institute of Jesuit Sources, 1970). A summary of Fr Futrell's teaching can be found in M. B. Pennington, "Communal Discernment," *Monastic Exchange* 2 (1970) 26–30, and a practical application to the Cistercians in *Rule and Life,* ed. M. B. Pennington, CS 12 (Spencer, Mass.: Cistercian Publications, 1971) pp. xix–xxiv.

38. Rogation Days, 36:1.

39. Cf. RB 2 with Guerric's Ser. for Rogation Days, 36:1.

40. 2 Pentecost, 39:4.　　　　41. Rogation Days, 36:1.

42. Mt 12:50.　　　　43. 4 Assumption, 50:2.

44. 3 St Benedict, 24:4f: "For it is the power and nature of true love that even when it does not feel affection it nevertheless contrives to make itself loved in return. Truth readily commends itself to everyone's good will even without any other support, unless it meets with the opposition of an evil and wicked mind ever ready to put a wrong interpretation on everything. For

The brethren are to help and support each other in their quest for Christian holiness. They should be able to find in one another the example of every virtue.[45] Their lives as well as their words are to express God's message. Guerric certainly had a deep faith in his brothers as channels of the Word of God and was conscious of the responsibility this entailed.[46]

But the community is not to be simply turned in upon itself. It has a role to play in the larger society, basically a role of witness, a witness that must be free from hypocrisy,[47] a witness that is a sign of hope.[48] However, for Guerric the social role did not necessarily

---

the commending of this holy love some have their own special gift from God, who makes their faces bright with oil, floods them with a gentle and pleasing graciousness, makes their every word and action agreeable in the sight of all. At the same time many who perhaps love not less but even more do not easily acquire that grace. But the obligation is the same for everyone. Taking thought for what is good not only in God's sight but also in men's, you must neglect neither a clean conscience through love of a good name, nor esteem of men through too much trust in a clean conscience. How can you possibly flatter yourself about a clean conscience unless you are without complaint among your brethren? Unless you show that you really are a brother among brothers in all your dealings with them?"

45. Ser. 45:4: "No mean repast this for the faithful soul . . . where it can take from them examples of all the virtues, one from one, another from another. This one is more solidly grounded in humility, that one has a more all-embracing charity. Another is more stalwart in patience, another quicker to obey. This one is more sparing and frugal, that one does more service by his work. This one is more devout in prayer, that one applies himself to reading more studiously. This one is more prudent in administration, that one is holier in repose."

46. 1 Purification, 15:4: "I reckon as God's own word, my brethren, whatever the Holy Spirit in his mercy sees fit to speak within you—every single word which avails to build up faith stirring up love. If you should start to use words that are as it were God's own, so that no bad word, even in private conversation, should cross your lips, but rather words that build up faith, gracious words for all who hear, that make them give you grateful thanks, then blessed indeed is the word upon your lips, for your word is a lamp to guide my feet, to illumine my path."

47. 4 Epiphany, 14:3.

48. 1 Pentecost, 38:2: ". . . We should be to them an example of hope . . . After a visit to one of the Cistercian monasteries Fr du Lubac penned at the top of a letter to them from his translator: "*Saint Joseph* (the name of the abbey), *c'est un signe d'espoir*."

end there. The contemplative life flows over into a mission of peace, a mediatorial role which may be exercised before God for all men and among men not only inside the monastery but even possibly in relation to those outside.[49]

Conclusion

It is evident that Guerric has not left us a complete treatise on community. We have only his pastoral Sermons and here he spoke of community in relation to a particular community, and a particular kind of community to which he was ministering.[50] He did touch upon many of the elements essential to any community and to Christian communities: stable sharing of life and love, ministering leadership, effective and affective fraternal concern. But the particular community he always had in mind is one with a specific goal. It is a gathering of men who have come together to strive to recapture the fullness of life.[51] And for Guerric this was to be found, in this life, in contemplation.[52]

CONTEMPLATION

Stages of Spiritual Growth

In a very real sense, to treat fully of Guerric's thought on contemplation it would be necessary to transmit the whole of his teaching because, for him, everything was ordered to this or flowed from it.[53] Several times in the course of his Sermons he traced out

49. All Saints, 53:2.

50. It might be well to call to mind a point made by Thomas Merton, namely that the monastic community is not the ideal Christian community; it is rather an abnormal celibate community, and, he adds, a state of penitential mourning. See T. Merton, "Christian Solitude," *The Current* (1967) 17.

51. 2 St John the Baptist, 41:2.

52. See below, "Stages of Spiritual Growth."

53. J. M. Déchanet in his Introduction to the *Golden Epistle* of William of St Thierry rightly says: ". . . for William, as indeed for all the writers of his period, asceticism only exists for the sake of the mysticism which controls and crowns it."—William of St Thierry, *The Golden Epistle,* The Works of William of St Thierry, vol. 4, CF 12 (Spencer, Mass.: Cistercian Publications, 1971), p. x.

the stages of spiritual growth beginning with the lowest, man still in sin, and reaching up to the contemplative experience. Perhaps the best and most complete treatment is to be found in the *All Saints Day Sermon* where he used the eight beatitudes as his paradigm.[54] Other examples using various Scriptural images are to be found in the *First Sermon for the Feast of the Epiphany* (11:7—the myrrh, incense and gold of the Magi[55]), the *Third Sermon* for the same feast (13:2ff—justice, knowledge and wisdom with a reference to the man gradually cured of blindness), the *Second Sermon for the Feast of St Benedict* (23:6—the upper and lower springs of Achsah[57]), the *Third Sermon for Easter* (35:5—Elisha restoring the child to life[58]), the *Second Sermon for the Feast of Saints Peter and Paul* (45:3—the valleys and shadows of the Song of Songs 4:5f) and the *Second Sermon for Our Lady's Birthday* (52:4—the knowledge, fear, hope and love of Wisdom personified[59]).

Universal Call to Contemplation

Guerric expected his monks to be contemplatives. For this they were "transplanted" to the Monastery.[60] All are invited to it.[61]

Some of his monks had already a deep experience of God,[62] an experience which they have shared with Guerric.[63] The others were urged toward it.[64] Indeed, Guerric believed that all the members of

54. All Saints, 53:2.

55. Mt 2:11.

56. Mk 8:22–25.

57. Josh 15:19.

58. 2 Kings 4:32–35.

59. Sir 24:44.

60. 2 St Benedict, 23:7.

61. 1 Pentecost, 38:4: " 'Everyone who thirsts,' he says, 'come to the waters.' Just that. He is no respecter of persons. He takes no cognizance of their rank, nor does he enquire into their merits: he only wants those who thirst to come to him."

62. See 2 Advent, 2:3f; 3 Easter, 35:4; 1 Pentecost, 38:4.

63. 3 Annunciation, 28:5.

64. See 2 Advent, 2:3f; 2 St Benedict, 23:6; 3 Easter, 35:4; 3 Assumption, 49:1.

his community had some experience of the mighty working of the Lord within themselves.[65]

There are passages in Guerric's Sermons which might lead one to conclude that he thought the contemplative experience was something rarely given.[66] But if the context is fully read one quickly perceives that the rareness is due, not to any lack of willingness to give on the part of God or an exclusive call to a few, but to man's lack of efficacious desire.[67] "For if you constantly attend through faith to the presence of the Lord, veiled though he be, eventually you will even contemplate his glory with face unveiled albeit in a mirror and an image."[68] And this is "quite often granted" to his devout friends.[69]

Preparation for Contemplation

Gift though this be, man has his preparatory role. "Happy the man who, in order to receive [this experience of Truth] more worthily and more often, prepares a fitting place for it in the interior of his heart."[70] This place is prepared by a quietness of soul,[71] a watchful faith[72] and ardent desire.[73] But one cannot enjoy interior quiet if he does not first confess his sins,[74] mortify himself,[75] practice

65. All Saints, 53:5: "Unless I am mistaken you have all experienced this taste and so realize that the business you are engaged in is good."

66. 5 Purification, 19:6: ". . . what is granted but rarely and to rare souls to experience as in a mirror and a confused reflection, that is, to be before the Lord in Jerusalem. . . ."

67. 3 Epiphany, 13:6.

68. 5 Purification, 19:6.

69. 2 Christmas, 7:3.

70. 3 Purification, 17:2. See also 4 Assumption, 50:4.

71. See 3 Purification, 17:3; 4 Psalm, 32:6; 3 Assumption, 49:4.

72. See 5 Purification, 19:6; 3 Easter, 35:3; 1 Peter and Paul, 44:5.

73. 3 Advent, 3:3ff; 1 Epiphany, 11:7; 3 Purification, 17:2f.

74. 3 Advent, 3:4: "Make a perfect confession of your past life, have a good will in respect to all else (for there is peace to men of good will), and in this way you will have prepared with right and justice a throne for the Most High." See also 1 Lent, 20:3.

75. All Saints, 43:3.

L

the virtues,[76] especially humility[77] and fear of the Lord,[78] and above all abide in silence.[79] However even while one is still busily engaged in this task of preparing for the Lord, he sometimes comes and manifests himself to his laboring servant.[80]

A Cistercian, Guerric was faithful to the Cistercian school in giving an important place to Christ the man in his spiritual doctrine: "Christ it is whom I desire to give you in my sermons.[81] For unless

76. 4 Advent, 4:3; 3 Purification, 17:3.

77. 3 Assumption, 49:5: "Who but the humble man can be quiet?"

78. 5 Purification, 19:6.

79. Thus we see that asceticism is not something negative but extremely positive, perfecting man's openness and responsiveness to God. Based on the experience of the brethren (3 Annunciation, 28:5) Guerric had a well developed positive theology of silence:

> Truly it is a trustworthy word and deserving of every welcome, your almighty Word, Lord, which in such deep silence made its way down from the Father's royal throne into the mangers of animals and speaks to us better by its silence. Let him who has ears to hear, hear what this loving and mysterious silence of the eternal Word speaks to us. For unless hearing deceives me, among the other things which he speaks, he speaks peace for the holy people upon whom reverence for him and his example impose a religious silence. And most rightly was it imposed. For what recommends the discipline of silence with such weight and such authority, what checks the evil of restless tongues and the storms of words, as the Word of God silent in the midst of men? There is no word on my tongue, the almighty Word seems to confess while he is subject to his mother. What madness then will prompt us to say: "With our tongues we can do great things; our lips are good friends to us; we own no master." If I were allowed I would gladly be dumb and be brought low, and be silent even from good things, that I might be able the more attentively and diligently to apply my ear to the secret utterances and sacred meanings of this divine silence, learning in silence in the school of the Word if only for as long as the Word himself was silent under the instruction of his mother. O brethren, if we listen devoutly and diligently to this word which the Lord has made and shown to us today, how much and how easily we can be taught by it."—4 Christmas, 10:2.

There must be a real correspondence between interior and exterior silence, see 4 Advent, 4:2.

80. 3 Easter, 35:4: ". . . often Jesus whom you sought at the memorials of the altars, as at the tomb, and did not find, unexpectedly came to meet you in the way while you were working."

81. 5 Christmas, 10:5.

he who is the Life, the Truth and the Way anticipates his own advent to us our way cannot be corrected. . . ."[82] If anyone is in the doldrums of *acedia* his solution is to "make his way to Bethlehem and there let him look upon that Word of God. . . . What so edifies behavior, strengthens hope, inflames charity?"[83]

If the contemplative is to begin his quest for the experience of God in the Sacred Humanity, it is not to end there. The Truth which is Christ whom Mary gives us clothed with flesh, grace gives us unclothed in the inpouring of the Spirit.[84] It is not easy for mortal man to see the face of supreme Truth, yet we do experience something of its naked self when the Spirit makes his entry into us.[85] Guerric set before us the example of St Paul: ". . . the gentle breeze of the Holy Spirit blew upon him, by force of which he was taken up to the interior passages."[86] Contemplatives have always been attracted to solitude as a place where they can listen to the Holy Spirit[87] but this must not preclude seeking guidance from the Scriptures and a spiritual director.[88]

The Contemplative Experience

But what is this contemplative experience for which one must so prepare, which is the crowning point of man's striving on earth?

Here Guerric showed himself very evidently a disciple of Bernard of Clairvaux. For him the contemplative experience is an "intimate visitation"[89] of the Word which plunges the contemplative into "a

82. 4 Advent, 4:2. See also, 2 Purification, 16:3.

83. 5 Christmas, 10:2. See also 4 Psalm, 32:5.

84. 3 Purification, 17:2. See also 4 Psalm, 32:1.

85. *Ibid.,* also 2 Christmas, 7:3.

86. 2 Peter and Paul, 45:5. See also 3 Advent, 3:3 and 3 Purification, 17:6, where Simeon is also proposed as an example.

87. 4 Advent, 4:1: ". . . solitude had always been dearly loved by the holiest of the prophets as a place where they could listen to the Holy Spirit."

88. 4 Advent, 4:4: "And so if you are wise you will not be your own teacher and guide in the way along which you have never walked; but you will incline your ear to masters and acquiesce in their reproofs and advice and give yourself to the task of learning and reading. . . ."

89. 2 Advent, 2:3.

sweet and happy state of absorbed admiration. . . ."[90] God is experienced as both wonderful and lovable, inspiring admiration and bringing consolation.[91] "However this comes about in various ways according to the capacity of the soul which receives it or according to the judgment of the mercy which distributes it."[92] And in every case, for the monk still on the way it is always an all too quickly passing experience.[93]

This experience is not limited to the times of formal prayer: "Often Jesus whom you sought at the memorials of the altars, as at the tomb, and did not find, unexpectedly came to meet you in the way while you are working."[94] These visits of the Word first of all bring enlightenment[95] and understanding of the Scriptures,[96] which move one to praise and love.[97] They bring comfort.[98] And finally the Spirit, who comes with the Word and is poured out in the heart, raises the monk above the shadows of earthly things.[99]

The matter does not end there. There is a social or ecclesial dimension:

> Tested and proven in this way both in the active [taken in the more traditional meaning of striving for virtue, disposing one's self for contemplation] and the contemplative life, he who bears the name and office of a son of God through his having become the father and servant of other men will then and only then be worthy to be a peacemaker between them and God. Thus he will fulfill the office of mediator and advocate, and be worthy to make peace among the brethren themselves and even among those who

90. *Ibid.,* 4.

91. *Ibid.*

92. 3 Purification, 17:2. See also 3 Peter and Paul, 46:5.

93. 2 Christmas, 7:3; 2 Epiphany, 12:7.

94. 3 Easter, 35:4.

95. 3 Advent, 3:4.

96. 4 Advent, 4:1; ". . . so places in Scripture which previously seemed fruitless and dry will quite suddenly be filled for you at the blessing of God with a wondrous and spiritual abundance. . . ."

97. *Ibid.* See also 3 Purification, 17:2.

98. 2 Christmas, 7:3.

99. 3 Peter and Paul, 46:7.

are outside the community.[100] The man who is faithful in this will even attain to the virtue and merit of the martyr.[101]

CONTEMPLATIVE COMMUNITY

We have seen briefly and in very summary fashion Blessed Guerric's teaching on community and contemplation. How did he bring them together?

For Guerric his men had gathered together in community precisely to seek with earnestness the experience of God, the return to Paradise: "You have come together to wrestle with the angel who guards the way to the tree of life."[102] The contemplative experience of God, intimate union with him, remains his gift, not something man can do more than prepare for, ardently desire and seek. It is therefore in the realm of preparation that one seeks to find advantage in entering into a community. Yet there a paradoxical question arises. As we have seen, preparation essentially lies in a quietness of soul and faithful attentiveness to the Word of God. The striving for self-mastery, for virtue, is to make this quietness possible. Silence, interior and exterior, is essential. Yet one enters a community where he commits himself to a Christian response to his brethren, to a life of sharing with them. How do these two dimensions, rather than crossing purposes, actually become one?

Guerric's most explicit answer is expressed in this passage:

By the wonderful favor of God's loving care, in this solitude of ours we have the peace of solitude and yet we do not lack the consolation and comfort of holy companionship. It is possible for each of us to sit alone and be silent, because we have no one to disturb us with interruptions, and yet it cannot be said of us: "Woe to him who is alone, since he has nobody to console him or if he should fall has none to lift him up." We are surrounded by companions, yet we are not in a crowd. We live as it were in

100. All Saints, 53:2.
101. *Ibid.*
102. 2 St John Baptist, 41:2.

a city, yet we have to contend with no tumult, so that the voice of one crying in the wilderness can be heard by us, provided only that we have interior silence to correspond to the exterior silence that surrounds us.[103]

In a world where most is rush and noise and striving for alien values men enter a contemplative community to find a "climate of monastic prayer,"[104] a climate that is produced by the common efforts of a community of like-minded men: "Let us all together then so make a point of being quiet that in our quiet we may always be occupied with meditation on eternal quiet. . . ."[105] A stable commitment to abide in such a community helps one to be faithful to his quest.[106] Moreover the brothers are channels of God's word to each other: "I reckon as God's own word, my brethren, whatever the Holy Spirit in his mercy see fit to speak within you—every single word which avails to build up faith, stirring up love."[107] From this it follows that monks must "start to use words that are as it were God's own, so that no bad word, even in private conversation, should cross one's lips."[108] This constant personal, loving and fraternal ministry of the Word is one of the things the monk seeks in community, where living in community ministers to his contemplative call.

The hard work necessary for the support of the community, its fidelity to Christian poverty, the other community services, the general strictness of life, all have their own very beneficial role in

103. 4 Advent, 4:2.

104. *Ibid.,* 1. This is the title Thomas Merton gave to the last book which he prepared for publication before his tragic death: *The Climate of Monastic Prayer* (Spencer, Mass.: Cistercian Publications, 1969).

105. 3 Assumption, 49:6. See also 4 Palm, 32:6.

106. 1 St Benedict, 22:4. See also 4 Advent, 4:1 and 5 Advent, 5:5. William of St Thierry says in his Golden Epistle: "It is impossible for a man faithfully to fix his soul upon one thing who has not first perseveringly attached his body to one place."—n. 95, tr. T. Berkeley, *The Works of William of St Thierry,* vol. 4, CF 12 (Spencer, Mass.: Cistercian Publications, 1971), p. 44.

107. 1 Purification, 15:4.

108. *Ibid.*

helping the individual member, through self-mortification and the practice of the virtues, to attain to that inner quiet which can expectantly await the coming of the Word.[109] Yet this is so only in so far as the monk enters into these with the proper dispositions of soul. Guerric expressed this well in his *Third Sermon for the Feast of the Assumption:*

> Happy is he who in all his labors and in all his ways seeks blessed rest, always hastening, as the Apostle exhorts, to enter into that rest. For desire of it he afflicts his body, but already he has prepared and disposed his spirit for that rest, being at peace with all men as far as it lies with him. Giving preference where his will is concerned to the rest and the leisure of Mary, to the extent that necessity demands he accepts the toil and the business of Martha, yet he does this with as much peace and quiet of spirit as he can, and he always brings himself back from his manifold distractions to the one thing necessary.
>
> A man of this sort is at rest when he is working. . . .[110]

Guerric said surprisingly little about community prayer. It was so much a part of the life it is perhaps taken for granted. He had little patience for the man "who prefers little prayers to the holy labors which he has promised to perform" or "a man, whose brother holds something against him offering at the altar" or one who "thinks the voluntary offerings of his lips are pleasing to God— those psalms and the prayers one offers secretly—if they prevent one from saying the number of psalms laid down in the Rule."[111] He undoubtedly has the Office in mind when he says to his monks:

> So too there are not lacking clouds which will raise up our spirits to higher things provided our hearts are not too lazy and tied to earth, and so we will be with the Lord if only for half an hour. Unless I am mistaken you know from experience what I say. For when the clouds sent out a sound, that is to say, when the voices of prophets or apostles sounded in the Church, your minds and

109. 1 Lent, 20:6; 4 Assumption, 50:4.

110. 3 Assumption, 49:2.

111. 5 Advent, 5:2.

hearts have been borne aloft as on a cloud to sublime things and
on occasion carried beyond even these, so that they have merited
to behold, in however small a degree, the glory of God.[112]

This is indeed the goal of community prayer.

Perhaps Guerric described some of the characteristics he would
find in the members of the contemplative community when he
spoke of Simeon and Anna:

> . . . not wedded but joined together, by a bond not of matrimony
> but of a more sacred mystery, peers in their faith, equal in
> chastity, alike in their devotion, partners in the proclaiming of
> grace, both advanced in age, both perfect in sanctity. Even
> before the Gospel they dedicated in both sexes the first-fruits of
> the Gospel's purity and devotion.
>
> These two have adorned your bridal chamber, Sion, with the
> varied beauty of their virtues, to receive Christ the King—they
> have adorned not the walls of your temple but the inmost
> recesses of their heart, the hidden places of their bedchambers.[113]

CONCLUSION

Guerric's teaching on contemplative life and community life
in no way veers from the tradition. What synthesis he offered can
hardly be called revolutionary. Yet it is worth pondering. He had
a very real understanding of the correlative role of community in
man's search for the fullness of the Christian experience, and a
true appreciation of it. Yet he did not *ex professo* explore it, nor
did he even touch on all its facets. The contribution he made
through his relatively few surviving Sermons must be said to be
valuable but limited. Arguments against the eremitical life could
possibly be drawn from the Sermons, but appreciation and affirmation of the values of one way of life does not necessarily preclude
the values of another.

Guerric's synthesis responds well to values we see as capital

112. 2 Advent, 2:3.
113. 2 Purification, 16:5.

today. He showed a deep respect for the individual even as he expressed the real value and role of communal life and sharing. In his talks the nature of the community and the reason why the men he was addressing had come together were always in evidence. He believed it was of value to keep the end, the goal always in view: ". . . look forward to the end to which it [the way] leads you. If you were to see how everything is to be attained, then you would say without hesitation: 'Broad indeed is your command.' . . . The man who dwells sufficiently on this end I think will not only make the way easier for himself but also grow wings so that he no longer walks but flies."[114]

Communities are groups of people linked together by shared beliefs and experiences. With Guerric there was no doubt what are the beliefs that are shared. He also relied heavily on lived experience; he frequently appealed to it. True contemplative community will exist only when the members have, in sufficient numbers, experienced in their own lives the complementary values and the healthy tensions that arise out of truly seeking the experience of God in a community.

Guerric's rather challenging idea of each member having a share in mothering Christ in the community[115] can well be pondered in these days of emphasis on co-responsibility. Co-responsibility does not end with debate, politics, and votes. Though all of these can have their legitimate place in the community as in any social body, the more theological approach of the Abbot of Igny is far more conducive to the attainment of the ends of the contemplative community: humble openness, lived witness to the values held sacred, confident that in the end by the power of the Spirit they will prevail.[116]

Guerric had no illusions about the type of men who make up a contemplative community; they are men of flesh as well as of spirit: "We live on two levels, partly according to the flesh, partly

114. 5 Advent, 5:5.
115. 3 Christmas, 8:5.
116. *Ibid.*

according to the spirit."[117] The highest tribute Thomas Merton could pay to the Zen monks was tersely expressed: "They keep working at it." Guerric would ultimately ask nothing more.

M. Basil Pennington OCSO

St Joseph's Abbey
Spencer, MA 01562

117. 1 Lent, 20:1.

A CHALLENGE FOR TODAY

THE PROBLEM OF CONTEMPLATIVE COMMUNITY AT THE END OF THE EIGHTEENTH CENTURY

Cyprian Davis OSB[*]

THE SUBJECT OF OUR SYMPOSIUM is contemplative community. This problem is being examined sociologically, psychologically, theologically, and in the context of history. The historical perspective is quite naturally that of the Middle Ages since it is in the High Middle Ages that most contemplative communities find their origins and the first formulation of their spirit. Nevertheless, contemplative communities are an historical reality existing today in a world vastly different from that which saw their beginning. We are faced today with the problem of the contemplative community in the modern world, prayer in a secular age, monastic spirituality versus service to others. The history of any institution is not only important for the insight that comes from a study of its origins and its growth but also that which is revealed in studying the periods of crisis and decline. Contemplative community as well as the very contemplative ideal has passed through periods of development and decline. It was especially with the demise of that medieval world, which had managed to survive into the eighteenth century, that Western

*Fr Cyprian Davis has just returned from Louvain where he earned his Licentiate in Historical Science. He also holds a STL from the Catholic University of America. Father is presently Assistant Professor of Church History at St Meinrad School of Theology. He has contributed some articles to the *New Catholic Encyclopaedia*.

Catholic contemplative communities met their own "dark night." Yet it was precisely with the period of the French Revolution with its destruction of the old society and institutions and its formation of a totally new society with its own patterns of thought and scale of values that our contemporary secular age truly began. Was the almost total destruction of contemplative orders in the aftermath of the French Revolution the result of the incompatibility of contemplative life to survive as a community structure in the present age? Must a community of contemplatives be a living anachronism? Was the demise of most contemplative life in the Catholic Church at the end of the eighteenth and the beginning of the nineteenth century the result of external force or internal weakness? In other words, could they have adapted to a different world and another atmosphere and survived all the while remaining faithful to their basic ideal? A very brief look at the male contemplative communities in France and in the Empire during the period between 1750 and 1789 might give an answer to some of these questions and a direction for discussion of contemplative community in our world today. We shall limit our discussion mainly to the Benedictines and Cistercians.

History is the study of man in time and place. We know what a man is by what he reveals of himself. But man or a group of men or a community reveals itself through communication. One communicates by what one says as well as by what one fails to say, by external show as well as by the act of concealing, by what one thinks of himself and by what his *milieu* thinks of him. It is a question of relationship, relationship of man to others and to himself. There is another relationship, which in the case of contemplatives is extremely important, namely man's relationship to God; but this relationship can only be known by the relationship that is had with others and with himself.

In the last half of the eighteenth century the relationships of the contemplative communities with themselves and with their world was in most cases extremely uneasy. There are various factors that reveal this to us.

First of all, there was the relationship with the great community that is the Church. In the latter part of the seventeenth century and the first part of the eighteenth, the ecclesiastical world was rocked by the controversies over Jansenism. Jansenism was a theological controversy, but it was also a political and a sociological conflict as well. This conflict spread much farther than the Cistercian nuns of Port Royal and its devout clientele. It spread farther than France. It created a mentality that was political and social as well as moral and theological. But important for us it affected in one way or another all of the contemplative communities at the end of the *ancien régime*. The reforms that it prompted and the divisions that it fostered all happened prior to 1750. In 1713 Clement XI issued the Bull *Unigenitus* which was the last in a long series of condemnations. The monks of the Congregation of St Maur, who were especially divided by the controversy, accepted it for the most part in 1736. Those who refused were scattered hither and thither in various houses and deprived of all posts of responsibility.[1] In 1725 fifteen members of the community of Orval[2] secretly left the monastery to avoid submitting to the Bull and found refuge as a Jansenist community in Utrecht.[3]

The passions raised by the Jansenist controversy left their mark on the various communities. There was a bitterness that remained as well as a certain lassitude. It would seem, moreover, that the aftermath of the Jansenist quarrels left little taste for mystical prayer and contemplation.

There was also the relationship between the contemplative communities and the other currents of thought of the time, namely

1. See P. Denis, "Le Cardinal de Fleury, Dom Alaydon et Dom Thuillier. Documents inédits sur l'histoire du Jansénisme dans la congrégation de Saint-Maur, (1729–1730)," *Revue Bénédictine* 26 (1909) 325–370. For a particular instance in how this crisis affected the Congregation of St Vanne, see J. Godefroy, "Figures de Moines: Dom Charles Chardon, Bénédictin de Saint Vanne, 1695–1771," *Revue Mabillon,* 34–35 (1944–45), 82–118. For a general picture of the intellectual climate in the monasteries of the period, especially for the Congregation of St Vanne, see by the same author: *Les Bénédictins de Saint-Vanne et la Révolution* (Paris, 1918).

2. Province of Luxemburg in present-day Belgium.

3. See N. Tillière, *Histoire de l'Abbaye d'Orval,* 6th ed. (Gembloux, 1958).

the rationalism of the Enlightenment. The monks, moreover, came under the influence of the attitudes of mind engendered by a nascent technology. It was the age that opened up the way for the technological revolution of the nineteenth century.[4]

Perhaps Dom Jean-Joseph Cajot (1726–1779), monk of the Congregation of St Vanne, who had published at Cologne in 1762 a work entitled, *Histoire Critique des Coqueluchons*, in which he ridiculed the variety of religious habits, and another work, *Examen Philosophique de la Règle de Saint-Benoît*,[5] in which he examined the Rule of St Benedict in the light of eighteenth-century rationalism and found it wanting, is not typical of the general mentality of all of the monks of St Vanne of the period. His brother, however, Dom Charles Cajot (1731–1807), who occupied the position of professor of philosophy and theology in the Congregation of St Vanne, did not consider prayer as the primary purpose of the monastic life but only a secondary aim. The primary end of monasticism was education. It was for this that society gave gifts to the monasteries; and if the monasteries failed to educate, then society could take back its gifts. He explained this idea in a work entitled, *Recherches Historiques sur l'Esprit primitif et les anciens collèges de l'Ordre de Saint-Benoît, d'ou résultent les droits de la société sur les biens qu'il possède.*[6] At the time of the suppression of religious houses by the National Constituent Assembly in 1790, Dom Ferlus, a Maurist, professor at the College of Soreze,[7] also suggested that the monastic orders be re-organized for the purpose of education and thereby insure their utility. It must be remembered that both the Congregations of St Maur and St Vanne maintained several secondary schools at the time. His

---

4. See the account of the inventions of Dom Jacques-Antoine de Maurey while he was still a monk in the article by J. Montier, "Les Moines de Fécamp pendant la Révolution," *L'Abbaye Bénédictine de Fécamp. Oeuvrage Scientifique du XIIIe Centenaire.* 658–1958, 3 vols. and a supplementary volume with notes and index (Fécamp, 1960), 3:204–18.

5. Avignon, 1767.

6. 2 vols., Paris, 1787.

7. Department of Tarn.

plan was rejected. In this latter half of the eighteenth century the great question was the reason or the utility of things. What was the utility of contemplative communities? This was a problem for many of the monks as well.

It was this inability of the enlightened thinkers of the age to see any value in the contemplative communities that brought about their suppression. Already Emperor Joseph II had suppressed in the 1780's many contemplative communities such as the Carthusians in his Austrian dominions, Hungary, Bohemia, and later the Austrian Netherlands. The Cistercian and Benedictine abbeys were forced to engage in the apostolate or to conduct schools in order to become useful. The Divine Office was no longer to be celebrated in public. This would be the origin of so many of the choir chapels of the Baroque period.

The extent to which the members of the contemplative communities were imbued with the mentality of their age is seen in the fact that many monks like many other ecclesiastics of the period belonged to the Freemasons. At the abbey of Fécamp in Normandy, which belonged to the Congregation of St Maur, the Masonic Lodge of Saint John of the Triple Unity was established in 1778. It was composed of nine monks, three musicians attached to the service of the abbey, one priest, and seven other laymen.[8] Despite the prohibitions of several popes membership in the Masonic Lodges was not infrequent in eighteenth-century Europe for members of the clergy, including bishops. This is not so surprising as one might think when it is remembered that the ideals and mentality of the Masons were also in evolution. In this new age of scientific thought, technological development and social upheaval the monks would have their part. Can one draw the conclusion that the contemplative community in one way or another will understand its vocation under the influence of the society in which it lives?

What was this contemplative community in the latter half of

8. See J. Montier, "L'Abbaye de la Sainte-Trinité de Fécamp au XVIIIe Siècle," *ibid.*, 2:17–44.

the eighteenth century? It is not easy to say. The first half of the century has left an abundant literature on spirituality, on theology, and on history. In the second half there is only the continuation of certain works of historical erudition. This very silence is eloquent, but the monastic orders made a statement by the way they lived. Almost all of the monasteries were rebuilt in monumental proportions in the style of the period in the course of the eighteenth century, as for example Cluny, Einsiedeln, etc. Cîteaux partly completed its conventual buildings in 1760 as did Clairvaux in the same year. Orval was rebuilt in monumental proportions in 1782. This was the case with many of the Cistercian abbeys in the Empire as well.

The communities, on the other hand, were generally small. In 1766, the year in which the Commission of Regulars began its work of suppressing many of the monasteries in France, the Congregation of St Maur had 41 houses in the province of Brittany. Of these only nine had more than nine monks. Many Cistercian houses had less than ten. Lecestre lists 228 Cistercian houses in France in the year 1766 with a total of 1,873 monks. Of these, 178 had less than ten monks. And of these, 100 had five or less.[9] The Camaldolese had six houses with only one, Grosbois near Paris, having more than three. Grosbois had seven.[10] This was also the case in the Empire, but in the Empire certain of the abbeys were limited exclusively to the nobility. This was true of Murbach, a

---

9. L. Lecestre, *Abbayes, Prieurés et Couvents d'Hommes en France. Liste Générale d'après les papiers de la Commission des Réguliers en 1768* (Paris, 1902), pp. 19–29. For further information on the personnel and the wealth of the Congregation of St Maur during our period, see the series of articles by Dom G. Charvin, "Bénéfices possédés par la Congrégation de Saint-Maur au milieu du XVIIIe siècle," *Revue Mabillon* 44 (1954), 152–188; "Etat Général du Temporel de la Congrégation de Saint-Maur en 1766, 1769, 1779," *ibid.,* 45 (1955), 43–60; "Contribution à l'étude du Temporel de la Congrégation de Saint-Maur au XVIIIe siècle (1730–1786)," *ibid.,* 45 (1955), 259–281; 46 (1956), 33–61; "Contribution à l'étude du Personnel dans la Congrégation de Saint-Maur," *ibid.,* 46 (1956), pp. 107–114; 213–230; 47 (1957), pp. 44–56; 115–129; 200–212; 278–290; 48 (1958), pp. 59–74; 152–164; 221–238; 269–281; 49 (1959), pp. 35–59.

10. Lecestre, *op. cit.,* p. 30.

Benedictine abbey in Alsace (by the end of the eighteenth century it was located on French territory), which in 1759 would transform itself into a chapter of canons. Fulda is another example of an exclusively aristocratic community. Several of the Italian monasteries were likewise in great measure aristocratic.[11]

The abbot in most cases was a commendatory abbot who like a parasite lived off the lion's share of the community's revenue. Many of the priories were benefices in the hands of the lesser clergy. Among the Benedictines, the monks themselves were usually titulars of priories that were nothing more than properties with a church. Other monks enjoyed as a benefice the posts in these fictional priories. The revenue of the benefices, both that of the priors and the titular officials, very often went to the support of the individual monk. In the case of many of the Benedictine Abbeys outside of the Congregation of St Maur or St Vanne, the monks had their own pension guaranteed by their family. In some instances they lived in their own dwellings with scarcely a semblance of community life. In France these unreformed Benedictines would in great measure be suppressed by the work of the Commission of Regulars after 1766.

All contemplative communities lived from the revenue from their lands, many receiving the feudal dues from the rural populace that were so bitterly resented by this period throughout Europe. Most of them received tithes from churches in their possession. Both Benedictines and Cistercians had parishes. Some were served by the monks; others by the diocesan clergy who complained about the insufficient portion granted them by the monks. It must be admitted, however, that many monasteries continued to aid the poor and the indigent in their area up to the eve of their suppression. Such was the case for Fécamp. The inhabitants of

11. More and more studies of the social *milieu* of the eighteenth century have been appearing. The same sort of work must be done in regard to eighteenth-century monastic history. For an example of such a study, see J. Salzgeber, *Die Klöster Einsiedeln und St Gallen im Barockzeitalter. Historisch-Soziologische Studie. (Beiträge zur Geschichte des Alten Mönchtums und des Benediktinerordens. Heft 28),* (Münster, Westfalen, 1967).

M

the town publicly acknowledged the charity of the community in its petition to the National Constituent Assembly.[12]

It must be admitted, however, that the image of the contemplative community or the statement that these communities made to their contemporaries was one of a gentlemanly style of life, led by landlords who in their leisure seemingly made little contribution to either Church or society. An institution which no longer fills its function is doomed to die. Might not our conclusion be that a contemplative community which does not make a positive statement about man's relationship to God so that the men of its time can clearly comprehend it no longer fills its function?

In regard to France it seems clear that the contemplative communities evoked a reaction of hostility on the part of the clergy. In 1766 the Commission of Regulars was set up by Louis XV to carry out the work of reforming the monastic and mendicant orders in France according to the recommendation of the General Assembly of the Clergy in 1765. Five ministers of State, five archbishops, four legal advisers, a notary, and a secretary made up the commission. The driving force in the commission and the spokesman was the Archbishop of Toulouse, Loménie de Brienne, a man of the Enlightenment, with very few religious scruples and even less faith. Pierre Chevallier in his two-volume study, *Loménie de Brienne et l'Ordre Monastique (1766-1789),*[13] has examined anew the documents of the commission as well as other documents that were in the possession of the family of Loménie de Brienne and hitherto inaccessible. His conclusions are that the work of the commission was done with care and that the documents show that in general the suppressions that were made were justified. He does not deny that some of the suppressions were ordered through venality on the part of some bishops avid for monastic property. Nor does he deny the ambition and the rationalism of Loménie

12. See J. Montier, "L'Abbaye de la Sainte-Trinité de Fécamp au XVIIIe Siècle," *loc. cit.,* p. 19.

13. P. Chevallier, *Loménie de Brienne et l'Ordre Monastique (1766-1789)* 2 vols. (Paris, 1959).

de Brienne who was not the best judge of what constituted a healthy monastic community.

It might be interesting to cite some of the evidence in regard to the state of the monastic orders that Chevallier has carefully collected from the Archives Nationales, particularly the records of the Commission and the personal papers of the Archbishop of Toulouse. Many addressed their observations to the Archbishop of Toulouse who carefully added each document to the *dossier* he formed in order to make his judgment. The bishops had been asked to respond to a questionnaire. They did not all do so, but out of 116 bishops, 88 replied in diverse manners.[14]

The observations revealed a hostility and a criticism of many of the contemplative communities. The parish priest of the town of Luxeuil complained about the dangerous doctrine of a certain D. Maignien, a monk of the Congregation of St Vanne, devotee of the new philosophers.[15] He disseminated their teaching in his parish.

Tragic was the state of the Celestines, a Benedictine reform congregation that dated back to Pope St Celestine V in the fourteenth century. By the end of the eighteenth century the abuses were so great that it seemed impossible to bring about a reform. All were agreed that the only remedy was suppression. A letter from the Prior of Verdelais[16] to the Prior General of the Order in France says the same: "I sense as well as any other the miserable state of the Congregation and the moral impossibility to strengthen ourselves in the type of life that we have embraced unless there is a total reform, which no one will accept, I among the first, because I feel neither strong enough nor virtuous enough to put up with the reform that would be absolutely necessary in order to keep us going."[17] The Celestines would disappear entirely before the Revolution.

All were agreed that the Carthusians, the Abbey of La Grande

14. *Ibid.*, 1:38ff.
15. *Ibid.*, p. 75.
16. Department of La Gironde.
17. Chevallier, 1:75.

Trappe, the Abbey of Sept-Fons and the Congregation of the
Feuillants had no need of reform. It is significant that the Trappists
and the Carthusians would survive the Revolution in a heroic
manner.

The Cistercians were divided by a conflict between the Abbot
of Cîteaux, Francois Trouvé, and the Abbots of Clairvaux, La
Ferté, Pontigny, and Morimond.[18] The General Chapter supported
the Abbot of Cîteaux, but the Abbots of the four principal
daughter-houses appealed to the Parliament of Dijon, a secular
authority, which in turn supported the Abbot of Cîteaux. The
four abbots then turned to the king. In this way it came into the
domain of the Commission of Loménie de Brienne. Thus in 1768
the principal Cistercian abbots fought among themselves with
acrimony and stubbornness.

The reputation of the Cistercian Order was not the highest.
The Bishop of Poitiers, Martial de Beaupoil de Saint-Aulaire,[19]
described in a letter to Loménie de Brienne the state of the Cistercian
monasteries in his diocese : "They are all located in small villages
and there is not a sufficiently large number of religious in order
to carry out the Office with decency. The Priors consider themselves as holders of a benefice. They are rarely changed and each
follows his own inclination. One gives himself to dissipation, loves
to spend money, and desires to live like a lord; the other hoards
money that he considers his own not the community's; none make
themselves useful in the diocese and are not employed in the
ministry.

Their churches are badly kept up and the main task of the
religious is the up-keep of their domains from which they draw
profit and which they exploit like careful farmers. . . ."[20]

There is one final relationship of the contemplative community

18. See the article by A. Presse, "Notes et documents sur les derniers temps
de l'Abbaye de Cîteaux," ASOC 10 (1954), pp. 169–207, for an account of
the quarreling between the abbot and the monks over the property at the
time of the suppression and expulsion of the community.

19. He was bishop from 1759 until his death in exile in Switzerland in 1798.
See Eubel, *Hierarchia Catholica Medii et Recentioris Aevi* (Padua, 1958), 6:337.

20. Chevallier, 2:11.

under the *ancien régime* that must be mentioned because it is crucial. All contemplative communities were under the tutelage of the state in one form or another. This was the result of a long process dating back to the beginning of the Middle Ages. It was the result of being under the patronage and the protection of the prince. This was not the fault of the monks, but the consequences were still ruinous. The sovereign had control in the final instance not only over the property or the feudal relationships but also over the internal affairs of the house. Thus it was only natural as well as legally necessary that the Maurists of St-Germain-des-Prés address a petition to the king for modifications in the habit, in the hour for Matins, in the number of fast-days, etc. And it was considered normal that in the wake of the protest from other Maurist houses contesting this request that the king should set up the Commission of Regulars to investigate the whole state of monastic life in France.

The same control was exercised by the Hapsburgs in their dominions. The monastic communities were corporations under the tutelage of the sovereign. The revolution in France and its spread through much of Europe would change the sovereignty but not the consequences. The new sovereign states merely withdrew that legality and protection that the old sovereignty had conferred and maintained. Moreover, the contemplative communities had been enriched by pious donations throughout the Middle Ages. In the minds of men of the time the communities existed to insure the acts of charity and devotion that prompted these donations. But what if other works were substituted in place of the alms and the psalms? What if the pious intentions were carried out by the creation of other works more in keeping with the times? Joseph II did not enrich himself from the property of the contemplative communities that he suppressed. The monies from this property went to a fund for the seminaries and other ecclesiastical needs. It was for less exalted reasons, however, that most of the abbeys in the Empire were suppressed in 1803. It was in order to indemnify the princes who had lost their domains to Napoleon on the left bank of the Rhine.

In the final analysis it could be said with some justification that the contemplative community as such no longer existed in the eighteenth century. What did exist was often no longer contemplative and no longer a community but a legal entity, a corporation. Speaking broadly, that vision of the Infinite, that thirst for union with God, that dedication to an ideal that brought men together and made them one with each other in mutual support and love to pursue this vision and satisfy that desire for union had practically ceased to exist. What did exist was a corporation that held a recognized place in society, enjoyed specific privileges in that society, fulfilled a formal function in that society, and bore witness to a tradition that was no longer vital nor seemingly important. But this legal institution was intimately connected with this society, and the destruction of this society meant inevitably the monasteries' destruction as well.

Is it correct then that contemplative life as such was incompatible with the new age ushered in by the French Revolution? We would say no. The form of that life, the external structure, even the mentality was no longer relevant; but a challenge to such a life had been levelled by the new age. Unfortunately, the old orders, apart from a few notable exceptions, no longer had the strength or the will to take up that challenge. Too often in the period of revival of the contemplative communities during the nineteenth century, the externals which had become anachronistic were also revived. Nevertheless, as we contemplate the picture of desolation presented by the contemplative communities at the end of the eighteenth century, we too are presented with a challenge in this period of upheaval and social revolution. It is in enumerating these challenges that we conclude this study.

No contemplative community can escape the influences of its age. No contemplative community can cut itself off from the mentality of its age. The tragedy of many monks in the eighteenth century, however, was their own self-doubt. The challenge that the contemplative community has today is to remain open to its age while remaining convinced of its own value.

No Catholic contemplative community can live apart from the Church or be estranged from the members of the Church. This estrangement was seen in the eighteenth century in the failure of many ecclesiastics and laymen to see any need to preserve the monasteries or the contemplative life. In the contemporary Church many see little place for the contemplative community which seems to them to represent all that is outmoded and medieval. Our challenge is how to make a statement to our contemporaries in a language that can be understood. A value forgotten or ignored is a value lost.

The contemplative communities of the eighteenth century were riven by dissension, by appeals of subjects to the secular courts against their superiors, by superiors in conflict with each other seeking adjudication from secular authority, by conflict over changes in discipline and observance, etc. The challenge to the contemplative community today is to permit differences without division, adaptation without relaxation, freedom without abuse.

Most eighteenth-century communities were small, the external observance mitigated or almost non-existent; at the same time there was often a breakdown in central authority. The larger communities were usually more fervent. Many today seek a form of contemplative life in small communities with less formality in prayer and observance. The challenge must be to overcome the dangers of isolation and the reduced resources of a smaller personnel.

Most eighteenth-century communities remained closed within a certain social *milieu* and formed part of a particularly privileged class. The challenge to monasticism today is to be part of the local community and yet not be imprisoned within the mentality or the pre occupations of one social group—to be neither minions of the Establishment nor camp followers of the revolution.

The final challenge is to us as individual monks. Whatever may

have been the failings of the monastic order at the end of the
eighteenth-century, many monks—more than is generally con-
ceded—remained or made a valiant attempt to remain faithful to the
monastic ideal as they understood it, even to the point of death,
imprisonment, or when possible clandestine ministry. Only later
history will tell how well we answered the challenge to fidelity
today.

Cyprian Davis OSB

St Meinrad Archabbey
St Meinrad, Indiana

CONTEMPLATION AND COMMUNITY

AN ANGLICAN PERSPECTIVE

The Love of Christ constrains us. (2 Cor V 14)

BENEDICTA WARD SLG*

THERE IS NO DOUBT about it: the contemplative life cannot be justified. In terms of what it produces, what it achieves, how it "relates," it is of no use whatsoever, not even as a sort of prayer-wheel for the benefit of other Christians. When "the poor man in Christ," to quote St Bruno's definition of a monk, is asked to justify his way of life, all he can say is "I am here to stand before God: the love of Christ constrains me; I can do no other." Perhaps it can be compared to ecology—forests are necessary to the world, just to stand where they are; by their mere existence they keep the air pure and breathable. So the monk stands before God for the life of the world. And the strange thing is, that such "trees" rarely remain alone; they grow in groups, in communities, until it is possible to speak of "contemplative communities," those groups where the constraining call of Christ has drawn men and women into fellowship in the Holy Spirit.

Such communities exist now in the Anglican Church, and the basic reason for their existence is, as always, the constraining love of Christ. But there are certain theological ideas and historical circumstances behind these communities that make them significant both

---

*Sr Benedicta Ward is a member of the Anglican Community of the Sisters of the Love of God. Sister has just done a year's work at Harvard and has returned to Oxford to complete her doctorate, having done a BA Honors in History at Manchester. Sister will shortly publish a translation, with introduction, of St Anselm's Prayers and Meditations and is presently working on Conrad of Eberback's *Cistercian Origins (Exordium Magnum)* for publication in the Cistercian Studies Series.

for Anglican theology and for monasticism. The historical facts are well known, but it is worth recalling them, to underline the difference between the tradition of the Anglican communities and that of other older institutions.

By the summer of 1540 the monastic houses of England were no more. With the exception of the communities restored briefly during the reign of Mary, there were to be no religious orders in the Church of England for three hundred years. The 1850's saw a remarkable revival of formal religious life in England, both with the re-establishment of Roman Catholic orders, and perhaps more significantly with the development of orders for women and for men within the Church of England itself. By 1900 there were twenty-seven active communities in the Church of England, and more were to come. The present century has seen the establishment of enclosed communities for men and women, wholly given to contemplative life. Finally, the last twenty years have seen also the development of the eremitical life, largely as an extension of the life of the contemplative communities. It is, incidentally, interesting to note how this reverses a more usual pattern of development; instead of the sequence: solitaries—communities of contemplatives—communities of active religious, we have the sequence: active religious—contemplative communities—hermits.

Here in a Church which has had no established communities for years, men and women have chosen to live out their contemplative vocation in communities, and to use many of the traditional ways of life, not in imitation or because they had to, but because the tradition was still living and viable. Before discussing this, however, there are two minor points to be considered concerning Anglican communities.

The first is that there is no such thing in the Church of England as an "active" community. Every community has some form of the Divine Office, some rule of silence and enclosure, some measure of community life. The active works they undertake are seen as the overflow of a life of corporate prayer, as the expression of the prior commitment to a life of holiness. The second point concerns the connection between the Anglican communities and those of other communions. When the first sisterhoods were formed, their founders turned naturally for help and advice to existing communities, especially those on the Continent. When it came to drawing up rules, Dr Pusey and Dr Neale, two of the tractarians most concerned with the religious life, borrowed from St Francis de Sales and St Vincent de Paul, with the unfortunate but perhaps inevitable result that the early communities copied many social as well as spiritual ways from the French communities of the eighteenth century. When the contemplative communities were formed, this borrowing was less marked. Some of the communities took the Rule of St Benedict, but it was the Rule itself and not the declarations or house-rules of any particular contemporary community that they used. Increasingly these communities felt free to live their life and form their rule from that, and from no specific model, drawing rather on the more general tradition of monasticism and using what was appropriate.

The new communities in the Church of England in the nineteenth century faced widespread misunderstanding and criticism, yet they continued steadily to assert their integral relationship with the worship and theology of the Anglican Church. Again and again in letters and sermons relating to the foundation of these communities, there is concern that they should understand themselves within the faith and liturgy of the Church of England: "We are not drawn out of the Church but drawn together within the Church;" "We are not gathered here because God was not with us before the Society was formed but rather because he was;" "The object of all religious societies is to gather up and as it were to focus the love which ought to animate the whole body of the Church catholic."[1] This conception of the religious society as a focus of the life of the whole Church, as part of the basic Christian commitment, is something present from the beginning in the Church of England; the communities in the nineteenth century only made this explicit. A latent "monastic" element, in which concern for the Kingdom of God was realized in serious and disciplined Christian living remained

1. R. M. Benson, *The Religious Vocation* (New York: Morehouse, 1939), p. 56.

after the Reformation as an integral strand in the theology and devotion of the Church of England.

From the beginning a way was left open for the positive re-evaluation of the monastic life. In the sixteenth and seventeenth centuries, Anglicans turned back to the undivided Church, the Church of the Fathers, and there they found both monastic life and the theology that had produced it. And so, instead of the condemnation of monasticism in principle which was the usual Protestant attitude, Anglicans saw the dissolution of the monasteries as a condemnation of their abuse and not of their ideals. As Launcelot Andrewes wrote: "Nor was it the King's intention to condemn the original foundations of monasticism but rather the monks who have long since fallen away from that foundation."[2] In the life of the Church in England in the seventeenth century there were clear reflections of monastic ideals; for instance, in worship, the offices of Matins and Evensong in the Book of Common Prayer were derived from the Breviary, but instead of being for the use of monks and clergy, they were intended to be the ordinary devotion of lay men and women, in churches and colleges and households.

The great households of seventeenth-century England were another and especially interesting expression of this basic monastic orientation. The most famous of these was that of Nicolas Ferrar at Little Gidding, where in 1626 Nicolas settled with his relatives to live out their commitment to Christ in a life of prayer and fraternal charity, not as a monastic house in the strict sense of the word, but as a family with a monastic, contemplative orientation. Nicolas' own dedication of himself echoes that of the monastic: "He promised that since God had so often heard his humble petition and delivered him out of so many dangers and in many desperate calamities had extended his mercy to him, he would now give himself up continually to serve God to the utmost of his power in the office of a deacon, to be the Levite himself in his own house and to make his own relatives, who were many, his cure of souls." The idea of belonging essentially to the Church of England, and of following

2. L. Andrews, *Responsio ad Apologiam Cardinalis Bellarmini* (Oxford: Parker, 1851), p. 394.

the charism God had granted to the founder is expressed, too, in this early description of Nicolas' last instructions to the community: "He would often exhort the family that they should steadfastly and constantly adhere to the doctrine of the Church of England and to continue in the good old way and in those they have been taught out of the Word of God, and to what he had accordingly informed them of, for it was the true, right and good way to heaven." This way of life which Nicolas so firmly believed to be Anglican, made others describe Little Gidding as "a nunnery of Protestants," "the nunnes of Little Gidding." Accounts of the daily life there contain those elements of discipline and prayer which are usually found only in religious and contemplative communities. Besides the routine of work and prayer, they had that essential eschatological dimension in their life, which perhaps most fully sums up the contemplative community: "They kept sentinel at all hours and seasons to expect the second coming of the Lord Jesus."[3] Here indeed was "a place where prayer has been valid," and although Little Gidding had no immediate continuity ("mid-winter spring is its own season") the same attitude toward Christianity persisted as an element in the Church of England, to emerge again in the nineteenth century in the more explicit religious communities.

This ideal can be expressed in the term "communion of the saints," the affirmation that our life is rooted in heaven, in the shared vision of God—like a Chinese tree which grows downwards with its roots in heaven. Or it can be expressed by saying that the monastic community focuses the understanding of the monastic element in the life of not only every Christian but of every man. The understanding that "no man is an island, entire in himself . . . he is part of a continent, a piece of the main," is fundamental to the idea of a community of contemplatives. I would like to go more deeply into this approach to contemplative life by referring to a monk who was also archbishop of Canterbury, St Anselm. In one of his earliest works, the *Proslogion,* he is concerned with this idea of the vision of God, which is to be found in association with other

3. B. Blackstone, ed., *The Ferrar Papers*(Cambridge University Press, 1938), p. 85.

men. The idea of contemplation as a mystical "state," as the private
concern of the individual, was foreign to St Anselm. Equally, our
idea of "community" as something horizontal, concerned only with
human relationships, at variance with the individual, vertical,
dimension of contemplation, did not come within his frame of
reference. And this understanding is that of the Anglican communities, in essence.

Eia, nunc, homunicio . . . . "Come, now, little man," he begins,
"enter into the inner chamber of your mind, exclude everything
except God and whatever will help you to find him; close the door
and seek him: Your face, Lord, will I seek . . . ."[4] The withdrawal
essential for contemplation could not be more clearly stated, and for
St Anselm, as for the rest of the Fathers, the fall, sin, is seen as a
failure in *theoria,* a fall from contemplation, from the vision of God.
This is also for him a failure to live in true *communitas,* a falling
apart into individuality and separation: "From home land into
exile, from the vision of God to our own darkness, from eternal joy
to the bitterness and horror of death."[5]

The restoration of the vision of God is therefore seen as a return to
true community, because, essentially, the vision of God is of a
community of Persons, of the shared love of the Trinity.[6] This
vision of perfect community in the life of God is also the vision of
heaven, the society of the saints, the new and eternal city of God.
So, after describing the shared love of God who is perfect community, Anselm gives his well-known description of the life of
heaven, the vision of God who fills and fulfills all things, where
"they love God more than they love themselves and each other
more than themselves; they love God in each other and each other
in God," and the more people there are who share in that love, the
greater will be the love of each one. *Gaudium vero quale aut quantum
est, ubi tale ac tantum bonum est.*[7]

This recognition of the unity between the vision of God for each
and its expression in community depends upon an eschatological

---

4. St Anselm, *Proslogion,* ch. 1; PL 158:225.
5. *Ibid.,* 226.   6. *Ibid.,* ch. 23, 239.   7. *Ibid.,* ch. 25, 241.

dimension in one's understanding. Community must be in some sense a realization of the community of love which is the life of God. For Anglican communities, this is focused most of all in the sacrament of the Eucharist. Here the mystery of love and unity is one, as we are united with Christ our God and with one another in him. "Christ in the holy Eucharist is the living root, and the Divine Office which we say daily is a blossoming of the tree which springs from it," wrote one of the Anglican monks of the last century.[8] With this approach to contemplative life, the dichotomy of community—contemplation enters a new ethos, and is freed from certain tensions. One result of this is a deeper understanding of the underlying unity in the different forms of life within the Body of Christ, where categories of "higher" and "lower" make no sense. This leads to a greater integration between contemplative religious and other Christians, or indeed with God-seekers in any tradition, a freedom to learn from others, to see all things as means and not as ends, to change, adapt and grow. At the same time, the life of the community can take on a new and vital role as a realized eschatology, in the life of the whole Church. This frees the individual instead of limiting him, and can lead to a rejoicing in the shared life in Christ of those who have chosen one another as brethren in him. This joy in community life is one of the signs of the indwelling Spirit—when, as St Anselm put it, the life is *non pondus importabile sed pondus cantabile*.[9]

I would like to conclude with a quotation from the Rule of my own community, which is within the tradition of the Anglican Church. It is another expression of the definition of St Ireneus, "the glory of God is a living man and the life of man is the vision of God," applied to the corporate community:

As the heavenly city is built of innumerable stones, each possessing its own intrinsic beauty and its own due place, so the living Church of Christ on earth is continually being built up by the

---

8. G. Congeave, *Christian Progress* (London: SPCK, 1934), p. 58.

9. St Anselm, Ep. 101: *ad Helinandum*, line 47; ed. F. S. Schmitt (Edinburg, 1946–61), 3:233f.

perfecting of individual souls and their due relationship to one another in the oneness of charity. This is especially true of the monastic family where all depend for their growth in holiness upon the perfection of their relationship to one another in mutual obedience and holy love. . . . While the spirit of silence serves to separate each individual life unto God, the spirit of love must ever be binding all together in God, that in the unity of the Spirit all may seek their perfection by holy charity.[10]

Sr Benedicta Ward SLG

Convent of the Incarnation
Fairacres, Oxford

---

10. *Rule of the Sisters of the Love of God* (Oxford: Fairacres Press, 1970), c.26.

LITURGY AND CONTEMPLATIVE COMMUNITY

RANDOM REFLECTIONS AND NOTES FOR DISCUSSION

CHRYSOGONUS WADDELL OCSO*

LET THE READER BE CLEAR about it from the outset: the sub-title, "Random Reflections and Notes for Discussion," is no mere space-filler. It has an explicit function, and is meant to serve as a warning not to expect more from this essay than what the sub-title suggests. Do not, then, proceed further in the hopes of finding a systematic treatment in which the sweep of the logic leads onward relentlessly, inevitably, triumphantly to a tidy series of practical conclusions. What you will find is something much less pretentious—a few occasional thoughts about various aspects of the topic, "Liturgy and Contemplative Community." That is all.

The sub-title serves also a less obvious function, and one more personal to the author. He would have preferred to offer his reader an orderly, logically developed and thematically coherent essay, rather than a series of "random reflections"; a well-balanced analysis and synthesis rather than mere "notes for discussion." Better, however, to be more realistic, admit one's limitations, and even insist upon them. Thus, the sub-title serves me as a preventive against guilt feelings, since I do not have to attempt more than I can honestly cope with. In the following pages then, I do not presume to

*Fr Chrysogonus is a member of the Liturgical Commission of the Cistercian Order as well as that of the American Region. He has published many articles on various aspects of the liturgy, including contributions for the previous Cistercian Symposia. He obtained his STL from the Benedictine International College at Rome.

N

act as teacher, but merely as someone who provides material for your own reflection and further discussion.

I propose, then, simply to offer you a series of *pensées* which might possibly lend themselves to fruitful discussion. Some of these thoughts I shall develop briefly, but only briefly.

A few words are used frequently in the course of these random notes. "Contemplative experience" is one. By "contemplative experience" I mean a direct, intuitive experience of God. (I see no reason for distinguishing here between mystical prayer and contemplative experience or contemplative prayer and mystical experience. Nor is there any need, I presume, to clarify further the terms "direct," "intuitive" and "experience." A rose is a rose is a rose is a rose . . . .)

Liturgy is another key word. I use it in the same sense adopted by the Fathers of the Second Vatican Council in the *Constitution on the Sacred Liturgy,* n. 7:

> Rightly, then, the liturgy is considered as an exercise of the priestly office of Jesus Christ. In the liturgy the sanctification of man is manifested by signs perceptible to the senses, and is effected in a way which is proper to each of these signs; in the liturgy the full public worship is performed by the Mystical Body of Jesus Christ, that is, by the Head and his members.

A few further introductory remarks. The context in which I write and in which I hope these notes will be read is limited in the extreme, since my direct experience extends to only a few communities of Cistercians, situated for the most part in the United States; and I myself am constantly becoming more aware of the fact that I really do not know my own community as well as I should like to think I do. About Carthusians, Camaldolese, or other groups of contemplatives, then, I do not presume to write. I also exclude explicitly nuns, partly because my contacts with these communities have been only occasional; but also because my general impression is that most nuns are in a rather privileged position relative to us poor benighted males. As a group, they seem (to me) to be remarkably vigorous, level-headed, and not very prone to compromise their ideals. I am quite certain that a great deal of what I have to write *does* apply to them; but a great deal probably does *not*.

Finally, I wish to alert the reader that, in *my* vocabulary, "monastic" connotes "contemplative." It is true, of course, that one can be a contemplative without in any way being a monk; but I am still much hidebound by the tradition of many centuries which holds that a monk in any serious acceptation of the term not only seeks God truly, but seeks to encounter him as directly and immediately as is possible here below: and this, I believe, is what contemplative prayer is about.

The liturgy of a contemplative community is the liturgy of a contemplative community

In the abstract, there should be nothing problematic about the liturgy of a contemplative community. Essentially, this liturgy is the same Mystery of Christ celebrated in any community of worshipping Christians. Evidently, it does not exist in a void, but is actualized in a concrete community of flesh and blood believers. Inevitably, the shape, form and style of the actual celebration will depend to a great extent on the shape, form, and style of the praying community. The Sunday Eucharist in a Bantu village, on a swinging university campus, in the private chapel of the Pope, aboard a Spanish ocean liner on the high seas—all these celebrations will differ enormously, even though the same *Ordo Missae* is followed in each instance with reasonable fidelity.

The liturgy of a contemplative community, then, will simply be the liturgy as celebrated in the concrete by a community of contemplatives. Whatever is proper to the community as a *contemplative* community will doubtless leave its imprint on the shape and style of that given community's liturgy. There is nothing the least bit mysterious about this.

Liturgy and community-identity

In the concrete, there is a great deal which is problematic about the liturgy of many Christian communities, the chief problem being that there are many communities whose sense of community identity is weak, very weak indeed. One can hardly have a community liturgy without a real community; more is needed for a living liturgy than a conglomeration of people without faces.

Hopefully, most Bantu villagers still experience a sense of community participation and community purpose. They belong to the same clan or tribe or family; they live in the same village; they share the same beliefs; they are heir to the same customs and traditions. Humanly speaking, it is relatively easy for them to celebrate as a community in a style suited to their situation and experience.

Students on a university campus are in a quite different situation, coming as they do from every conceivable regional and ethnic milieu, and representing a vast spectrum of interests, aspirations, and levels of experience. But as students, they also share a great deal in common; and the liturgical celebrations of such pockets of campus Christians are often marked by a powerful sense of community-identity.

But whatever elements enter in to foster disaggregation within such community groups, necessarily affect the quality of such a group's liturgy, inasmuch as the culture of any given group somehow affects the whole fabric of its mode of life. As the UNESCO report, *Cultural Patterns and Technical Change*,[1] expresses it,

> The culture of each people is a living unity in the sense that a change in any one aspect will have repercussions in other aspects. This is true even in those cultures which, while in the process of very rapid change, are torn by conflicts and contradictions.

Liturgy, community-identity, and contemplative ideals

If the contemplative experience imports, as it does, some kind of an immediate, intuitive experience of God, and if a given community is made up of men whose life-thrust finds its dynamism in and through this sort of experience, it is normal that such a given community adopt a life-style which is in harmony with this kind of experience: a life-style which supports this experience, fosters it,

1. Edited by Margaret Mead in the UNESCO series printed by Mentor Books, New York, 1955, p. 288.

helps deepen it. Obviously, in the context of liturgy, the liturgical forms, style of celebration, choice of texts and music (if any) should all fit in with this general fabric.

Community-identity and crisis in contemplative ideals

To be a bit blunt about it—the first problem with regard to liturgy and contemplative community is finding a community which, in the concrete, can be said to be really contemplative in an unemasculated acceptation of the word; a community whose members are deeply committed to a common ideal of contemplative prayer, and who actually share (or desire very much to share) in the same sort of experience.

Most communities of monks can rejoice in at least a few men for whom contemplative prayer is a basic exigency of their very being; and most communities can point to even larger numbers of the brethren whose efforts are seriously directed toward entering more deeply into this sort of experience. But such men do not always represent a sizable majority; they do not always represent, indeed, a significant minority. The truth of the matter is that some, perhaps many contemplative communities, are passing through an identity crisis which bears on their understanding of contemplative life. Everyone is ready to agree on a few broad principles: we really ought to try to be fully human; and our monastic life is certainly nothing unless it is really an authentic expression of the Gospel. But as for "contemplation" . . .

An extreme statement of position—extreme, but held by growing numbers—was well expressed by Fr Nivard Kinsella ocso of Mount Saint Joseph Abbey, during the course of a Symposium on Prayer held at Mount Melleray Abbey, September 21–25, 1970:

> We must question . . . our acceptance of the primacy of con-templation. This notion is essentially Greek. . . . The Greek ideal was canonized and taken over by the Christian writers, and it was not free of Gnostic and Manichean influence. It passed into the inheritance of the Middle Ages and it was finally worked out in a synthesis by St Thomas. . . . It must be said that the classic teaching on the primacy of contemplation has to a large extent

ignored the realities of human life, and to some extent has detracted from the simplicity of New Testament religion, which is summed up in the two great commandments.

The fact is that contemplation seems to be largely dependent on temperament, and this fact has been almost entirely ignored in monastic life. To characterize a religious body or a monastery as contemplative is wrong. . . . This word can be properly applied only to an individual, except in so far as one can talk about the general thrust of the activities of life of the institute. The use of the phrase "contemplative institute" is misleading.

Further, to propose contemplative prayer as a general ideal seems to me to be unwise, in that for some people it leads to a degree of introspection that is unhealthy, and for others it leads to disappointment. . . . The number of persons for whom contemplative prayer is a reality that can fill their lives and at which they can spend long periods, is quite small . . . smaller, I think, than has been recognized or admitted in the past.

. . . The acceptance of the primacy of contemplation as anything other than an academic statement that has little relevance to life, seems to me to be misleading . . . (yet) the degree to which this . . . notion of the primacy of contemplation has influenced us can be seen in the altogether foolish and misplaced adulation that we give to the ideal of the hermit.[2]

As for the further question of the monastic ascesis as a preparation for contemplative prayer:

The idea that one must prepare oneself for contemplation by a long hard asceticism is true only to the extent that asceticism is identified with unselfishness. . . . Renunciation has its importance, but in general it will be much slighter than has been claimed in the past. . . . I think the emphasis on asceticism was entirely overdone and misdirected.[3]

Such statements have been extracted from their total context, in which Fr Nivard is admirably and explicitly concerned for the deepest realities of Christian life: love of God and neighbor. I am sorry that lack of space prohibits a more ample *in extenso* citation of

2. "Prayer Toady", *Hallel 2*, Special Issue 2, Symposium '70, pp. 30 and 31.
3. Ibid., pp. 32–33.

the passage, and emphasize this point by including this remark, not in a foot-note, but in the body of the text.

Here I am not at all concerned with the correctness of Fr Nivard's remarks. Whether he is quite right or all wrong or somewhere in between is simply not *ad rem*. What is *ad rem* is this: that, to a greater or less degree, the position adopted by Fr Nivard makes sense to some if not many monks of an Order which, in times past, had no difficulty in identifying itself with the device: Primacy of Contemplation. The contemplative nature of monastic tradition and its relevance to the present age is not always a self-evident pro-position even to monks committed to monastic life by solemn vows. In any given community of monks where there is an appreciable amount of discussion in progress relative to goals and contem-plative ideals, the liturgy is bound to be affected.

Liturgy in contemplative communities in crisis

Painful as an identity crisis at the community level usually is, it would be wrong to exaggerate its import on the community liturgy. One simply goes ahead and does the best one can. At the same time, one hopes and prays that the tensions created by the various currents of thought and experience may become fruitful and life-giving tensions which lead one deeper into the Mystery of Christ. Ultimately, an identity crisis can be a great thing for the community liturgy.

Besides, it would be fatal to draw a clear line of demarcation between the liturgy of contemplatives and the liturgy of the *massa damnata* of non-contemplatives. Without taking the trouble here to reject with reasoned argument such a division between contem-plative and non-contemplative, I should simply like to state my persuasion that, liturgy-wise, the contemplative is in exactly the same situation as everyone else. The Word of God present and acting in word and sacrament is to be received, interiorized, lived. Whether the setting is a Harlem storefront chapel or the lonely windswept oratory of St Martin perched on a crest on Mont Canigou in the Pyrenees, the situation as regards participation and celebration is identical. Everyone who celebrates the liturgy has got to be something of a contemplative, because the whole thrust of his being should be moving in the direction of a personal encounter with the living Word—an encounter as direct and immediate as possible. Thus, no matter how one articulates one's spiritual ideals and life-program, if, in the celebration of the liturgy, one tries to be receptive to the Word of God, the experience will not be alien to that of the "full-time contemplative." Indeed, the "professional contemplative" frequently makes rather much of a mess of his liturgical life, attempting, as he so often does, to create within himself a self-induced state of interiority which has no reference to the texts proclaimed or the mystery being celebrated. The ritual action simply becomes an irritating background against which one tries to celebrate an independent, interior liturgy. Often enough such individuals would do better if they directed their conscious efforts toward something as prosaic as singing on pitch.

But my real point here is that a community in crisis should turn its apparent disadvantage into advantage. If the suffering is born of honesty and authenticity in seeking God as a community, then chances for a vital contact with the Lord present and acting are all the greater than for a group of possibly somewhat complacent individuals who sometimes, and for what mysterious reason I know not, turn to poor account the grace of infused passive prayer. The beatitudes are for everyone. If you are poor, if you weep, if you hunger and thirst after justice, if you long for peace, you can celebrate the liturgy.

Liturgy in communities of contemplatives not in crisis

The word "contemplation" etymologically derives, I understand, from the Latin word *templum*[4]—but not from *templum* understood in the sense of a building set apart for the worship of the gods. It refers rather to a clear, open space from which one can view the broad sweep of the heavens for the purpose of observing auguries. This is illuminating. Our monasteries by right should provide such

---

4. Ernout and Meillet, *Dictionnaire etymologique de la langue latine,* under the word *Templum* (Paris, 1939); reference given in P. Philippe OP, *De contemplatione mystica in historia* (Romae, 1955), p. 1.

clear, open spaces. The monk should find within the cloister the ideal, clean, uncluttered place from which the man intent on God can gaze upon the full broadsweep of heaven. This is why our life style has got to be simple and liberating. Ideally, everything should open as directly as possible upon God's horizons.

This is also true of our liturgy, which should form a single piece with the fabric of the rest of community life.

Now, the contemplative experience, as I understand it, is not usually felt as a sudden irruption of the divine in total discontinuity with everything that had gone before. Though the experience is wholly gratuitous, totally beyond our own power to conjure up at will, and quite literally ineffable, perhaps it would not be wholly wrong to describe a common form of this uncommon experience as simply the Word of God becoming living and active and transforming within one's deepest being. It is a matter of empirical fact, however, that no one seems to live habitually and consciously at the deepest or highest point of intensity of one's peak experiences. But the monk whose interior being has begun to be transformed by the living presence and action of God normally develops a kind of connatural response to the Word of God wherever encountered, and no matter what the modality of its presence; so that Word somehow merges into the Word.

In the context of the liturgy, then, the mature contemplative is generally sensitive about mere wordiness or excess verbiage. Literary cleverness falls flat, and verbal pyrotechnics repel. Anything that might tend to overlay and obscure the simple, direct Word of God is out of place.

Whoever, then, has anything to do with liturgical renewal in a contemplative community should direct his efforts first and foremost towards creating a context in which the Word of God can be proclaimed with such simplicity and immediacy that it can effectively resonate in the hearts of the listeners.

In some communities, the presence of a few readers who can read with genuine understanding, slowly, and with a sense of interiority, would probably do more to spark a contemplative revival than a three-week community work-shop on prayer.

Along the same line of thought, music—if music there is—should always be in the service of the word. *Sensum litterae non evacuet, sed foecundet*[5]—"Let music not void the text of meaning, but render it fruitful." This text of St Bernard writing to Abbot Guy and the brethren of Montieramey has for many years been a source of great delight for me; and I know of no better program to direct the efforts of anyone concerned with music in the liturgy of contemplatives. This principle by no means excludes instrumental music; indeed, I should think that music as a means toward the practice of the sort of *Contemplatio physica* or *theoria physike* described so well by Maximus the Confessor, should have a privileged place in the contemplative community; music, pure music that springs from a source deeper than words and goes beyond mere verbal expression. In a sense, the jubilus should be in a special way characteristic of a monastic liturgy. At the same time, the grace of contemplative prayer is not always accompanied, alas, by the grace of musical appreciation.

St Bernard has sometimes been quoted as saying that the proper music for monks is *planctus, non cantus*—"dirge, not song." This is a hilarious statement for anyone who knows Bernard and the tradition he represents. It is true that, like every other person who takes the spiritual life seriously, Bernard excludes trashiness and frivolity. In the letter just quoted above, he specifies that the chant used in church should be "full of gravity"—*plenus sit gravitate.*[6] But "gravity," to his way of thinking, is not gloominess. A whole book could be written on *gravitas* and the Benedictine experience: a contemplative mode of experience which sees things as they are, which feels the order and proportion and rhythm of the phenomenal world and of life. Only the monk with a sense of *gravitas* is capable of real play; only the monk with a connatural feel for the harmony of things can enter fully into the dance of life.

Bernard further writes, in the same Letter, *Nec lasciviam resonet, nec rusticam*—our music should "smack neither of the sensuous nor

---

5. Ep. 398, PL 182:610 BC, tr. M. B. Pennington, *The Works of Bernard of Clairvaux,* vol. 1, CF 1 (Spencer, Mass.: Cistercian Publications, 1970), p. 181.
6. *Ibid.*

of the clumsily constructed." By "sensuous" or "lascivious" he by no means intends to negate the emotive aspect of the aesthetic response: in fact, quite the contrary is true. He insists that the music should be *suavis*; that it should "so strike the ears as to move the heart; that it should lighten sorrow and mitigate wrath." In other words, the praying monk has got to be open to the music; he has got to let it "work" on him and enter deep into his inner being. This is why the music should be neither frivolous nor superficial, since it is not something which the monk is expected to ignore, but rather is an element of a transforming nature—hopefully transforming for the better. Bernard's monk is a man who is wholly alive. *Nec rusticam.* "Rustic," clumsily constructed," *gauche.* . . . It is rather difficult to find the right word or combination of words to do justice to Bernard's thought. He is asking for an *integrity* of music. Badly composed, clumsy music is as bad as music that makes a direct appeal to superficial emotions. It lacks inner truth, and its effect can only be enervating. Too many of our communities have had to suffer on this score. Good will and a sincere enthusiasm cannot always supply for the lack of technical competence in musical composition. A few years ago, a large group of our French monasteries called upon several professional composers for help in precisely this area. Out of several hundred examples of various chants composed by our burgeoning monk-composers, only a single one proved acceptable to the critical musician who knew the tools of his trade. Our present historical context provides us with a magnificent scope for real creativity. It also provides us with unlimited opportunity to deluge our long-suffering communities with insubstantial pseudo-music which has its adverse effects even though no one can quite articulate what is actually happening. There is, of course, the simple fact that we have to make do with whatever talent we have—and, potentially, there is a good deal of talent at hand. But much of this talent is still in a rather raw, crude state. It would be in the interests of contemplation if a few of our burgeoning liturgical poets and musicians were to submit themselves to the serious discipline of cultivating their muse in an intelligent, systematic program of study.

We have immense need of poets and musicians. I have often heard it said that the monastery should be the ideal place for the creation of liturgical texts and music, because contemplative monks are supposed to be men attuned in a special way to the Word of God. This is quite true. But a contemplative can be attuned to the Word of God without necessarily having the charism of creative expression. Indeed, the contemplative experience is something that goes beyond words. A fellow who is colorblind is still going to be colorblind after a peak experience of contemplative prayer; and if his aesthetic responses were minimal, they are likely to continue to be minimal. We need contemplatives who can both see deep into the things of God, and can speak and write about the deep things of God and man in such a way that the community as a whole can recognize this as the expression of their own experience.

Perhaps it would be easier simply to avoid all such problems by eliminating as much as possible everything that touches on music and other art forms as so many complications and distractions. I wonder. Lama Anagarika Govinda, who had spent many years in Ceylon in a Southern Buddhist (Theravada) milieu in which music was entirely absent (on account of the view that music is merely a form of sense-pleasure) notes that, in consequence of this, "the religious life had taken on a dry intellectual form of expression, in which together with the lower also the higher emotions were suppressed and all negative virtues were fostered to the extent that no great personality could arise. . . . For the last 1,500 years the Buddharma in Ceylon had existed only in theory, or at the best as a belief, since (according to the Sinhalese themselves) Ceylon had not produced a single saint during this long period and it was no longer possible to enter into the higher states of *dhyana* or direct spiritual insight."[7] Evidently, the mystical experience is not bound up with a musical tradition—at least, not what *we* think of in terms of the mystical experience; and most of us would hesitate to see a direct casual influence between lack of music and mystical experience. Still, most of us do not live day in and day out absorbed in

7. *The Way of the White Clouds,* 3 ed. (London, 1969), p. 31.

an uninterrupted peak experience. And people who are pure brain or who turn into walking zombies as a result of cultural exinanition are not usually apt subjects for the higher graces of prayer, though for reasons best known to God.

Liturgy, community, and "pure" and "impure" contemplation

There is a "pure" form of contemplative experience that unifies a man and makes him whole. His divided inward being is brought together into unity; his outer self and his inner self begin to sing together in harmony; and outer and inner life are all of one piece, springing forth as in a single thrust from the same living source of life. The shattered mirror finds itself whole; and the light it reflects is no less Pure than the light it receives. The man who shares in such an experience is caught up in it in the totality of his being, so that his entire life in all its aspects is renewed and made whole at the very source of his being. In such a man, the New Creation is well on its way to consummation.

But there is also an "impure" form of contemplative experience. Perhaps "impure" is not the right word for an experience which begins with a genuine and positive grace of contemplative prayer. But what begins as an authentic experience of God ends, as a result of one's own egoism and selfishness, in a kind of pseudo-mysticism in which the individual manages effectively both to aggravate the divisions already present in his own heart and to isolate himself from all that is best and most meaningful outside himself. What I am talking about begins, I insist, as a genuine grace of deep prayer. This grace, however, is of its nature an inchoative kind of experience, meant to lead on to something deeper and more vital. In its initial stage, it lacks a wholeness and fullness, so that it sometimes co-exists with elements of a more ambiguous sort. The pattern, all too familiar to many of us, runs as follows:

We receive a "touch," an intuitive experience of longer or shorter duration, which leaves us in a state of exhilaration. For a moment, perhaps for a much longer while, our life has taken in a new dimension, a deeper quality of truth. This is sometimes (but not always) an experience of unalloyed happiness, and it is normal enough that we should wish to deepen and stabilize such a type of experience; in fact, we would like to turn it into as permanent a state as we can. A flash of joy; a torrent of rich, red wine. Who would blame us if we get a little drunk?

In spite of the spiritual hang-over which often accompanies such an experience, we want nothing more than more of the same; and, unless we receive the special help of the Holy Spirit and the enlightened counsel of an experienced spiritual director, we are liable to do all sorts of questionable things in mis-guided attempts to conjure up and re-create our "experience." Inevitably, we toss up defences against anything which might stand in the way of a repetition of this too-brief experience; and our sensitivity and touchiness increase in proportion as our attempts to produce our own spiritual experience end in frustration. Many of us succeed marvellously well in blocking out permanently whole areas of our human, spiritual dimension. And it is always easy enough to attach the blame to things so earth-bound and material as the liturgy or the community.

In brief, having had a taste of vintage wine, anything less smacks of vinegar; and we much prefer to spew it out rather than settle provisionally for wine of a less inebriating bouquet. Instead of becoming progressively unified and made whole in our deepest being, we become more and more torn apart interiorly and alienated from our brothers.

Writing in a different but related context, Rainer Maria Rilke had this to say to a young would-be poet of feeble gifts, who was experiencing difficulty in bringing his outer and inner life into harmony:

All emotions (read: forms of contemplative experience) are pure which gather you and lift you up; that emotion (read: contemplative experience) is impure which seizes only *one* side of your being and so distorts you. . . . Everything that makes *more* of you than you have heretofore been in your best hours, is right. Every heightening is good if it is in your *whole* blood, if it is not intoxication, not turbidity, but joy which one can see clear to the bottom.[8]

The problem is that, in the beginning of the contemplative experience of so many of us, we are seized in only *one* side of our being. The heightening or deepening or whatever you may wish to call it, is not in our *whole* blood. And the joy is not always a clear joy, but one mixed with a turbid intoxication.

And the tragic element in all this is that some of us make the gravest of decisions out of the poverty of our experience rather than out of the fullness of our experience. It is normal that a person exposed to a few deep but transient graces of contemplative prayer should experience, and keenly, difficulties on the score of community and of prayer shared in common. But it is also suicidal if a budding would-be mystic decides at this critical juncture to resolve his tensions by opting for contemplation as opposed to liturgy and community. Such a monk rarely totally eliminates liturgy or community. But community, he will tell us, is merely the *matrix* within which contemplative prayer is to be fostered; the community is for the individual monk; the community is there simply to make it possible for the contemplative to do his own thing. As for liturgy, its chief function is to provide grist for the mill-stones of contemplation.

Perhaps there *are* instances in which such a choice is called for. (Let the individual and his ghostly father see to it.) All I wish to suggest here is that too many begin much too early in the contemplative life playing contemplation off against liturgy, community, and everything else. To such a one I should like to say:

"Well, what you are experiencing is important; and if you're serious about contemplative prayer, it could become one of the best things that could happen to you, *if* you handle it in the right way. But don't be so foolish as to think you are feeling the present conflict because you are a great contemplative. You experience this conflict because you have just begun the life of serious contemplative prayer. If you were really a contemplative you would

8. *Letters to a Young Poet* (New York, 1954), p. 74.

realize that what you call the community is only the husk of the community, the outer shell; and when you talk about liturgy it is only about outward signs and words, and not about the deep reality of Christ living and present in and through the celebrating community. You can certainly try to resolve your tensions simply by eliminating liturgy and community from your perspectives, but I doubt if this is going to contribute much to any kind of an immediate, intuitive experience of God. The only *real* way to resolve your tensions fruitfully will be to attain the spiritual growth needful to find Christ present and acting in your brother, in the worshipping community, in all that passes through your experience. Quite possibly you'll never resolve fully whatever tensions you feel at present. But the simplistic sort of solution you propose is certainly no honest answer—not, at any rate, within the context of the Cistercian monastic tradition. (There *are* other traditions, and perhaps you are called to a different form of life.)

"At any rate, do not expect to hit upon some simple solution which explains away all your tensions at a merely intellectual level. Your conflicts will be resolved in proportion as you live more deeply and richly in Christ. You have made some small beginning; simply continue from the point where you are now."

Words of Thomas Merton, from a little noticed, dry, but rather important minor *opus*, *Symbolism: Communication or Communion?*:

The temptation of modern pseudo mysticism is perhaps one of the gravest and most subtle, precisely because of the confusion it causes in the minds and hearts of those who might conceivably be drawn to authentic communion with God and with their fellow man by the austere traditional ways of obedience, humility, sacrifice, love, knowledge, worship, meditation and contemplation. All these ancient ways demand the control and the surrender, the ultimate "loss" of the empirical self in order that we may be "found" again in God. But pseudo mysticism centers upon the individualistic enjoyment of experience, that is, upon *the individual self experienced as without limitation*. This is a sublime subtlety by which one can eat one's cake and have it. It is the discovery of a spiritual trick (which is sought as a supremely valuable "object") in which, while seeming to renounce and deny oneself, one in fact definitively affirms the ego as a center of indefinite and angelic enjoyments. One rests in the joy of the spiritualized self, very much aware of one's individual identity and of one's clever achievement in breaking through to a paradise of delight, without having had to present one's ticket at the entrance. The ticket that must be surrendered is one's individual, empirical ego. Pseudo mysticism on the contrary seeks the permanent delight of the ego of its own spirituality, its own purity. . . ."[9]

Harsh words. Too harsh, I think. St Bernard was just as realistic; but he was perhaps a bit more compassionate. "A great thing is love," he wrote, "but it has its *degrees*. The Bride stands at the highest."[10] He took it as self-evident that love and the contemplative experience admit of degrees, and that one advances from what is imperfect to that which is more perfect. Nor was he unaware of the fact that the generality of beginners in the spiritual life often manage to lace their life of prayer with substantial doses of egoism and self-love. But Bernard never called such persons pseudo-mystics or fakes. They had made a beginning; they still had a long way to go. It was a question of purifying a genuine love from all that was devious and perverted.

My impression is that a number of spiritual directors are so impressed with the indications that this or that spiritual son has received a genuine gift for prayer at a deep level, that they tend to consider him as already "arrived" when, in point of fact, the fellow has just begun. They canonize as full-fledged contemplatives newly hatched nestlings who are just beginning to flap their featherless wings. We need, and need desperately, spiritual directors who have not only a deep life of prayer, but who also have and exercise the gift of discernment of spirits. Such spiritual fathers can do much to protect their spiritual adolescent sons from shaping up a speciously attractive life-style which effectively relegates community and liturgy to an extremely peripheral position, while

9. J. Laughlin (ed.), *New Directions* 20 (New York, 1968), p. 14.

10. As quoted in E. Gilson, *The Mystical Theology of Saint Bernard* (New York: Sheed and Ward, 1940), p. 138.

apparently according contemplation its full primacy. What frequently happens is all too evident. A period of sustained difficulty or aridity in prayer discourages the erstwhile enthusiast, who has effectively insulated himself from contact with Christ through community life and participation in the liturgy. Usually he is able to shape up some kind of a foot-dragging *modus agendi*; but life in general becomes a rather dull affair.

While insisting that some individuals might very well be called upon by God to grow in a single direction, I remain hopelessly convinced that a truly deep contemplative experience leads more often than not to mature growth in every meaningful direction. For most of us, this entails a progressive rousing and purification of consciousness, so that everything that passes through our experience takes on a deeper, richer dimension. Something of what I am trying without much success to formulate is suggested in the lines written by Dame Edith Sitwell, where she speaks about "growth of consciousness":

> Sometimes it is like . . . a person who has always been blind and who, suddenly endowed with sight, must *learn* to see; or it is the cry of that waiting, watching world, where everything we see is a symbol of something beyond, to the consciousness that is yet buried in this earth sleep.[11]

Or again, it is like the phenomenon described in some of the books by C. S. Lewis, where he uses the symbol of an enclosed garden. Two things are proper to this garden enclosed: 1) from the outside, the area enclosed seems small, whereas, from the inside, the garden is bigger than the outside; 2) all that is most real about the outside is recapitulated within the garden in a more intense, deeper level of reality:

> "The further up and further in you go, the bigger everything gets. The inside is larger than the outside."
> Lucy looked hard at the garden and saw that it was not really a garden at all but a whole world, with its own rivers and woods

11. *Taken Care Of: Edith Sitwell's Autobiography* (London, 1965), pp. 44-45.

and sea and mountains. But they were not strange: she knew them all.

"I see," she said. "This is still Narnia, and, more real and more beautiful than the Narnia down below . . . I see . . . world within world, Narnia within Narnia. . . ."

"Yes," said Mr Tumnus, "like an onion: except that as you continue to go in and in, each circle is larger than the last."[12]

I do not believe that we shall do youngsters in the monastic life much of a service if we let them think they really see when they have really only caught a brief flashing glimpse of Truth; if we let them think they are in the garden enclosed when they are still at the bottom of the hill on which the garden is perched. Perhaps this is as far as they will get in this life. But if so, the reason should lie in the mysteriousness of God's predestinating action, and not in our own failure to help them along into a *fullness* of monastic experience in which one does not have to pick and choose between this or that aspect of our life, but can rather live a deep, integrated life where liturgy, work, contemplative prayer, relations with the brethren, and everything else are all deeply connected and mutually enriching.

Hence, I suggest a certain firmness when dealing with the bright-eyed youngster who for the first time has tasted a drop of the prayer of quiet, and decides that liturgy and community are not for him. The situation is a bit like that described by Flannery O'Connor with regard to teenagers who are turned on by contemporary literature, but could not care less about literature of past centuries:

The high-school English teacher will be fulfilling his responsibility if he furnishes the student a guided opportunity, through the best writing of the past, to come, in time, to an understanding of the best writing of the present.

And if the student finds this is not to his taste? Well, that is regrettable. Most regrettable. His taste should not be consulted; it is being formed.[13]

12. *The Last Battle* (New York, 1956), pp. 170–171.
13. *Mystery and Manners* (New York, 1969), p. 140.

Obviously, this principle should not be applied too brutally to the novice on a spiritual binge. The novice's taste *should* be consulted. But it also is in the process of being formed. Should it turn out that God really is leading a tyro along a special path in which community and liturgy are peripheral, I should think that, as a normal thing, that person would be called to a life so structured.

The wisdom of despair in things human

The mature contemplative should be experienced enough not to demand *too* much from community or from liturgy. If he has really tasted God in a direct experience, he knows very well how poor (though rich), how fleeting (though meaningful for eternity) everything else is.

The final pages of J. R. R. Tolkien's great Ring Cycle strike deep in the heart of any serious contemplative, who, like the Ring-bearer Frodo, has been called on a quest that leads to the ultimate, a quest hopelessly beyond one's frail capabilities. In the moment of deepest truth, Frodo is wounded; and though he returns to the comfortable world of the Shire, his wound, which is an interior one, cannot heal. He is no longer whole, and knows that his wholeness and final happiness lie beyond, over the High Sea, past the Grey Havens, into the West. Others are whole, unwounded; and theirs it is to live richly and fully on this side of the High Sea—like Frodo's faithful man Sam:

"Where are you going, Master?" cried Sam, though at last he understood what was happening.

"To the Havens, Sam," said Frodo.

"And I can't come."

"No, Sam. Not yet anyway, not further than the Havens. . . . Your time may come. Do not be too sad, Sam. You cannot always be torn in two. You will have to be one and whole, for many years. You have so much to enjoy and to be, and to do."

"But," said Sam, and tears started in his eyes, "I thought you were going to enjoy the Shire, too, for years and years, after all you have done."

"So I thought too, once. But I have been too deeply hurt, Sam. I tried to save the Shire, and it has been saved, but not for me. It must often be so, Sam, when things are in danger: someone has tó give them up, lose them, so that others may keep them."[14]

And that's the way it is with us. We cannot be too demanding with regard to the various things that make up our life. We cannot expect to find peace and full happiness in the things which bring peace and deep happiness to others less wounded than ourselves. We can rejoice with and for the others. And we can and should be in earnest when it comes to liturgical renewal and structural changes in community and so forth. But deep down, we know that this is not enough and can never be enough; and a certain peace comes with this realization. Hence, there is a sure wisdom in accepting our present situation as somewhat hopeless. Perhaps this is what St Paul meant when he wrote about using the things of this world as if we use them not. Because a fellow who has really felt the direct touch of God has been wounded, and he has a home-sickness which admits of only one cure. So my final remark is this: Though we should be very serious about all that touches on liturgy and community, we should not be overly serious.

Then Frodo kissed Merry and Pippin, and last of all Sam, and went aboard; and the sails were drawn up, and the wind blew, and slowly the ship slipped away down the long grey firth. . . . And the ship went out into the High Sea and passed on into the West, until at last on a night of rain Frodo smelled a sweet fragrance on the air and heard the sound of singing that came over the water. And then it seemed to him that . . . the grey rain-curtain turned all to silver glass and was rolled back, and he beheld white shores and beyond them a far green country under a swift sunrise.[15]

Chrysogonus Waddell ocso

Gethsemani,
Trappist, Ky.

14. *The Return of the Ring* (New York: Ballantine, 1966), p. 382.
15. *Ibid.*, p. 384.

THE THEOLOGY OF CONTEMPLATIVE COMMUNITY

Tarcisius Conner ocso[*]

IT MAY BE ASKED from the outset just what is meant by "the theology of *contemplative* community." Does this indicate an essentially different type of community or does it merely indicate a particular form of community? It must be clearly stated that this paper maintains the latter. "Community" is, first and foremost, *Christian* community; it is that community to which we have been granted access through the Blood of Christ and the sending of his Spirit. No qualification of this community life can change its essential nature.

This was already indicated during the discussions at Vatican Council II regarding the Decree for Religious. The Union of Major Superiors of Germany proposed in their remarks of December 4, 1963, that

> the distinction not be made between the various forms of religious life: *vita contemplativa, vita activa, vita mixta,* since grave misunderstandings result from this distinction. . . . Religious life, according to the evangelical counsels, is a witness to the redemptive work of our Lord Jesus Christ, and this is manifested in various ways, whether by a life of silence, prayer and expiation in a radical withdrawal from the world, or by an active apostolic life in the field of education or charity.[1]

[*]Fr. Tarcisius Conner is Professor of Theology at Gethsemani Abbey, Trappist, Kentucky. He holds an STL from the Pontifical University of the Gregoriana, Rome. Father has published a number of articles in *Monastic Exchange* and *Review for Religious.*

1. J. M. R. Tilard, "Les grandes lois de la rénovation," *L'Adaptation et la rénovation de la vie religieuse,* Unam Sanctam, 62 (Paris: Cerf, 1967), p. 130. See also *Lumen Gentium,* 44.

And the German and Scandinavian bishops commented that

> all religious institutes must, in accord with their proper mission, unite both contemplation, by which God is sought alone and above all, and apostolic zeal by which they strive to carry out the work of Redemption and extend the Kingdom of God.[2]

Religious life, under whatever form it is looked at, is simply the manifestation of the Christian's total adherence to the Father as realized in the baptismal event. This event constitutes us as "sons in the Son"; but it is necessary that we assimilate this gift as our own and strive to give it full expression in our lives. The *filii in Filio* is the initial and radical consecration, the primal sanctification which comes from God as the gift of *Agape* in Baptism, by which God takes hold of our very being in his Son. Religious profession, on the other hand, is the free act, coming from the Christian, by which he commits himself to center his entire life in a generous effort at perfect response to this adopted sonship.[3] Hence at the center of all religious life there is the risen Christ, and in the Spirit of Christ the religious enters into Communion with the Triune God.

This clearly shows that "there are not several religious lives, but one religious life; while it appears under various forms, it remains fundamentally one in essence, that is, in its theological and ecclesial dimension."[4] Christian tradition recognizes this and sees the differences as coming from the fact that the various types of religious life result from the way that each is structured predominantly around one or the other facet of the life of the Church.

"Contemplative community," then, is simply Christian community structured around the direct search for God alone. It expresses the life of Christ praying on the mountain ; it offers to God a service of praise and fulfills a particular function within the Church.[5]

2. *Ibid.,* p. 132. See also *Perfectae caritatis,* 5–6.
3. *Ibid.,* p. 135–136.
4. *Ibid.,* p. 139, n. 178.
5. *Lumen Gentium,* 46; *Perfectae caritatis,* 7.

At the same time, each contemplative community realizes the fullness of the life of the Church within itself. In the letters of St Paul, words such as *Ekklesia, People of God, Koinonia* and *Body of Christ* often refer in the first place to the local community of Christians. Recent Scripture studies have renewed this understanding. It was brought out in a speech during the Council. Bishop Edward Schick, of Fulda, Germany, made the following statement :

> This Church of God and of Christ truly exists in the local Church. . . . In such Churches God gathers together the faithful through the Gospel of Christ. In each of them the mystery of the Lord's Supper is celebrated, something so great that the whole universal Church can perform nothing greater. It is a mystery by which the complete Christ, present everywhere among his own in each community, manifests himself as the symbol of that unity and love in which he wanted all to be joined together among themselves. In these communities, even though they be small and poor, the whole Christ is present through the one Spirit by whom all are filled with life and united among themselves. He is the Spirit of love, of consolation and of hope, who gives his charisms to each individual, so that they make one Body with those varied gifts and bear witness before the world to the hope they have by their calling. . . . Each local Church is a true representation of the total and universal Church, which itself carries on its own life in these local Churches.[6]

From this we can conclude that "contemplative community" is essentially the Church of God as realized and manifested in a particular group of persons who join together in order to further their search for God in a more intense and exclusive manner. Hence the nature of "contemplative community" will be essentially the same as the nature of the Church. This nature can best be summed

---

6. Council Speeches of Vatican II (New York: Paulist, 1964) pp. 37-38. *Lumen Gentium,* 26, expresses the same notion. See also, *Lumen Gentium,* 11 and *Sacrum Concilium,* 2. This has been developed by G. Baum, "The Ecclesial Reality of Other Churches," *Concilium* 4 (1966), pp. 76-81 and E. Corecco, "The Bishop as Head of the Local Church and its Discipline," *Concilium* 38 (1969), pp. 88-104.

up in the phrase *Koinonia:* fellowship of mankind in the Father and the Son through the Spirit.

Statement of the Problem

During the Regional Meeting of the American Cistercians in 1968, the question of what constitutes the essence of monasticism was discussed.[7] Some placed this in the search for a life of prayer, while others saw it in the efforts to establish community. In reality, it would seem that both sides were deficient in their definition. It will be the purpose of this paper to show that true Christian community, and hence true contemplative community, is to be found in the element of *Koinonia*, which involves a true life of prayer and contact with God as a basis for one's relations with other men; but likewise that any life of prayer must, by its very nature, tend towards the establishment of community.

This has always been the contention of monastic tradition itself. Two recent studies on this matter have centered around the Rule of St Benedict.[8] It is the conclusion of both of these studies (which were carried on independently) that the Rule of St Benedict made a conscious and deliberate effort to develop the theology of community for his monks. Sister Augusta Marie concludes her study as follows :

> When the historical manifestations of the vision of Benedict for his monks are viewed from the standpoint of his *biblical theology*, his ideal shines forth. It is seen to be the Christian life of *Koinonia:* men gathered together in the love of Christ, having it, sharing it, and giving it.[9]

And Philip Hickey concludes :

7. Report of the Regional Meeting of the American Cistercians, Genesee Abbey, May 26–June 1, 1968, *passim*.

8. Sr Augusta Marie osb, "Koinonia: Its Biblical Meaning and Place in Monastic Life," *American Benedictine Review* 18 (1967), pp. 189–212. P. E. Hickey, "The Theology of Community in the Rule of St Benedict," *American Benedictine Review* 20 (1969), pp. 431–471.

9. Sr Augusta Marie, *ibid.*, p. 211.

For the early Eastern cenobites charity was one virtue among many and the ideal was to grow in virtue as an individual and to come to practice contemplation in a face-to-face relationship with God. . . . In other words, these monasteries cultivated the life of the community as a means to growth in individualist perfection in a spirituality which saw salvation in contemplation and in subjection of the body. Benedict did not see these emphases in the Scriptural roots of cenobitic life (i.e., the apostolic community). He had some intuition of the value of community in itself, that community was an essential element in salvation and an essential means to salvation. There is in the RB a deliberate effort to imitate the early Christian community in all of its aspects. . . . For Cassian community life is secondary. It is helpful to live and associate with wise spiritual directors until one's training is well advanced. Then one should go alone into the desert and cultivate contemplation. . . . For Benedict community life is essential. The meaning of Christ's obedience and humility effects the formation of a community of people. Eternal life in heaven is a community life. The cenobitic community lives that heavenly life in its communitarian life on earth. Community for Benedict is not simply a means to enable one to grow in virtue. It is already living in heavenly community.[10]

Using these conclusions as a starting point, we will try to study some of these communitarian themes in an effort to see how they relate to the real essence of "contemplative community."

The Nature of Community in General

It will be beneficial, however, to first look at the nature of community in general. A community of persons can be looked at from radically different viewpoints. Community may be conceived as an end in itself or as a means to something else. In the latter case, we have what may be called "functional society." This is not a formal unity of persons, but of actions and functions. It arises from the coordination of functions performed by members of the group. Such coordination is intended to achieve some further good which can be attained only by their concerted efforts.

10. P. E. Hickey, *ibid.,* pp. 465, 470.

In such communities, persons are united not as persons but as workers or functionaries.[11]

In contrast to this, we have "personal community," where the unity of persons is seen as an end in itself. Persons are now united, not in terms of their functional relationships, but in terms of their reality as persons. The ultimate good they seek is loving inter-relation as persons, the good of communion and fellowship. To this end, everything else is subordinated. Any functional relations will be determined by the demands of communion.

It might seem to some that contemplative community would be more in line with "functional society." In this light, persons would come together not to form a unity of persons, but rather for the purpose (or function) of creating an environment conducive to contemplation. Once this environment is created, each one would then be free to pursue his own life in a spirit of solitude. There are certain elements of truth in this. However this does not alter the fact that contemplative community, like any truly Christian community, is essentially "personal community." Community is the union of human beings by means of a profound bond. This bond unites the members in their very persons, and not merely in their activities or material goods, and enables them to know and love one another.

In 1966 a "communal weekend" was held in Belgium in an effort to study the meaning of community. After much discussion the following definition was formulated:

A Community is an organic and stable fraternal association of persons accepting responsibility for one another through sharing both what they are and what they have in order to bring about the unity of mankind.[12]

Some of these elements need explanation.

11. R. O. Johann, *Building the Human* (New York: Herder and Herder, 1968), pp. 85f.

12. M. Delespesse, *The Church Community: Leaven and Life Style* (Ottawa: Catholic Center, 1969), p. 4.

Fraternal association. This expresses a relationship based on a " life principle " which is common to all the members. Christians recognize themselves as brothers because they live by the same life of Christ and are sons of the same Father, God. The fraternal nature of a communitarian grouping implies the necessity for mutual knowledge and profound love among the members.

Organic association. Community is a living body. In a living body, the whole is greater than the sum of the parts. Community is a being which is higher than the sum of its members. It has an existence of its own, an autonomy. Just as a living body, the community is composed of various organs and members, each with a particular place and determined role for the good of the whole. The organic nature of community does not destroy the persons; on the contrary, it develops them and brings them to true fulfilment by recognizing their particular role, based on their aptitudes, desires and needs. The good of the whole body brings about the good of each member.

Stable association. Community is not formed by accident, as for example the underground forces or prison camps. Community unites the beings for better and for worse. It implies fidelity. But it can give birth to other new communities as a multiplication of cells, or it can receive some members who are not " stable " but dwell there only for a time, though the community itself remains firm in its inner cohesion and fidelity.

Association of persons. While "organic community" (or "functional society ") unites only in relation to certain activities or goods, personal community involves the person in his very being and enables him to build himself up in perpetual sharing with others.

Realizing a mutual responsibility. Co-responsibility is not merely assistance ; it is the action by which each bears his brother including both all his riches and all his misery. This continual action can exist only by means of mutual knowledge and love which express themselves in a physical, moral and spiritual support, fraternal correction, mutual dialogue, advice, encouragement, etc. It presupposes a "common life" which is very real, involving common meals, periodical common work, a common form of correction, and common prayer. "Common life" is something more than merely a number of "get-togethers" which unite activities or discussions rather than persons. It is by means of "common life" and co-responsibility that a true collective and personal responsibility develops.

Sharing what they are and what they have. Not only is each one co-responsible for the others, but he shares with them spiritually and materially. Each one brings to the others his very being, with its riches and poverty, as well as his material goods, in order to achieve the fullest possible balance. The "sharing of what they have" is possible only by means of sharing "what they are." The sharing of goods in community is merely the extension of the sharing of persons. Such sharing implies availability, a detachment from what one is and has; it relinquishes all demands.

In order to bring about the unity of all men. By perfecting unity in this way, the Community bears within itself the salvation of mankind. Community thus pertains to the order of end rather than means. At the same time, it must be aware of its vocation to extend itself to all men. A community that turns in on itself falsifies its own very nature ; it will no longer be a community. This "universal" character can be expressed in different ways and with varying intensity according to the circumstances of each community ; yet it remains essential. It expresses something of the eschatological nature of the community of the Church and the universality of salvation willed by Christ.

Using this definition as a basis, we can study the various theological elements of community.

Fraternal Association

This element is brought out most clearly in Number Fifteen of the Decree *Perfectae Caritatis*. It has been said that these lines are among the richest of the Decree.[13] They state that common life is the actualization of the fraternal *Koinonia*, by means of the presence

13. J. M. R. Tillard, *op. cit.,* p. 153.

of the risen Lord Jesus himself. The manifestation of charity, mutual regard and the desire to bear one another's burdens are simply the manifestation in human acts of that profound and mysterious reality which is communion of life with the Father in Jesus. This was begun by Baptism, enriched by the Eucharist, and is to be brought to its fulness by means of Profession.

Religious community is seen as a *mystery* within the heart of the Mystery of the Church. It is a *sacramentum,* that is, both a reality and a sign, which reveals first to the Church Itself and then to the world that the *Mysterion,* in the full Pauline sense of the word,[14] has already taken root within the history of mankind, as planted by the Lord Jesus.

This thought of Paul shows that ecclesial communion (*Koinonia*) is a reality which has already been perfected by the Paschal Mystery. Paul continually tells us that, by means of the Cross and its completion in the Resurrection, Jesus has recreated that unity which was broken asunder by sin: unity of men with the Father, unity of men with one another.[15] This was expressed by Bonhoeffer in the following way:

> [Christ] wants to be the center; through him alone all things shall come to pass. He stands between us and God, and for that very reason he stands between us and all other men and things. He is the Mediator, not only between God and man, but between man and man, between man and reality. . . . The path to the "God-given reality" of my fellow-man or woman with whom I have to live leads through Christ or it is a blind alley. We are separated from one another by an unbridgeable gulf of otherness and strangeness which resists all our attempts to overcome it by means of natural association or emotional or spiritual union. There is no way from one person to another. However loving and sympathetic we try to be, however sound our psychology, however frank and open our behavior, we cannot penetrate the *incognito* of the other man, for there are no direct relationships,

14. Rom 16:25-7; 1 Cor 2:7-16; Eph 1:3-14; 3:7-13; Col 1:25-28; 2:2-3
15. Eph 2:14-18; Col 1:21-3; 3:14-5; Gal 3:28.

not even between soul and soul. Christ stands between us, and we can only get into touch with our neighbors through him.[16]

The risen Lord bears within himself the fraternity of all men, their communion with the Father and with one another. The Holy Spirit whom he gives has precisely the mission of spreading within humanity this *mystery,* the source of which is the Lord Jesus and none other. When we enter into the mystery of salvation through Baptism, it is into this communion and this fraternity that we enter. We became "adopted sons" of the Father while becoming "members of the Church," "brothers of the saints." Communion and fraternity—which express the horizontal dimension—thus appear essentially as a gift, the gift of the *Agape* of the Father. It is the preeminent sign of the love of God for us; it freely introduces us into the fraternity of Christ Jesus, his only Son. The Eucharist, which draws us into sacramental communion with the Risen Body of the Lord, deepens and expands within us this *mystery,* it roots us in the fraternity.

But the Eucharist is a passing rite; it must express itself in the daily lives of men. The ecclesial *Koinonia,* the religious community, appears in this light. Community is to be the manifestation of the fact that in Jesus Christ, and in Him alone, God the Father has already given the fundamental gift to mankind. He has placed within the world that seed of true *fraternity,* based on belonging to the only Son of the Father. Its effects are frequently veiled due to the daily tasks. *Community* strives, by means of a special way of life,

16. D. Bonhoeffer, *The Cost of Discipleship* (New York: Macmillan, 1966), pp. 106–110. See also "Community," *Life Together* (New York: Harper, 1954), p. 23–24: "Without Christ there is discord between God and man. Christ became the Mediator and made peace with God and among men. Without Christ we should not know God, we could not call upon him, nor come to him. But without Christ we also would not know our brother, nor could we come to him. The way is blocked by our own ego. Christ opened up the way to God and to our brother. Now Christians can live with one another in peace; they can love and serve one another, they can become one. But they can do so only by way of Jesus Christ. Only in Jesus Christ are we one, only through his are we bound together. To eternity, he remains the one Mediator."

to render this actual presence of fraternity more living and perceptible. It is thus to be a sign of ecclesial communion in as much as this is the gift of the Father as expressed in Jesus and in his Spirit.

Koinonia

Reference has been frequently made already to the notion of *Koinonia*. It will be well to study this more in detail before proceeding further. The term itself is a basic word that is used in the New Testament to convey the Christ-Christian relationship. The central core of meaning of this term is sharing, that is, a voluntary, bilateral covenant of mutual, reciprocal having and giving. Besides frequent use in its ordinary non-religious sense, *Koinonia* is used in a specifically religious way in the New Testament.[17] It is most common in Paul, where it means the religious fellowship (participation) of the believer in Christ and Christian blessings, and the mutual fellowship of the faithful with one another. Specifically it is used for the fellowship arising from the Lord's Supper, the Eucharist, where the fundamental fellowship with Christ through faith is realized and lived in a higher sacramental form.

In St Paul, community or fellowship with Christ imparts to the Christian a share in the individual phases of Christ's life. These always involve a personal relation with Christ and inclusion in the mystery. These include: the Christian in Christ (Gal 3:28; Eph 2:4–6; 3:6), and Christ in the Christian (Gal 2:20; 4:19; Col 1:27; 3:11). This fellowship with Christ's sufferings, etc., is not restricted to individual believers. It broadens out into the spiritual fellowship in suffering of the whole community both within itself and with Christ. Similarly in 2 Cor 1:5, 7, Paul deduces from the participation of the Corinthians in his sufferings that they will also be

17. Forms and their meanings include: *Koinos*—common (ordinary, profane); in common (shared); *Koinonos*—a sharer, companion, partner; *Koinoneo*—to share, participate (both active and passive: to have a share, or give a share); *Koinonis*—(abstract noun), a sharing participation; hence, an association, fellowship, communion, close relationship; also a sign or proof of this (more concrete). Gerhard Kittel, ed., *Theological Dictionary* (Grand Rapids: Eerdmans, 1964) 3:789f.

P

fellow-participants in the divine comforts allotted to him. He expects this as a fulfillment of the law of fellowship.

Another element of Christian *Koinonia* is a communion in the Spirit (sometimes in the sense of a giving or sharing of the Spirit; sometimes a fellowship in the Spirit). Again community with Christ leads necessarily over into community among Christians themselves. This is the fellowship of the members of Christ's body with one another (sometimes in the passive sense of having Christian blessings, love, faith, fruits of the Spirit; at other times in the active sense of giving a share, especially with reference to collections of money for the poor).

In 1 John, *Koinonia* is a favorite term to describe the religious union of life in which the Christian lives. To be a Christian means to have community with God, with the Father and the Son (1:3–6) which results in a community of the faithful brethren themselves (1:7). John's gospel principally uses the verb *Menein* to express mutual abiding which begins in this world and reaches into the world to come, where it finds its supreme fulfillment (3:2).

The New Testament relationship of having and giving, of relationship in community, is a relationship between Christ and the Christian, and of Christians themselves in Christ. Numerous references in the New Testament make it clear that the bond of this relationship is love, *Agape,* in fraternal relationship, *Philia.*

Koinonia as an Expression of the Trinity
This shows us that *Koinonia* or Christian community ultimately springs from and expresses the life of the Trinity itself. Christ prayed that "they may all be one; even as You, Father, are in me, and I in You, that they also may be one in us" (John 17:21). Christian community is the fruit of this prayer. In this sense it is always a gift of God to man. It reflects in time the life of the Trinity itself.

The Cistercian Father, Baldwin of Ford, saw this and spoke of the common life as a copy or reflection of the life of heaven. "God is life; the holy and undivided Trinity is one life. The Father is not one life, the Son another, and the Holy Spirit yet another; but these three are one life."[18]

It should be obvious that this life of the community is not merely a reflection of the imminent Trinity in the sense of expressing unity in plurality. The community is an extension of the very life of the Trinity. It was "handed down to us to preserve it; in order that here on earth, through the common life we might begin to be formed in the likeness of the angels of God, so that we will be equal to and resembling them in life eternal to come."[19] The great revelation of Christ is to equate the charity of the Father and the Son and that of the disciples. There is not simply a question of a parallel or some comparison. It is the love which is proper to God himself that belongs to man by the mediation of Christ, to such an extent that they are the object of it, participate in it, and really live in it.[20]

The Trinity is not for us a reality which can be expressed only as a doctrine. The Trinity itself is with us, it is not merely given to us because revelation offers us statements about it. Rather these statements are made to us because the reality of which they speak is bestowed upon us. Karl Rahner speaks of the "Economic Trinity" (in the sense of the Greek *Oikonomia*—the Plan of Redemption) and says:

> The Trinity is a mystery of *salvation* otherwise it would never have been revealed. . . . This mystery is essentially identical with the mystery of the self-communication of God to us in Christ and in his Spirit. Man understands himself only when he has

18. Baldwin of Ford, *De Vita Communi*, PL 204:546D–549D.

19. *Ibid.* See the study of Charles Hallet, "La communion des personnes d'après une oeuvre de Baudouin de Ford," *Revue d'ascétique et mystique* (1966), pp. 405–422.

Compare Baldwin with Pachomius: "It is by a favor of God . . . that the holy *koinonia* appeared on earth . . . by which he made the apostolic life known to men desirous of modeling themselves after the apostles. . . ." quoted by H. Bacht, "Pachôme et ses disciples," *Théologie de la vie monastique* (Paris: Aubier, 1961), p. 67.

20. Ceslaus Spicq, *Agape in the New Testament* (St Louis: Herder, 1966), 3:34f.

realized that he is the one to whom God communicates himself. Thus we may say that the mystery of the Trinity is the last mystery of our own reality, and that it is experienced precisely in this reality."[21]

This shows that our own reality, our own inner depths, are united with the Holy Spirit as given by Christ. By his resurrection, Jesus possesses the Spirit so fully that he can share it with the Church (Acts 2:33) and thereby share with the Church that knowledge of the Father that he himself has in the Spirit. This same Spirit is the expression of the risen Christ's relation to the Father, and derivatively of the Christian community's expression of its filial identity (Gal 4:6). It is this same Spirit that the early Christians experienced as the very atmosphere of their life of shared faith and hope and love. The Spirit of Christ bound them together in a community of outlook and missionary energy.[22] The Spirit of Christ became their own spirit, their own vital force which united them to Christ and to one another.

Christ himself had compared the relation between himself and his disciples to that of the vine and the branches (Jn 15). The organic unity and common life between the vine and the branches, which are known to us as natural phenomena, are *realized* in a preeminent way in the relationship that exists between Jesus and his disciples. It is even here alone that they are *realized* to their perfection: the vine is a sign, a symbol, a sensible representation of this sublime and unique reality.[23] To abide in Christ (15:4) is to abide in his love (15:9) just as Jesus abides in the love of the Father. Just as the sole condition for the existence of the branches is to "abide" in the Vine, so the sole law of life for the disciples is to love one another. At the time of separation, Jesus gives his "new"

21. Karl Rahner, *The Trinity* (New York: Herder and Herder, 1970), pp. 46–47.

22. Bernard Cooke, *Beyond Trinity,* Aquinas Lecture, 1969 (Milwaukee: Marquette University Press, 1969), pp. 51–52.

23. W. Grossouw, *Pour mieux comprendre S. Jean* (Paris: Aubier, 1946), pp. 21–22.

commandment which comes from the future world, and which transports in some way the disciples into this divine world by isolating them from the "world" of hate. Charity is to distinguish the disciples from all others who know only hate (Jn 13:33-35).[24] God, by engendering us, communicates to us his nature and his life. For John, "he who is born of God" and "he who loves" are equivalent ways of designating the Christian. This charity does not stem from any moral fittingness or ideal perfection; rather it is a vital movement issuing from the new nature. The Christian who truly loves his neighbor could have this love only if God had given it to him. This love is a participation of that love by which God loves himself and by which he loves men. In other words, the *Agape* establishes a community of nature and life between the "one born" and his Divine Father, and it is by the experience of *agape*— lucid love—that the believer realizes what God is. The fraternal charity of the disciples of Jesus Christ springs from their divine nature as a pure spontaneity, after the manner of the love of their Father. It is consequently the unquestionable proof of their divine filiation. Men are capable of loving with a devotion and exquisite delicacy, even to sacrifice themselves for those who are most dear to them (see 1 Cor 13:3); but they cannot love *as* God loves. It is not only a question of greater or lesser quality or extension, a difference of degree. Rather it is a difference of *nature*. *Agape* is something different than what humans possess or even conceive. It is only God who can love in this way, with this fullness, this power of giving, independently of the amiability of the object.

The *redamatio* of the Christian cannot have the characteristics of priority, gratuity, spontaneity which characterize pure *Agape* (1 Jn 4:10). However, when proving his love toward his brethren, the child of God takes the initiative in regard to a neighbor who perhaps is not sympathetic, and with an effective beneficence which he could never exercise in regard to the Author of all. It is in loving his brothers that the disciple can love *as* God (see Eph 5:1-2),

24. Lucien Cerfaux, "La charité fraternelle et le retour du Christ," *Recueil L. Cerfaux*, vol. 21 (Paris: Gemblous, 1954), pp. 38–39.

manifesting a charity which is the source and plenitude at the same time as the pure gift (1 Jn 3:16). It is fraternal love, divinely poured forth in the soul of the Christian (1 Jn 3:1; 4:7–8) which constitutes the *Koinonia*. So long as one possesses and exercises charity in regard to neighbor, God is there, in us, just as the Savior promised (Jn 14:23). But an essential mark of fraternal love will be that it loves "not in word or in speech, but in deed and truth" (Jn 3:18). It will dedicate itself in a humble and fervent service after the example of the Lord who washed the feet of his disciples (Jn 13:15). Hence, simply an intention does not suffice. One must truly give himself to others, must unite a cordial love and sacrifice of self.[25]

This shows clearly that supernatural love of one's brother cannot be merely an "idealized" love. It is false to believe that the union of Christians in the one Body of Christ involves merely the mysterious higher-part of our being. The Christian belongs fully to Christ with every fiber of his being and every part of his desire. The Christian community, the perfect community, is the perfect place for "primary" relations, that is to say, relations of person to person in mutual knowledge and love. It has been well said:

> We must take care not to think of the relationship between Christians as purely supernatural. Grace does not destroy nature; it presupposes it and, we might say, builds on it so well that it pushes nature beyond its own limitations. Between Christians of the same community there are bonds of knowledge, love and sharing which are all the more profound because they have been lifted up to the divine level. . . . But because of this life in Christ that we have in common we necessarily seek to know the others and to share spiritual and material goods among communities.[26]

In the same way, Karl Rahner remarked:

> There must be real love, not merely fulfillment of a command that protects the other from brutal egoism. "Love for the sake of God" does not mean a love that uses one's neighbor as the

25. Ceslaus Spicq, *op. cit.,* pp. 130–137.
26. M. Delespesse, *op. cit.,* p. 11.

"material" for pure love of God alone, but real love of the neighbor himself. In its ultimate roots this love is made possible by God and reaches the neighbor to remain with him.[27]

This need for a real and personal love which attains to concrete persons springs from the nature of the Incarnation. God has entered into this world body and soul and has identified himself with the nature of man, so that now all those who bear that nature are also bearers of the divinity. This means that man can find God expressing himself in the brother and he can respond to God in responding to the brother. But again this takes place only through and in Christ. We are called to truly deal with the brother, but in a new way. Man can have no immediate relation to his brother except through Christ. This breach with all immediate relationships is inescapable. It can be either external and evident, or it can be hidden and secret. But in the last resort it makes no difference. Bonhoeffer explains this by using Abraham as an example:

Abraham is an example of both. He had to leave his friends and his father's house because Christ came between him and his own. On this occasion the breach was evident. Abraham became a stranger and a sojourner in order to gain the promised land. This was his first call. Later on he was called by God to offer his son Isaac as a sacrifice. Christ had come between the father of faith and the child of promise. This time the direct relationship not only of flesh and blood, but also of the spirit must be broken. Abraham must learn that the promise depends on God alone. No one else hears this call of God, not even the servants. Once again, as when he left his father's house, Abraham becomes an individual, a lonely and solitary figure. He accepts the call as it comes; he will not shirk it or "spiritualize" it. He takes God at his word and is ready to obey. At that very moment all that he had surrendered was given back to him. He receives back his son, but henceforth he will be his son in quite a new way— through the Mediator and for the Mediator's sake. Since he had shown himself ready to obey God literally, he is now allowed to possess Isaac though he had him not—to possess him through

27. Karl Rahner, "The Love of God and Love of Neighbor," *Theology Digest* 15 (1967), pp. 87–93.

Jesus Christ. No one else knows what has happened. Abraham comes down from the mountain with Isaac just as he went up, but the whole situation has changed. Christ has stepped between father and son. Outwardly the picture is unchanged, but the old is passed away, and behold all things are new. Everything has had to pass through Christ.[28]

This brings us to the new element of the particular call of God.

The Call of God to Community—Ekklesia

"It is not for us to choose which way we shall follow. That depends on the will of Christ. But this at least is certain: in one way or another we shall have to leave the immediacy of the world and become individuals, whether secretly or openly."[29] This brings us face to face with the Call by God which is called a Vocation. If there be anything specific to the contemplative community, it is in the way that the Word of God is received and the demands that it places on that community. This is something, however, which cannot be determined *a priori* or on a universal basis. Bonhoeffer has spoken of a breach which is either open or secret. But between these two, there will be varying degrees. The breach between the hermit and others will be more "open"; that of the Christian in the world with business and family, will be less "open" and more "secret." The breach also of the monk in his coenobium will be more "open," even though that breach between himself and the other cenobites will be more "secret."

But the same Mediator who makes us individuals is also the founder of a new fellowship. He stands in the center between my neighbor and myself. He divides but he also unites. Thus although the direct way to our neighbor is barred, we now find the new and only real way to him—the way which passes through the Mediator.[30]

28. Dietrich Bonhoeffer, *The Cost of Discipleship*, pp. 111–112.
29. *Ibid.*
30. *Ibid.*

Each one must face God alone, and in this confrontation learn what is the call of God for himself. We are to face him in the nakedness of faith, willing to abandon all things—to "leave all things for his sake" (Mk 10:28). In this spirit, we are to hear his Word. This Word is always something of a revelation, since a word in its higher essence is the means by which two interior beings reveal themselves to one another in view of a reciprocal relationship.[31] If God means to reveal himself this can only be in order to establish bonds of friendship and love with man and associate us in his own divine life. For the Word of God puts the meaning of our personal existence at stake, as well as the meaning of all human existence. It is not a question merely of modifying our system of values in one or another detail. It is our whole person which needs a different orientation. If Christ is God, who is Truth in person, then his Word becomes the basis, norm, criterion for everything. Human thinking and conduct are subject to the judgment of this Word.

It is in this spirit that history has viewed the question of vocation. The "canonical" question of the obligation to follow a religious vocation has tended to obscure the basic issue: does this vocation, this call, come from the Word of God and if so, what does this Word ask of me? Since Jesus Christ is a Person and since each man is a person, there will be many varied ways of responding to the Word. The exchange between two persons is never the same as that between any other two. The encounter, the call, the proposal, the orientation of life, the service are each unique. As Jean Leclercq remarks in a study:

> Anthony heard a word, he received a grace: he had a vocation; this is a charism. A charism is a gift of the Spirit who was in Christ and who acts within the Church. The same Spirit communicates various gifts to each one, different ways of participating in his one, unique action. And each gift must be received,

31. René Latourelle, *Theology of Revelation* (New York: Alba House, 1966), develops this theme at length, referring to the works of Karl Buhler, H. Noack, M. Heidegger, M. Merleau-Ponty, M. Nedoncelle, L. Lavelle, G. Gusdorf, H. Delacroix, A. G. Robledo, *et al.*

accepted. The call, if it is heard and answered, determines the
conduct of him to whom it is addressed, it points the direction
for his life and action.[32]

This call always asks one to follow Christ, and this following
leads in directions that one cannot foresee. But the Word also
carries with it the strength to carry out whatever God may ask.
Certain ones may be invited by God to accept the total renounce-
ment which is implied in the act of faith, without any hope of
compensation within this world. In this way, certain ones may be
asked to live, in a certain way, apart from this world and within
the Kingdom in order to point the direction for others. Like
Abraham, this direction is given, not from within the Promised
Land, but from the land of exile, in that obscure but ardent search
which constitutes the life of faith. It is in virtue of this that the
religious community, and particularly the contemplative community, is an eschatological sign within the Church. The contemplative community relinquishes certain elements which may be
necessary and beneficial for those who are more directly involved
in establishing the beginning of the Kingdom upon this earth. The
way in which the monk responds to the call of God determines
his place within the larger community of the Church. It determines
his mission and purpose in relation to the whole.

It is this call of Christ which brings the man to the monastery.
St Benedict developed the whole of his Prologue within this
context. The monastic community, then, like the ecclesial community, comes about because of their personal encounter with the
risen Lord. In this way it can truly be said that the monastic life
is a life of prayer. However the call does not end there. Men bind
themselves together in response to a common encounter with the
Lord. The very encounter itself is not merely a "one-to-one"
experience between the man and the Lord. Already within this
experience there is an impetus toward an encounter with others

32. Jean Leclercq OSB, "Pour une théologie de la vie contemplative," *Le
Défi de la Vie Contemplative* (Paris: Editions Duculot-Lethielleux, 1970) p. 33.

who have similarly heard the call of the Lord and seek to respond to it. Hans Küng expressed this in regard to the Church:

> The common experience of personal communion with the living Jesus, in addition to the common experience of the resurrection, would inevitably have led to a new alliance between the disciples. It was their common allegiance to Jesus, to the "man" now hidden, but who would soon reveal himself in glory, which would remain a constant factor for the disciples, even after his death, and would continue to bind them together. . . . As soon as men gathered together in faith in the resurrection of the crucified Jesus of Nazareth and in expectation of the coming consummation of the reign of God and the return of the risen Christ in glory, the Church came into existence. . . . Not the words and instructions of Jesus in the time before Easter alone, but the action of God in resurrecting the crucified Christ and in pouring out the Spirit, turned the group of those who believed communally in the risen Christ into a community of those who could claim to be the new eschatological people of God.[33]

It is thus their common experience of the Lord which unites the early disciples into a community of believers. We can see something of the reason for this by looking briefly at the nature of "experience." In the sense in which we are using this term, "experience" cannot be merely equivalent to sense data. It must be seen in relation to the contemporary view which defines "experience" as "the whole range of the self's active relationships with the other."[34] Within man's response to the risen Lord, there is already contained the whole of his response to the rest of men and to the whole of reality. Consequently his response to the Lord impels him to respond to others; to form with others into that community of persons which will enable them to further their mutual search for the Lord.

It is this which links the community with the true notion of the Church—the *Ekklesia*. In the Bible, the notion of *Ekklesia* is always qualified by the phrase "of the Lord." It implies a process of congregating a group, but not just any arbitrary group. The *Ekklesia*

33. Hans Küng, *The Church* (New York: Sheed & Ward, 1967), pp. 75–76.
34. Robert O. Johann, *op. cit.*, pp. 87–88.

of God is a congregation of those previously chosen by God, who gather around God as their center. By taking over the term, the early Christian community made its claim to be the true congregation of God, the true community of God, the true eschatological people of God.[35] This notion of *Ekklesia* means both the actual process of congregating and the congregated community itself. Both of these are important. The former shows that the *ekklesia* or community is not something that is formed once and for all and then remains unchanged; it becomes an *ekklesia* by the fact of a repeated concrete event, people coming together and congregating, in particular congregating for the purpose of worshiping God. On the other hand, the community remains as the constant source of the constantly repeated event of congregating.

Applying this to our notion of community, we can see that the Christian community is likewise congregated by the action of the risen Lord, through the call of his Spirit. He himself remains ever the source and life of this community. Precisely because the community confesses Jesus as Lord, it has confidence that the Lord himself will lead the community during this period between his resurrection and his final coming. The contemplative community is particularly in line with this aspect of community. It seeks to remain in contact with the risen Lord through a spirit of continual prayer, waiting in expectation for his return. The monastic community in general has traditionally fulfilled this function within the Church of serving as the "watchman of the night" who strives to ever seek the face of the Lord. This is the meaning behind the traditional practice of nightly Vigils and recitation of the Psalms. It is this which expresses the living faith of the concrete community. This faith is the experienced response to God's self-revealing Word. The Bible itself becomes fully "Word of God" only when it is proclaimed to a community of believers. This Word of God is never communicated exactly the same to any two Christian communities. "The experience of hearing the Scriptural expression of the Word of God, the sacramental experience of enacting the

---

35. K. L. Schmidt, "Ekklesia," *Theological Dictionary*, ed., Kittel, vol. 3.

very mystery of which Scripture speaks, the experience of confronting the realities of daily life with the vision of Christian faith and hope;" all of these fashion that particular way in which the Word of God is received by a particular community.[36] All of these serve to constitute the particular nature of the community in question. Hence, all of these will have particular influence in determining what makes "contemplative community."

The contemplative community strives to center its life around the Mystery of Christ in the full sense of this term. It follows the example of the early Christian community which St Luke referred to not by terms such as "friends" or "brothers," but simply as "the believers."

> By this manner of address, Luke seems to be inviting us to understand the early Christians' conduct and personal relations in terms of the faith which unites them to each other in their common attachment to Christ. This faith grounds their joyous experience of community. The reality of love is present in the early Christians' fraternal love and concern for one another. Friendship binds them together, but in a much deeper sense than Greek philosophy would have conceived it. Acts testify to a strong brotherly feeling of union, which manifests its genuineness in a selfless concern for one another's welfare and happiness.[37]

Once again we see that, as Bonhoeffer expresses it, "Christian brotherhood is not an ideal, but a divine reality; and secondly, that Christian brotherhood is a spiritual and not a psychic reality." It takes place only through and in Jesus Christ. It ever remains essentially a Gift of God's mercy to man.[38] "We have no claim upon such experiences, and we do not live with other Christians for the sake of acquiring them. It is not the experience of Christian brotherhood, but solid and certain faith in brotherhood that holds us together."[39]

36. Bernard Cooke, *op. cit.,* p. 50.

37. Paul J. Bernadicou, "Christian Community According to St Luke," *Worship* 44 (1970), p. 216.

38. Dietrich Bonhoeffer, *Life Together,* pp. 26f.

39. *Ibid.*

Christ thus gives us the community as an expression of his own love for us. It is through and with the community that we are able to accept his Love and respond to it. "Only in a community can man learn, in terms of his own experience, what it means to know and to be known, to love and to be loved. Without such experience a man is left with abstract concepts of a God who is remote from him. It is in and through community that God reveals to man something of his own love and concern and tenderness."[40] No one believes alone; we believe only in and through others. To believe is to enter into community with those who trust and are trusting. Faith is always relational. It looks out on the other; but it also looks in to oneself as known, in relation to others.

Faith is also purified through community. The believer needs to look at who he is and to re-examine the content of his faith. This search, which is particularly the search of the contemplative, is aided by community. Individualistic reflection can end up in unreality. Community reflection and community conviction can be a valuable asset in such a search. Man cannot reveal himself and his own deepest doubts to an unbeliever. But within community each man is freed to be himself, to be with others and enter into a faith relationship with them. The believer feels very keenly his own unbelief and so desires to be made firm in the faith of his brothers. This supportive role between believer and community is emphasized in Jesus' words to Peter: "I have prayed for you, Simon, that your faith may not fail and once you have recovered, you in turn must strengthen your brothers" (Lk 22:32). Unless faith is shared, no true community is possible. For it is this communality of faith which underlies common understanding and gives rise to consensus in decisions.

Sharing of all things in common—The Apostolic Community

The notion of sharing one's goods and one's person should not be seen merely as the result of a theoretical definition, however. It

---

40. Sister Marie Beha OSF, *The Dynamics of Community* (New York: Corpus Books, 1970), pp. 137–138.

must be explicitly connected with the early Christian community and its expression as seen in the Acts of the Apostles. Early monastic writers all referred to the pentecostal community which was structured around two pivotal points, as emphasized by the "Summaries" which are inserted into the structure of the Acts of Apostles (2:42–47; 4:32–35; 5:12–16): *koinonia* with the Lord, heard in the word of his witnesses and nourished by his mysterious presence in the midst of those who are gathered in his Name; and service of the Gospel, accomplished either by the witness of the community itself or by the preaching of the Good News by certain ministers.[41]

These texts contain two values which we have already seen in previous sections. First, the affirmation that the presence of the Lord is experienced in the hearing of the Word, the prayer and liturgy, and particularly his own Memorial. Secondly, that this presence of the Lord "in the Spirit" at the heart of the community of disciples constitutes the unifying point which binds them all in true fraternity, in the same way that the physical presence of Jesus constituted the unifying point for the group of those who followed him during his earthly life. This life of fraternity around this presence of Jesus normally tends to express itself in total *koinonia*. The Church of Jerusalem was identified by the fact that "no one said that the things he possessed were his own" (Acts 4:32); he abandoned them, but for the sake of the fraternal community in which all were "but one heart and one soul." The words of Jesus to those who must leave all things in order to follow him are thus applied anew to the pentecostal ecclesial *koinonia*. One leaves everything; but this very detachment becomes fruitful. It is not merely a negative despoilment. Concretely, it builds up *koinonia*: what is given up is given to the poor of the community.

This relation with early monastic community can be seen in the

41. L. Lefort, ed., *Les vies coptes de S. Pachôme* (Louvain: Museon, 1943), pp. 60–61 and 276f. See also John Cassian, Conf. 18, ch. 5, *Library of Nicene and Post-Nicene Fathers,* 2nd Series, vol. 11 reprinted (Grand Rapids: Eerdmans, 1955), pp. 480–481. See also in general the article by Tillard, "Les fondements evangeliques de la vie religieuse," *Nouvelle Revue Théologique* (1969), pp. 916–956, as well as Thomas Barrosse CSC, "Religious Community and the Primitive Church," *Review for Religious* 25 (1966), pp. 971–985.

one who has been called "the founder of cenobitism." In the *Rule
of Pachomius* everything is centered on *koinonia:* "the law of holy
and true *koinonia,* whose author, after the Apostles, is the Abba
Pachomius."[42] This law enables a multitude to become "a single
spirit and a single body."[43] This same insight was carried on by
Horsiesius, the first successor of Pachomius, who wrote:

> The Apostles teach us that our community and the *koinonia* which
> unites us is from God when he says: "As regards good deeds and
> the *koinonia,* do not overlook them, for it is from such sacrifices
> that God takes pleasure." We read this also in the Acts of the
> Apostles: "The body of believers had but one heart and one
> mind, and no one among them said: this is mine, for all things
> were held in common." And the Psalmist is in accord with this
> when he said: "Behold, how good and how pleasant it is for
> brethren to live in unity." We likewise who live in the *cenobia*
> and are united by mutual charity, act in such wise that, as we have
> merited to share the lot of our holy fathers, so likewise in the
> future life we may have part with them.[44]

The relationship between this sharing of goods and community
life can also be found in the *Rule of St Benedict.* Both of the studies
already referred to[45] show how the New Testament references
throughout the seven chapters on ownership and work contribution
are the key to the relationship of these chapters, and therefore, of
poverty, to the total ideal of the Rule. Common ownership sustains
and expresses brotherhood in Christ, *koinonia.* Hence for Benedict
the stress is not on the absence of possessions, but on sharing and
giving common possessions in Christ, the concrete *koinonia* of
the Gospels.

The same can be said for the other elements of religious life. The
vows of religious life express not merely a consecration to God, but

42. Th. Lefort, *Oeuvres de S. Pachôme et des ses premiers successeurs,* CSCO
160 (Louvain, 1956), p. 38.

43. Th. Lefort, *Le vies,* p. 212.

44. A. Boon, *Pachomiana Latina* (Louvain, 1932), p. 142: *Liber Patris nostri
Orsiesii.*

45. See note 8. Sr Augusta Marie, *ibid.,* p. 206; P. L. Hickey, *ibid.,* pp.
435–438.

also a dedication to *koinonia*. By the practice of chastity the entire community professes that the love which directs it comes not from the flesh but from the action of the Holy Spirit within the hearts of each. If the community is to grow in love each day, this is not merely because the persons are humanly pleasing, but because the Father himself gives to each the grace of communion.

Obedience is promised, both to the superior and to one another, not merely as a denial of one's own will, but as an expression of inserting oneself into a community. Instead of seeking primarily to promote good order through rules (as might be the case in functional society), authority in personal community looks to the promotion of consensus—a genuine thinking, feeling and willing together of all the members. And it should be obvious that stability and conversion of manners are connected with community.[46]

Community of Sinfulness

Our sharing in all things extends not only to the good that one is or has, but also the evil, the weakness, the frailty of one another. The early Christian community was not entirely the idyllic reality portrayed in the Summaries just considered. This is proven by the incidents of Ananias and Sapphira, the frictions between Hebrews and Hellenists, and particularly the letters of Paul. Yet, in spite of this, a great spirit of charity and realism prevailed. Paul's simple exhortation was: "Bear one another's burdens, and so you will fulfill the law of Christ" (Gal 6:2). Bonhoeffer shows that one cannot approach Christian community in a visionary manner. To do so means that one comes to it with his own demands, sets up his own law, and judges the brethren and God himself accordingly. In such a case it is impossible to humbly receive the gift of community. "He who loves his dream of a community more than the Christian community itself becomes a destroyer of the latter, even though his personal intentions may be ever so honest and earnest and sacrificial."[47]

46. P. L. Hickey, *ibid.,* studies the communitarian nuance of *conversatio* at length, pp. 447–458.

47. Dietrich Bonhoeffer, *Life Together,* p. 27.

Q

The community that we share is the *real* community, the existential community made up of persons who may not be perfect or agreeable or likeable. Community means accepting all that is included in a person's nature, individuality, endowment. It means working with each person's weaknesses and oddities, which are such a trial to our patience, everything that produces frictions, conflicts and collisions among us. But it means accepting these just as Christ did: in a redemptive way.

Hesed is the Hebrew word for love as benignity or benevolence. It refers not primarily to a disposition, but to a helpful act which demonstrates assisting-faithfulness in mutual dealings. In the Old Testament *Hesed* rests on the covenant by which Yahweh has freely bound himself to the people (1 Kings 8:23; Is 55:3; Ps 89:49). Closely related is the Hebrew word *rahamim* which is best rendered love of pity or sympathy and may be used to denote gracious action. *Rahamim* is sometimes used in the Old Testament for the grace of forgiveness (Ps 51:1; Ps 79:8). *Hesed* is rendered by the Greek *eleos* or Latin *misericordia*, and English *mercy*. No English word adequately translates its meaning.

In the New Testament *eleos* is often used for the divinely required attitude of man to man. It is used to describe the act of the Samaritan (Lk 10:37) and to indicate Christ's attitude toward sinners. It signifies breadth and tolerance shown as the measure of what a person may expect from God (Mt 5:7; 18:33). The use of the word in the New Testament most frequently implies the will to save, moving the Christian to confer life in Christ (Eph 2:4; 1 Pet 1:3). In men *eleos* comes very near to the significance of *agape*. The revolutionary conception of love in the New Testament places a deeper motivation behind *eleos* than is evident in the Old Testament. The new feature is based on knowledge of God in Christ.[48]

This redemptive love has come from the Father in Christ. It has been shown to all men through the Cross and Resurrection and now infused into their hearts through the same Spirit who pours forth the *Agape* of the Father into our hearts. It is now to be spread

48. Kittel, *Theological Dictionary*, 4:479ff.

abroad by men themselves. This redemptive aspect of human love is concretized in life by men mutually giving and sharing acceptance which enables each to have the courage to be himself and to be a member of the *Koinonia*.

Paul Tillich has shown that every man needs a close relationship in which he feels acceptance and is, therefore, able to accept weakness in himself. Man to man acceptance-of-the-unacceptable in the other is the source of self-affirmation.[49] Tillich uses the word "acceptance" in place of forgiveness, for forgiveness humiliates while acceptance equalizes. Another is accepted not because he is good, but because he wants to be so. Acceptance includes forgiveness and is therefore redemptive.

It is necessary that one maintain fellowship with the others not only as believers and sharers in the divine life, but also as sinners. To accept one's sinfulness is a liberating thing, which enables one to put away the mask of untruthfulness. And once this mask is removed, one can truly be himself both before God and his brother. Man is ensured against all self-deception by opening himself to his brother. But he is also created anew in this act. Brother loves brother not *because* of their qualities, but *in order* to engender deeper qualities or to awaken qualities which are already present. Jesus saved us by loving us in the name of his father. We also, by loving our brothers, are to heal them spiritually and physically. Louis Evely has said that "a man can only increase his spiritual stature for those who love him. If we want to condemn others to sterility, it is sufficient merely not to love them." In community, forgiveness is not only a matter of accepting the mistakes a brother makes; it is accepting the brother who makes mistakes. This is why forgiveness can never be limited.

Bonhoeffer shows the necessity of real brotherly acceptance of the sinner when he says:

Anybody who lives beneath the Cross and who has discerned the utter wickedness of all men and of his own heart will find that

49. Paul Tillich, *The New Being* (New York: Scribners and Sons, 1955), pp. 10f.

there is no sin that can ever be alien to him. Anybody who has once been horrified by the dreadfulness of his own sin that nailed Jesus Christ to the Cross will no longer be horrified by even the rankest sins of a brother. Looking at the Cross of Jesus, he knows the human heart. He knows how utterly lost it is in sin and weakness, how it goes astray in the ways of sin, and he also knows that it is accepted in grace and mercy. Only the brother under the Cross can accept the sinner.[50]

Community and Communion

From the fellowship in sinfulness, one naturally passes to a deeper communion with the brothers on a level where all are most perfectly one: namely, on the truest level of who each man is. At this level, communication is not necessary in order to maintain community. All are truly one in the Christ who is the deepest center of our being. At this level, communion is experienced and expressed through prayer, through silence and solitude. Communion is first and foremost communion *with one another in a common value*. This value is primarily an ontological value, namely, the *Koinonia* in the very life of the Trinity, as has already been seen.

A French philosopher has expressed this very well in the following definition of communion:

The idea of *communion* in and through *love* is presented as that of a privileged form of union between the *I* and the *You* in which, without any rational mediation, verbal or discursive, the persons not only enter into immediate contact, but experience a reciprocal penetration of existences, through a participation or fusion which

50. Dietrich Bonhoeffer, *Life Together,* p. 118. See also p. 119: "In the presence of a psychiatrist I can only be a sick man; in the presence of a Christian brother I can dare to be a sinner."

The same thought is developed by Thomas Merton in *Seasons of Celebration,* "Community of Pardon" (New York: Farrar, Straus & Giroux, 1965), pp. 216–231: "If the unity of Christians in One Body makes the Church a sign of God in the world, and if men tend unfortunately to conflict and division by reason of their weakness, selfishness and sin, then the will to reconciliation and pardon is necessary if the Church is to make God visible in the world. Nor can this pardon, this communion in forgiveness remain interior and invisible. It must be clearly manifest. So the mystery of the Church demands that Christians love one another in a visible and concrete way—and that they love all men." p. 216.

creates a sort of *community* (a *We*) which is ontologically deeper and axiologically stronger than the association usually resulting from the intercourse of thinking subjects through intelligence and reason. Communion is consummated beyond language. There is a demand for silence and even obscurity, which are the atmosphere necessary for authentic communion.[51]

It is on this level that specifically "contemplative community" is formed. Other levels of community must spring from this and serve to lead the members back to this. There is obviously set up something of a dialectic between the proper form of communication and the proper form of silence and solitude; the right way to know and love another brother and the right way to respect the obscurity and the mystery of his own person. That community which is formed only on one of these two poles will inevitably remain shallow and fragile. It will not truly be a "personal community" in the deepest sense of the word.

Bonhoeffer shows the necessity of both poles when he says:

Let him who cannot be alone beware of community. . . . If you refuse to be alone you are rejecting Christ's call to you, and you can have no part in the community of those who are called. . . . But the reverse is true also. *Let him who is not in community beware of being alone.* Into the community you were called, the call was not meant for you alone. . . . If you scorn the fellowship of the brethren, you reject the call of Jesus Christ, and thus your solitude can only be hurtful to you.[52]

A true spirit of prayer can enhance the life of the community. It deepens the life of God within the heart of man and thus enables him to share more fully in that *Agape* of the Father which alone enables man to form deep community. It is this which enables man to accept his brother, not as he appears to the surface-viewer, but as he aspires to be before God. It is this, in fact, which enables us to have communion with the brother as he is before God and as we

51. G. Bastide, *Traité de l'action morale* (Paris, 1961), 1:54–55.
52. Dietrich Bonhoeffer, *Life Together,* "The Day Alone," p. 77.

are before God. The true "We" of community can be formed only in the presence of God and in contact with our own deepest and truest self.

In order to find the center of his life, the monk must separate himself to some extent from the ordinary concerns of man. This is not a flight from reality, but a thrust into a new kind of reality. The monk strives to deepen the clarity and the truth of his own inner awareness and thus live a life in which he can more readily and more simply and more naturally live in an awareness of his direct dependence upon God. It is this recognition of one's dependence on God that gives man's life its basic authenticity. It is only in contact with such authenticity that man can hope to authentically love his brother in a free way.

The Cistercian writer, Thomas Merton, expressed this very well in many of his writings.[53] He saw that man is called to share in the life of God, to the restored Image of God in Christ, and that this can only be attained by a total transformation of oneself. It is only such transformation which conditions us for communion with our brother on the truest level. This communion is a common listening to the call of God in the heart of each man and in the world at large. Man must always remember that: "He who attempts to act and do things for others or for the world without deepening his own self-understanding, freedom, integrity and capacity for love, will not have anything to give others. He will communicate to them nothing but the contagion of his own obsessions, his aggressivity, his ego-centered ambitions, his delusions about ends and means."[54] Hence, the love of God must remain the source of any true knowledge and any ordered love of ourselves as well as all living and authentic love for other men.

It is in solitude that man grows in an awareness of his own unwavering love for man and thus finds his true communion with

53. The following remarks and quotations depend heavily on John J. Higgins SJ, *Merton's Theology of Prayer*, Cistercian Studies Series 18 (Spencer, Mass.: Cistercian Pub., 1971). See esp. pp. 91–112..

54. Thomas Merton, "Contemplation in a World of Action," *Contemplation in a World of Action* (New York: Doubleday & Co., 1971), p. 164.

his fellow man. "We do not go into the desert to escape people but to learn how to find them; we do not leave them in order to have nothing more to do with them, but to find the way to do them the most good."[55]

But the truest solitude is not merely something outside of oneself—the mere physical state of aloneness apart from noise and other men. Rather, it must be primarily something within oneself, "an abyss opening up to the center of your soul" where you come face to face with yourself in the lonely ground of your being.[56] Here man is stripped of any illusory image of himself and realizes the true inner dimension of his being—the self that is created in the Image of God. By discovering this sense of his own personal integrity and his true reality, man is then more ready for the gift of himself to others. Solitude thus means not necessarily a withdrawal or separation from one's union with other men, but rather a renunciation of all the deceptive myths and falsities that can only alienate a man from God, from himself, from others, and thus prevent him from finding them in the truest sense. For this reason, Christian solitude is never a solitude *from* people but a solitude *for* people. Because of it, man can reach a new relation with his fellow man, one that is on a higher and more spiritual level, namely, the mystical level of *Koinonia*.

In this way, man is *really* united with other men, not on the superficial level of that intimacy which is often called "togetherness," but in the true relationship which God intends to exist between men. Merton wrote: "The life of every man is a mystery of solitude and communion: solitude in the secrecy of his own soul, where he is alone with God; communion with his brethren, who share the same nature, who reproduce in themselves his solitude, who are his 'other selves' isolated from him and yet one with him."[57] This communion implies an awareness, not only of

55. Thomas Merton, *Seeds of Contemplation* (Norfolk, Conn.: New Directions, 1949), p. 58.

56. Thomas Merton, *New Seeds of Contemplation* (New York: New Directions, 1961), p. 80.

57. Thomas Merton, *The Living Bread* (New York: Farrar, Straus & Cudahy, 1956), p. 141.

a participation in a natural love for one's brothers through direct activity, but also of a participation in God's love for them through a purifying of one's own heart. Hence it is not something that can be reduced to mere communication, to a simple sharing of ideas, or of knowledge of truth. Merton said: "It is in deep solitude that I find the gentleness with which I can truly love my brothers. . . . Solitude and silence teach me to love my brothers for what they are, not for what they say."[58]

To live in communion with others, man must come to respect his fellow man in his own authentic personal reality. And this he cannot do unless he himself has attained a basic self-respect and a mature identity by means of interior solitude. For it is in solitude that one establishes the union with Christ in God which is the foundation of his communion with others. This solitude then becomes something which is the monk's own responsibility to other men. As Merton said: "My solitude is not my own, for I see how much it belongs to others—and that I have a responsibility for it in their regard, not just in my own. It is because I am one with them that I owe it to them to be alone, and when I am alone they are not 'they' but my own self. They are no strangers."[59]

From this it becomes apparent that the true life of community demands an equally true life of prayer. One cannot say that he is living out Christian *Koinonia* merely by the fact that he is living in a single house with other men and communicating with them over the dinner-table. Man must always be striving for self-transcendence. This is the whole purpose of seeking God and it is likewise the whole purpose of seeking community. Both of these must serve to lead us out of ourselves to meet the living God.

The philosophical basis for this has been developed by Robert Johann.[60] Human activity is a matter of *responding* to meanings. A

58. Thomas Merton, *The Sign of Jonas* (New York: Harcourt, Brace & Co., 1953), p. 261.

59. Thomas Merton, *Conjectures of a Guilty Bystander* (New York: Doubleday & Co, 1966), p. 158.

60. R. O. Johann, "Developing Community," *The Way* 10 (1970), pp. 95–103.

man's choices are not sound simply because they are his. They are sound only if supported by the world beyond him in which they take effect. Man's self-transcendence thus means that man is true to himself as man only in the measure that the activity which is his life has its roots not only in himself but in "the other" as well and is actually a synthesis of both. "To live as a man is to be continually going beyond oneself in response to the other, so that one's life becomes progressively the expression, not of self merely, but of all that is, of the inclusively real."[61]

Beyond this, however, man must not only react to existing conditions, but he must transform existing conditions, both internal and external, in favor of something genuinely new. In this way, man's horizon extends beyond the order of the limited realities within which he finds himself, and reaches to Being itself. Man's openness to Being is precisely what makes him man. Man's essential vocation is to promote Being. But this search for Being cannot be realized by the individual man. Since Being as value transcends man on every side, man is unable to respond fully so long as his activities are only *his*. They must be his—and yet something more.

"A genuinely conjoint activity is a doing not merely of what *I* want, but of what *you* want. As willed not only by me nor only by you, but by *us*, it is born of being as transcending each of us and enveloping us both. It is thus more nearly an expression of Being itself than an act of mere self-assertion ever could be. To be able to be oneself in a common undertaking is thus to experience oneself confirmed in one's very being by transcendent reality."[62] But for this to truly be an expression of transcendence into the realm of Being, the community itself must in turn transcend its own limitations of space and time and remain open to the other dimensions and other manifestations of Being. "Community is a continually developing affair, both internally and externally, or it represents no advance at all."

Applying this to the terms of Revelation, we can see that the authentic realization of Being is to be found only in God and in the

Eschatological Kingdom. The Christian community must remain
ever open to these realms and realize that its perfection can never
be found merely by being self-contained, nor even merely by being
open to any other human community. For that Christian community which turns in on itself ends in destroying itself. True
community can be found only in expressing its own self-transcendence and that of all men in Christ.

Bringing all men to unity

This already introduces us to the final note of Christian-
contemplative community. The Christian community serves to
bring men to unity, to further the reality of *Koinonia* within this
world. There is a descending scale of participation. In the high-
priestly prayer of John 17 it descends from the Father to the
Incarnate Son and from the Incarnate Son to the eye-witnesses of
his glory. From them in turn it passes on to all believers in Christ;
and finally through the Church as a whole it passes to those who
are as yet outside the Common Life. For the ultimate goal of this
communication of divine life to man—the ultimate goal of all
Christian community—is nothing less than God's embrace of that
world which he created and which he loves (Jn 17:20–26). The life
common to Christ and his Church does not exist for its own sake.
It has a mediatorial character.[63]

The community must always transcend itself in order to attain
to that fullness which is found only in Christ. Every community,
just as every vocation within the Church, justifies itself only in so
far as it is a service, a *diakonia*. The contemplative community must
likewise be seen in this light. The contemplative life is basically to
be an affirmation of the absolute value of human life and of the
person who is a transcendent being. The monk "abandons the world
only in order to listen more intently to the deepest and most
neglected voices that proceed from its inner depth."[64] He seeks to

63. L. S. Thornton, *The Common Life in the Body of Christ* (London: Dacre
Press, 1942), final chapter, pp. 443–444.
64. Thomas Merton, *The Climate of Monastic Prayer*, CS1 (Spencer, Mass.:
Cistercian Publications, 1969), p. 35.

be liberated from the excessive demands of the "world" in order to be free. This enables him by that very fact "to be more truly present to his world and to his time by love, by compassion, by understanding, by tolerance, by a deep Christ-like hope."[65]

But this love, compassion and tolerance will normally be expressed in a very hidden way. For the specific role of the contemplative community within the Church is not so much "being-*with*-others" as it is "being-*for*-others."[66] This does not exclude the aspect of "openness" to the world, but it does qualify it. As Merton expressed it: "(The Christian monk's) function in the Christian community is the paradoxical one of living outwardly separated from the community. And this, whether he is conscious of it or not, is a witness to the completely transcendental character of the Christian mystery of our unity in Christ. . . . He testifies to the essentially mystical bond of unity which binds Christians together in the Holy Spirit. Whether he is seen or not, he bears witness to the unity of Christ by possessing in himself the fullness of Christian charity."[67]

Conclusion

The task of contemplative community today is to ensure that it itself and all its members are in contact with this Mystery of Christian Charity, of *Koinonia*. The fullness of the Plan of God (the *Oikonomia*) is contained therein. This means that the members must be able to attain to the fullness of Charity by fully responding to their own personal call from God. It is their response to this call which will lead them to self-transcendence and introduce them into the fullness of the Mystery of Christ. Not all will attain to self-transcendence mainly through solitude and formal prayer. Some

65. Thomas Merton, "Dialogue and Renewal," *Contemplation in a World of Action* (New York: Doubleday & Co, 1971), pp. 92–93.

66. Jean Leclercq, "Monasticism in a World in Transformation," *American Benedictine Review* (1971), p. 192. On this same question see Thomas Merton, "Openness and Cloister," pp. 129–143 and "Notes on the Future of Monasticism," pp. 218–225, *Contemplation in a World of Action.*

67. Thomas Merton, *Disputed Questions* (New York: Farrar, Straus and Cudahy, 1960), p. 191. See also p. 182.

will be called to attain this precisely through their service to the community or through this own spirit of penitence and humble charity. This is what St Bernard developed when he spoke of the monastic community which always contains the Marthas, the Marys and the Lazaruses. What is necessary is that each one see his own place in the light of the whole, as well as see his community in the light of the whole Church, and this in turn in the light of all mankind throughout all history. For these are the dimensions of the *Koinonia* which we are called to share and to manifest. "Oh, the depth of the riches and wisdom and knowledge of God!" (Rom 11:33).

This will demand an element of creativity for each community in order to discover what is its own particular mode of expression. It demands a spirit of *communication* between the various members of the community and the various communities. This "communication" cannot be identified merely with speech and dialogue nor with common participation in various activities. Robert Johann shows a deeper meaning:

Communication is precisely the continual establishment of community, the continual coming to agreement in action on the part of all the members. The way "community" has often been understood in the past, practically all the stress has fallen on structure, the need for a common pattern. It was thought that the very essence of community consisted in the conformity of individuals to an established program. The acceptance by the individual of this "common way" was precisely what made him a member of community. Unfortunately, what was not realized is that such a conception of community corrupts it from the start and prevents it from ever being an achievement of self-transcendence. A "community" so conceived can integrate the self not as a self, that is, as a genuine initiative, but only as a kind of automaton. That is why, for all their yearning for community, young people are little moved by such ideals of community life as have been inherited from the past. For the important thing is not the acceptance from others of a common pattern of behavior, but the continual creation *with others* of conjoint action. The forms of human association are genuinely human goods only as they are continually being instituted by the parties concerned.

Only so is the self as self caught up in the common life. Thus community in its only important sense is not the mere having of, and adherence to, common structures as given; it is rather the communicative *process* itself as continually giving rise to these structures and modifying them as needed.[68]

It is precisely here that the various other sciences will enter in to show communities how to construct and modify these communal structures. Contemplative community will always be based first and foremost, however, on these theological bases, on these onto-logical realities. For, as Bonhoeffer again says: "Christian com-munity is a spiritual not a psychic reality." At the same time, it does express itself within the psychic and human realm and it does share in the incarnational order. Consequently, the deepest type of communion must be complemented and clarified by communication between intelligences and collaboration in actions. Communion in solitude must at times be assisted by communication in word. The way in which this takes place must be expressed by the concrete community, according to its own needs. This introduces the need for that "fruitful equilibrium between silence and communication, asceticism and human development, obedience and co-responsi-bility." It is in this way that each community will hear its own *call* and give its own *response*, and the whole will be that perfect response of the Bride (Rev 22:17). This response is the response of Love.

The spirit of this response can be seen in the words of the dying monk, Fr Zossima, to his disciples in *The Brothers Karamazov:*

"Love one another, Fathers," said Fr Zossima. "Love God's people. Because we have come here and shut ourselves within these walls, we are no holier than those that are outside, but on the contrary, from the very fact of coming here, each of us has confessed to himself that he is worse than others, than all men on earth. . . . And the longer a monk lives in seclusion, the more keenly he must recognize this fact. Else he would have no reason to come here. When he realizes that he is not only worse than others, but that he is responsible to all men for all and everything, for all human sins, national and individual,

68. R. Johann, "Developing Community," *The Way* 10 (1970), p. 101.

only then will the aim of our seclusion be attained. For know, dear ones, that every one of us is undoubtedly responsible for all men and everything on earth, not merely through the general sinfulness of creation, but each one personally for all mankind and for every man. For monks are not a special sort of men, but only what all men ought to be. Only through that knowledge, our heart grows soft with infinite, universal, inexhaustible love. Then everyone of you will have the power to win over the whole world by love and to wash away the sins of the world by your tears. . . . Each of you keep watch over your heart and confess your sins to yourself unceasingly. Be not afraid of your sins, even when perceiving them, if only there be penitence; but make no conditions with God. Again I say: be not proud. Be proud neither to the great nor to the little. Remember them in your prayers thus: 'Save, O Lord, all those who have none to pray for them. Save too all those who will not pray.' And add: 'It is not in pride that I make this prayer, O Lord, for I am lower than all men.' . . . Love God's people."[69]

Tarcisius Conner OCSO

Gethsemani
Trappist, Ky.

---

69. F. M. Dostoevsky, "The Brothers Karamazov," tr C. Garnett (Chicago: Encyclopaedia Britannica, 1952), pp. 83–84.

APPROACHES TO
A THEOLOGY OF SOCIAL DYNAMICS

WITH AN APPLICATION TO CONTEMPLATIVE LIFE

Valentine Walgrave op*

THE RENEWAL OF CHURCH and religious life is in fact confided to men who enjoy an ever increasing autonomy due to their increasing domination over nature. This autonomy, a consequence of the immense advance in science and technology, concerns also our psychic and social structures. In fact, the sciences of psychology and sociology enable us to forecast and to direct to a great extent human development, even in the sphere of moral and religious life. Consequently sociological knowledge and method can be a notable help toward the development of a worthwhile religious community.

The trend toward "Sociologization"

While it is necessary to make use of the findings of sociology—in itself a magnificent task—serious risks accompany the undertaking. In applying sociological methods and in interpreting the results of research we are always influenced by a definite image of man. Insofar as we do not acknowledge the implied image we

*Fr Valentine Walgrave is well known for his excellent study on the Dominican Order which looked deeply into its monastic and contemplative dimensions. Father did his doctoral studies at the Pontifical University of Thomas Aquinas (Angelicum), Rome. Besides editing the review *Emmaus*, he lectures on theology at Lumen Vitae, Brussels, and in spirituality at the Louvain School for Novices and at the Catholic School for Social Workers at Ghent. He had formerly served as Director of the School for Social Workers at Louvain.

only observe a seeming neutrality toward values. Our use of sociology then actually makes us deduce conclusions from incorrect premises which are not even mentioned.[1] This surreptitious way of usurping the role due to philosophical or theological reflection may be called a "sociologization" of thinking. Some examples are:

The way practical conclusions are drawn out at the end of a sociological study often suggests that predominant trends in society are the norms of human conduct. One cannot be blamed for acting under the pressure of public opinion.[2]

It is also often suggested that the ongoing evolution in moral or religious matters follows a definite curve as a matter of course. ("In 1970 the last religious will enter Dutch convents," sociologists prognosticated six years ago. Cf. also the use of figures about overpopulation.)

Sociological group-study easily leads to thinking that the psychological integration of the individual or of a community is the top value of human life and is the condition for any valuable way of being or achieving.

It seems to me that at present the tendency to "sociologization" exerts a heavy and detrimental pressure on the life of the Church and of religious communities and that this is a serious threat to successful Church renewal as outlined by Vatican II.

The necessity of understanding social dynamics

To free us from this obnoxious influence of "sociologization" we shall clarify in the light of faith the meaning of the human dynamics which are the object of psychology and sociology.

It is extremely important to see how the basic facts revealed by Scripture affect human structures and the way they function. Apart from this approach psychological and social dynamics cannot be understood, our image of man becomes unreal (no matter how much it calls on realism) and the use we make of sociological knowledge nourishes utopian expectations.

1. Cf. K. Stern, *The Third Revolution* (Garden City, NY: Doubleday, 1955), ch. 4: The Mechanics of Society, pp. 50–64.
2. Cf. the criticism of the Kinsey report by H. Schelsky, *Soziologie der Sexualität* (Hamburg, 1955), pp. 51–59.

As we will see further on, some results of sociological research in fact confirm this view, at least on particular points. However, as regards the ultimate understanding of the problems we are coping with in the matter of social dynamics, the sociologist does not give us the decisive answer. We need a "theology of social dynamics," clarifying their meaning at the level of creation and also at the level of the Fall and Redemption.

TRANSCENDENT COMMITMENT AND COMMUNITY LIFE IN THE LIGHT OF THE FACT OF CREATION

Primacy of transcendent commitment in the making of community

According to the Bible, man is called to enter the realm of divine life, to live in intimate *companionship with God* and to collaborate in his enterprise. He must collaborate as a creature, in an obedient and respectful way. But he should act at the same time as a son of God, an image of the Father in heaven, in that free and creative way which belongs to the very nature of love.

"God-directedness" is the spiritual axis of truly human life, even at the level of the profane task, which only finds its ultimate meaning when it is performed for God and with God. In this sense one becomes man only by transcending man. Union with God presupposes that the Divine Partner is the ultimate point of reference at all levels of human life.

In the case of a *community of men,* things are different. Here the partner we love is not the ultimate point of reference. We only become real brothers in uniting with one another at the point where full human existence is achieved, in the transcendent commitment to God and to spiritual values. As de Saint-Exupery says: "To love does not mean simply to look at one another, but to look together in the same direction," and in this looking we shall finally meet the personal God.

The readiness, however, to join together in a response to God and absolute values is a fact of grace. Therefore the community itself is a work of God, moving the hearts of men to transcend themselves.

R

It follows from this primacy of self-transcendence that the *call to contemplation* is the most specific characteristic of man.

Contemplation is a state of mind by which man lives primarily in the reality above and beyond himself, being absorbed by its presence and its spiritual qualities. Contemplation shows that man by definition is an "openness" to what is beyond him. He waits to be filled by God (and by created reality as it is willed by him and directed to him), to consciously assent to him and to love him. This loving presence to reality, whereby we are "absorbed" by the beloved, is the constitutive moment of man's actualization.

Activity and transformation of reality will necessarily follow as a requirement of love because man is a being able to shape things and to rule situations. But such activities will have true human value only insofar as they share some contemplative moment, however short and weak it may be, insofar as they share the disinterested directedness of love to something beyond itself.

Transcendent commitment and social integration

The foregoing explains why in fact for the integration of the community the common commitment to a transcendent goal (a social service, a life consecrated to the Lord) is the decisive factor. It is, first of all, *more important than the mutual choice of the members.* When people join together for the ultimate purpose of self-fulfillment or the satisfaction of one's own affective needs, the level of true community is not yet reached. Some results of sociological research may illustrate the thesis:

> Friendship is more frequently based on similarity of ideals than on similarity of personality. Frequent contacts make people often seek unanimity in the matter of values and norms.[3]
> Homogeneity of outlooks, rather than permissiveness, makes people feel happy within the group.[4]
> A statement by psychiatrists: In the Western World the stress on human autonomy and the exaltation of so-called creative spon-

3. J. Klein, *The Study of Groups* (New York: Humanities, 1956), p. 106.

4. P. Lazarsfeld and W. Thielens, *The Academic Mind* (New York: Collier-Macmillan, 1958), p. 147.

taneity lead more and more to the neglect of absolute norms and to the disruption of links with the realm of the transcendent. Neurosis arising from inhibition of instincts is thereby vanishing, but another, more terrible neurosis is spreading now: that of the metaphysically lonely man who has been taught to expect all from human community but who is ever less able to make the necessary contacts.[5]

In the light of this some widespread positions might be questioned:

> . . . that the mutual choice of the members constitutes and stabilizes the community of religious.
> . . . that respect for the various opinions and patterns of behavior within the group is at the heart of any religious brotherhood.

A further deduction from our main position is that the more the members of a group are in search of a life lived in solitude and silence, the more the integration of the group will depend on the homogeneity of outlooks and on the palpable presence of these outlooks in community life. This can be applied to the life of monks at different levels: common spirituality, liturgy, symbols, etc.

Communion at a transcendent level is also more important for the integration of a community than fitting external structures. As we shall see, structures play an important role in the unification of a group. They support and express the common goal of the members. But the decisive factor for unification is the common commitment itself. It can be largely operative even when to a certain extent the structures are antiquated or in some ways stand in need of change.

A sociological statement: In a religious community the deeper the unanimity at the level of spiritual intention, the more this community is able to integrate large numbers. (G. B. Mailhiot)

The role of structure in the transcendent commitment of the individual and of the group

5. V. Frankl developed this idea in *The Doctor and the Soul* (New York: Knopf, 1965) and *Man's Search for Meaning* (Boston: Beacon, 1963).

By reason of his nature, man's spiritual orientation demands embodiment in physical structures which function on the one hand as a *support,* on the other as a *means of expression.*

There are various levels of "structuration":

1. The *structures of personality:* patterns of thought, systems of association (representations, feelings, aims, etc.), degrees of sensitivity to various values, established value-choices. The complexus of all these creates a definite type of person.

When one makes a commitment to a contemplative life he should become a contemplative type of man. One may "grow into" contemplative life, he can also "grow out" of it. Such "growing" involves changes in personality structures.

2. The *socio-psychological structures:* a collective consciousness in the matter of sensitivity to values, ideas, spiritual aims, etc., from which results as it were a collective personality.

We are so deeply social beings that we can scarcely be committed to spiritual values without the support of a community. This does not mean submitting to the pressure of socio-dynamics. In the case of the truly transcendent commitment, one freely and discerningly chooses the support of the contructive trends in the group, maintaining full independence toward the destructive trends found there. Occasionally one may feel called to move to another group in order to have the required support for his commitment.

In this area there are serious problems concerning the resolution of fundamental disagreements within a religious community, the desirability of provisional compromises—their nature and duration, the eventual regrouping of people and the methods of procedure.

3. The *external social structures:* customs and laws, language, a definite ideology, sciences, arts, cult, etc. In regard to religious life: rule and observances, spirituality and forms of prayer, historical antecedents, etc. All this should form an organic whole which expresses and supports the inner structuring of the person and the community. It is really the body of the common commitment.

The spiritual assimilation of external structures is assured by a double and recurrent movement: a movement of *proiecting* spiritual feelings and aims into new or adapted structures, and a movement of *reappropriating* existing structures through reopening oneself to their original meaning.

Macro-dynamics:[6] human culture fashioned by history

Till now we considered structures insofar as they are required and formed by individuals or particular groups in support of their commitment to values. The dynamics of these structures constitute the object of psychology and sociology. But in addition there are what we may call "macro-dynamics" which rule the human community on the larger scale of civilization or culture and explain along with other phenomena the major changes (transition periods) and the all-embracing movement of history.

At the level of macro-dynamics Christianity presently is experiencing its most decisive confrontation. It is face to face with evolutionism in general and with Marxism in particular. Nothing will have more effect on Christian renewal than the stand taken in the area of "macro-dynamics." No stand influences more our daily judgments and options, no matter how academic the problem. What people think about changes to be made or not to be made is often unconsciously inspired by evolutionistic and Marxist thinking.

Our spiritual or transcendental commitment is basically directed to lasting values, hence its embodiment involves some lasting structures: perennial moral principles, basic religious symbols, ascetical practices. But our need to accept the changes imposed by history is equally essential. We always enter the realm of lasting principles and ideals from a particular perspective which is determined (1) by the *external conditions* of the times (today, for example, by automation) and (2) by the specific *sensitivity* of contemporary society (the need, for instance, of existential thinking and dialogical openness).

6. We use this word analogically to divide sociology into micro-sociology (the study of the basic patterns of social relationship), sociology of the group, and macro-sociology, this last being concerned with culture as such and also with the dynamics of history as a whole.

Apart from this particular and contingent perspective, contemporary people cannot pursue the perennial vocation of man in a valid and authentic way. Now, this "perspectivation" of ideals implies that we should accept and live by some values which respond to the situation and the sensitivity of the times. This does not mean we should consider such values as necessarily higher than others, but they are for us a gateway to the objective order of values. To the engineer the special attention he pays to the technical side of things does not make this the top value of human life for him. Likewise, while monks may give more attention today to the dimension of fraternity, it should not be to the detriment of their living in solitude and silence but rather it should lead to greater fidelity.

To be sensitive to a definite value as a call of the times does not require that we should always go along with the particular trend which is typical at the moment. One may also feel called to contradict it, judging that it represents not a gateway but an obstacle to entering into the objective order of life. Sometimes we may choose to structure our life more particularly in function of some values which are complementary to those one-sidedly overstressed in order to save their contribution for our times. Thus, monks may be anxious to restore (with the adjustments required) the paternal role of the abbot before a world that suffers from the loss of any father-figure. Or they may give their attention to making their withdrawal from the world more effective in order to assure a more penetrating presence at the heart of the times.

The meaning of periodical changes in the structures of culture

We saw that the "perspectivation," characterizing a period of history, always represents a gateway but at the same time a limitation as regards our approach to perennial ideals—and we made the comparison with the choice of a profession. The fact of going a particular way may lead to over-emphasis of certain chosen values, causing at the same time the neglect of complementary ones and the "frustration" of corresponding but ignored needs. When frustration becomes unbearable, the neglected needs take their revenge, enforcing a transformation of structures in which the will be more largely satisfied.

At present we are sharing such a process of transition. The way religious life is taking part in this process has been already the topic of countless publications. Very often, however, the authors neglect a theological consideration of the dynamics of transition: what is the meaning of the "historicity" of human life, leading humanity through successive periods of civilization? Two questions ask for an answer:

1. Does the birth of a new civilization always mean that the *structures of the past have no longer any value?* E.g. the dogmatic formulae coined during the first centuries of church history, the Rule of St Benedict, the essentials of St Thomas' metaphysics, the spirituality of St Ignatius, or even the meditation methods of Buddhist monks, etc. When history leads the basically same man through successive perspectives, which are limited but also completing one another, should then the new period not be lived as the recapitulation of the past within a new perspective, rather than as a break with it? If so, then the most pregnant views and expressions of each period will be saved for the future, and be renewed from within through contact with the new trends.

2. Does the development of history as a whole follow *necessarily an ascendent line?* If in fact history represents a dialogue between the free God and a free man, then progress can never be assured by the dynamics of the process as such. Hence progressivism in the strict sense becomes a quite unrealistic attitude of mind.

This last question puts clearly in relief the irreconcilable opposition between Christian thinking and any strictly evolutionistic view of life. To the latter, history is a necessary and ascendent "process" whose dynamics simply determine our future. Our managing of structures should only be a conscious moment within that unavoidable development.

But there is no place in Revelation for such a view. Human dynamics are conditioned by the successive free options of man. In fact, bad options have disturbed them as the Bible clearly teaches. The computer is still intact, we could say, but the programming we incorporated was inspired by disordered aims. However, the God of mercy has come to help us in renewing aims and dynamics. Actual human structures can be rightly understood and constructively managed only in the light of what God revealed about the Fall and Redemption. Sociology cannot suffice. Particularly in this matter we need a "theology of social dynamics."

DISTURBED SOCIAL DYNAMICS AND CHRISTIAN LIFE

Our experience with disturbed dynamics

We mentioned the origin of our difficulties: called to a community of love with God within a freely adopted divine project, man disdained his position as a creature. Right from the very beginning he reached for the godlike position of an absolute autonomy. He refused obedience and lost love.

The disturbance by pride of the transcendent commitment was not confined to a transient moment but embodied itself as a lasting feature of disorder in the human personality-structure. This disorder concerns first of all our sensitivity or spontaneous way of feeling. Doubtless, conscience is not extinguished, as St Paul underlines, so that we still feel called to obedient and disinterested love. But this voice is almost smothered by anthropocentricity. Spontaneously indeed we rather tend

(1) to take man himself, his development and fulfillment, as the *ultimate goal* of life;

(2) to strive for earthly goods in a *demanding and possessive spirit*, unaware of the endowing God, source at each moment of their existence and their qualities;

(3) to rely on man's own forces as the *ultimate guarantee* of success.

Thus our *heart* speaks two contradictory languages: the language of self-transcendence and the language of self-centeredness.

This ambiguity of the heart makes *all created goods,* however good in themselves, ambiguous in actual fact. They can be grace or temptation, depending on how we approach them. If the inner ear receives the sounds emitted by things in a distorted way, this falsifies God's message and narrows or conceals man's vocation to transcendent commitment.

Since sensitivity to values and free response are the basic principles in shaping structures, sin must finally lead to the formation of *an ambiguous "world"* in which all cultural patterns (usages, arts, literature, etc.) and the whole resulting "climate" are ambivalent, now attracting in a good sense, now in a bad one. The culture reflects the ambiguous dynamics of man's own heart.

Because of this ambiguity in man's spontaneous tendencies the pursuit of what is good and the refusal of what is evil make him live with a psychological gap between his moral commitment and a part of his spontaneous tendencies. This is experienced as *an inner split of personality* and a lack of authenticity and may cause a profound *feeling of frustration*. But the psychological unity gets gradually restored as far as one existentially renounces those deviating tendencies (conversion of heart) and accepts the fact that he must live with a certain split or tension at the peripheral level of spontaneity.

It is proper to sin, as being self-exalting and demanding, to refuse such a scant existence and to *claim full identification* with spontaneity, at the level of both individual feelings and collective trends. Lack of authenticity, however peripheral, is considered as unworthy of man and frustrations as an unacceptable obstacle to happiness.

This attitude leads to the denial that one's heart, one's sensitivity, one's spontaneous tendencies, can be essentially wrong. One has "to be oneself." Sin can only be a mistake or a lack of maturity. As regards the level of collective behavior it is said that the present times have to develop purely and simply according to the specific contemporary tendencies for these are considered normative.

From all this follows a *disruptive conception of the renewal of society*. The thus privileged values, ideas and practical tendencies become idols and determine our structures in a way so absolute that we have no longer a normal change of value-stresses. The overstressing of the new trend causes in the end abnormally deep frustrations which in turn must lead to merely antagonistic changes, carried through in an often subversive way.[7]

Some modern philosophical trends are expressions of this. Thus the existentialist (in a more restricted sense) calls for simply creating the values and norms by which one's life shall be shaped in a particular situation. Thus also the evolutionist who holds that the main trends which emerged from the times are the normative way to progress. ("So contemporary man feels now, or thinks now," the evolutionist says.) Both are ignoring the ambiguity of the actual social dynamics and push people to identify with the sinful trends in life.

It may be noted that similar judgments are currently used nowadays in discussions on moral problems and on Christian or religious renewal.

Christ and the redemption of human dynamics

Redemption covers the whole of human life, but it begins with the transformation of man's heart from which all disturbance comes. Thus the heart is conquered by the way God scores off our disdain of divine Majesty, i.e., by revealing himself in the Son as the God of mercy and the astonishing acceptance of man into the mystery of God's intimate life.

To those who believe, Christ presents *social structures of a higher, supernatural order* which achieve and support this new life. These structures consist first of all in some major deeds of God which, just as creation, are forever actual as *mysteries* and within which we come to life and take part in Salvation History: Christ's Incarnation and Nativity, his Life, Passion and Death, his Resurrection and Ascension to the Father. The incorporation of human life into Christ's mysteries happens within the *Sacramental Church,* a whole with visible structures, in which Christ comes to us, in order to allow us to share his own transfigured life in the center and the core of the Trinitarian mystery. Central here is the *Eucharist* which is the liturgical celebration of Salvation's mysteries. But at the same

7. To see how Marxism illustrates this tendency and influences the present Christian renewal, see below, pp. 271ff.

time that our life is transfigured by Christ, we again accept the original state of creature, united to God by an obedient love (with full acceptance of the commandments), and to our fellow-men by a spirit of brotherhood. Grace restores nature.

"Reconversion" of dynamics through conversion of heart

But this thoroughly positive happening calls for a negation, necessitated by sin. To become linked again by love to the holy designs of the Father and the interests of the human family, our heart must be *freed from every demanding attitude and pride*. It has to become as the Heart of Jesus himself meek and humble. Then we can imitate his filial confidence and abandonment toward the Father in all circumstances. Life is no longer a possession but a continuous and wondrous endowment. But our heart, because in a degree still possessive, must experience this foresaking of possessiveness as a state of "poverty." *Poverty of spirit* creates the pure air and serene skies we need to be absorbed by transcendent reality into the ecstasy of a love contemplating the personal God. Conversion of heart cleanses human dynamics, so that they can be "reconverted," developing within us a God-centered, rather than a man-centered consciousness. This change in depth changes history. Toward this change the contemplative life makes its contribution.

The Church, the presence of the Spirit in history's macro-dynamics

The Church operates in history as the *leaven in the dough*. Under the Old Covenant the People of God were set apart at the level of civilization. They had to be a nation apart from the other nations. This was needed in order that they might be tempered by God and become true, obedient, abandoned—the "poor of Yahweh." The leaven had to be prepared. With the New Covenant it is put into the dough. All nations are called to become the People of God.

Western history shows Christian community, and through it the Gospel, leavening men's potentialities (the restoration of values such as reason, liberty, labor, etc., and the humanization of worldly structures). The successive rise of new ideas and experiences completing one another providentially enable the Church to come to an

increasing understanding of faith (dogmas) and to develop a number
of more adequate patterns in the realm of morals and spirituality.

But Western history also reveals the *continuous estrangement of
the new trends* from their Christian origins and even the tendency
for them to penetrate again, in a paganized form, into the bosom
of the Church distorting Christian thought and life. To this move
the Church will always be tempted to react in either of two opposite
and inadequate ways:

—to completely keep out of the new trends it once generated,
preventing in this way its own growth (*closed fidelity*).
—to go along indiscriminately with the still unsifted new trends,
calling them the voice of the Lord in our times and in this way
place itself in danger (*untrue openness*).

In order to be open to the times while remaining in the Spirit
(*open fidelity*) we must, (1) continuously abide in *spiritual poverty*
and renounce what disturbs the dynamics of Church: a proud and
demanding identification whether with existing structures or with
new and even lofty ideas; (2) in this way exercise *spiritual discernment*
in regard to trends and practical proposals, saying "yes" or "no"
according as they answer to the "Christian sense" inspired by the
Spirit. This means a continuous "testing" by the Gospel of ourselves and of our times. As Christ predicted, the world will tend to
maintain a proud identification with its ambiguous and unpurified
way of feeling and thinking. Therefore its dynamics will be predominantly ruled by sin, and "the world"—not as it is by nature
but as it has been shaped by man—will oppose the presence of
Christ and the Christian.

As a result, Christians and the Church as a whole, will always find
themselves led into *opposition to this "world"* by their very fidelity
to Christ, and by their effort to save the contribution of the times
from the deterioration caused by the disturbed cultural dynamics.
They have to do this humbly, realizing that they themselves are
part of this world called to conversion. They have to act with
that gentle mind of Christ as it has revealed itself in the Good
Shepherd and his meeting with Judas in the Garden. This is the

"war" with the wicked, which Christ will definitively win when he comes back.

External social structures assuring our link with the Holy Spirit

To go through history in the spirit of open fidelity is a task beyond human power. In this matter, however, the Church enjoys the special assistance of the Spirit through appropriate structures. Doubtless, the immediate organ of charismatic understanding is the People of God themselves. But we only join together as a charismatic people insofar as we accept to live within the external social structures the Lord has provided. They link, in an infallible way, our openness to the times with obedient fidelity, bringing about true integration of the new with his message.

The faithful recognize as normative sources of thought and conduct: (1) *Scripture*, which is the special repository of what the Spirit confided to the people of God; (2) *Tradition*, i.e., Faith and Christian sense as it unfolds through living and feeling with Scripture through successive historical experiences; (3) the *hierarchical guidance of the Church*, charismatically assisted for discerning and publicly authenticating what comes from the Spirit among the words and deeds of the faithful, and for giving the decisive commands and directives.

The fact that the People of God only become a charismatic body under this threefold charismatic authority is the expression, at a social level, of our true condition as Church: a humanity returning to love and truth through the purification of self-will.

Newman expatiated at length on this subject and stressed how the sovereign intervention of a charismatic central authority is most wanted in the Church when enthusiasm for new ideas and concern for neglected needs are damaging the charismatic community by tending toward an integration bought at the price of true faith and morality. At such a time obedience may be unusually difficult.

Out of this can come some conclusions concerning *group discussion on renewal:*

1. Exchanges on community life are normal. The Council restored the true meaning of the Christian community as a

"Church," hence as a charismatic organ of reflection. At the same time, contemporary knowledge of group dynamics is a providential gift we have to use, at least in its main guidelines.

2. For the Christian validity of these discussions it is necessary that the participants fully accept to meet within the structures here developed. It is amazing how often this requisite is neglected. Moreover, for getting out of the ensuing confusion, many call upon peace and love in a way which demolishes the unity of faith and obedience which constitutes the Church-community.

EXCURSUS

If today, as we have said, the Church has to cope in a special way with Marxism, this is so not only because of the social tensions throughout the world which are being exploited by Marxist agitation, but also, and primarily, because of the tensions rising within the Church itself from the overall change it is going through. On the one hand there is the feeling that the Church's structures are not sufficiently adjusted to the present sensitivity of the faithful, and on the other new theology is making it clear that the Church has to adjust to the call of the Lord in the signs of the times. Both of these make the Christian community particularly sensitive to Marxist ideas which are undiscernibly spreading throughout the Church.

Marxism indeed seeks, by its belief in the dialectic process of history, to justify a disruptive transition, and thus it makes the Christian's care for "open fidelity" meaningless. Therefore when the monk with an attitude of open fidelity seeks to discern the Christian value of any particular renewal, it is eminently useful for him to be able to discern those patterns of thinking which are Marxist distortions of Christian thought. In the following two columns there is presented some Marxist thought on changing society and parallel Christian thought on renewal, applied here to monasticism, which has been influenced by the Marxist thought. It would have been useful to have added a third column indicating the part truth that is found in each statement.

Marxist Thought	Marxist Trend in Christian Thought
(*a*) Our image of the world and man, and consequently our ideas about morality are right insofar as they flow from the socio-economic situation and as they are able to back the convenient social structure. With the rise of a new socio-economic period the former structures become worn out as does the supporting philosophy.	(*a*) Monastic structures are a religious derivative from an agrarian economy connected with feudal society. By their very nature they need to be backed by sacralized, hence perennial rules and usages and by spiritual paternalism. With the rise of an industrial and at the same time democratic age, the whole has lost its meaning, together with the old theology from which it is living (often to be understood as: the traditional propositions of faith . . .).
(*b*) All evil in the world ensues from maintaining antiquated structures which block change demanded by evolution. This makes people suffer from dehumanizing "alienations" and frustrations.	(*b*) Renewal is a question exclusively of structures to be adjusted to the sensitivity of a new generation no longer at ease within them. (NB One is unmindful of the fact: 1. that any new sensitivity is ambiguous and first calls for being purified; 2. that otherwise unrestricted adjustment inevitably leads to errors in faith and the loss of the religious vocation.)

N.B.—Psychologists and sociologists called to assist often confine their study on renewal to the relationships between existing structures on the one hand and actual needs and judgments on the other. Since their final figures generally reveal that structures no longer fit the new generation they end with discreet suggestions about adjustment to the new generation as required for the integration of the group.

Their conclusions, however, would often be different if they performed the other part of their task: to investigate to what degree the negative consequences (disturbance of the personality and frustration, experience of a non-monastic life) may be due not only to maintaining certain structures but to the loss also of the sense of values involved and to the fact that basic options have not been made. The omission of this inquiry is generally due to an evolutionistic view of man which leaves no place for the authoritative call of lasting principles. Neither is it seen that there may be a free and justified conversion to laws and structures—against one's spontaneous tendencies—which is an eminently effective way to the integration of personality.

(*c*) Because such a heavy pressure is exerted in favor of preserving existing structures by people behind the times, especially by the rich and those in power, the only way to liberation is to impose by revolution an unrestricted adjustment of structures to the needs of the frustrated masses.

(*d*) To come to revolution the consciousness of suffering from alienations has to be stirred up by showing on every possible occasion how all the daily difficulties proceed from the outdated nature of structures. The latent revolutionary will of the people, which represents the voice of conscience, is awakened.

(*c*) Because of the little understanding by Roman authority (bishops, major superiors), unacquainted as they are with the real situation and stiffened in outdated views by old theology, we have to accept full responsibility according to our charismatic vocation and to enforce the change we need.

(*d*) In every typical clash between Church authority and members, the latter refer to antiquated structures (e.g., celibacy, the hierarchical principle, vows, etc.) which no longer answer to our changed feelings and view of man.

Christians and religious have to be "helped in a respectful

way" to formulate their thoughts and needs and to enter into common decision-making, as an essential self-expression of the charismatic People of God, answering to the call of the Spirit. (This means very often, if we look at the whole context within which it is said, that, in the name of the Spirit, identification with the "man of the flesh," the unconverted person is fostered.)

(*e*) People shall be freed from the ideological pressure (religion and morality) which backs the maintaining of the outdated social structures. They shall be instructed in the Marxist views on society and on their own situation.

The members of the communist party shall express in appealing formulas what the people are unconsciously longing for and help them to set up effective campaigns for change.

(*e*) Structures considered as unfitting are interpreted as flowing from an old, antiquated theology. New theology is taught to justify the fittingness of the various disruptive changes propagated. This "assistance" sometimes takes the form of an intensive spoken or written teach-in. In this way, just as in communism, the new trends are, practically speaking, provoked (at least as regards their radical and disruptive form) and a majority is artificially concocted. In this case interviews, questionnaires and votes rather put into figures the results of an intellectual and affective management, now called the charismatic voice of the "People of God."

(*f*) The making of revolution presupposes "praxis," i.e., an active involvement in the daily life of the masses which allows a planning of structures uniquely inspired by the situation and the aspirations of these masses, and free from any a priori idea or norm.

(*f*) The true renewal of a religious institute (of the Church) asks for an "experiment" in its purest expression. It shall be free from all existing rules, laws or constitutions and safe from every intervention of authority; it shall start outside of the established structures and be involved in a profane environment, as typical as possible of the times.[8]

MONASTIC LIFE AS A REGULATING FACTOR IN THE DYNAMICS OF THE CHURCH

Theological reflection on human dynamics as conditioned by the Fall and Redemption shows the decisive part played by the "structures of Salvation," i.e., the Sacramental Church within the dynamic framework of the Mysteries of Salvation, and an attitude of dependence to assure fidelity to the Holy Spirit.

But this embodiment of the Church's involvement in Salvation History ought to be brought about in ways that are in accord with the definite needs of human nature. Actually spiritual values can hardly have an assured impact on the life of a group if there are not people so attracted by them that they finally dedicate their whole life to them, making their pursuit the main theme of their daily life. Just as the artist and the man of pure science assure in society a certain sensitivity to the beautiful and the true, so the radiation of the sacred calls for people whose life is thoroughly shaped by it.

8. For an extreme expression of this theory, see the articles of M. Xhauffaire: "L'Analyse d'un symptôme: le movement de Lorscheid" in *Supplément de la Vie Spirituelle*, 1970, pp. 353-384.

Such a life is not only an eloquent sign but it also fosters the radiation of inner religious conviction and experience.

In this way "charismatic" persons and communities develop at the heart of the Church. In fact, communities of religious, especially contemplative ones, raised up by the Spirit according to Christ's invitation, offer to those called by the Lord a more developed form of the structures of Salvation, deepening both one's penetration into divine mysteries and the process of *kenosis* or self-emptying.

In the following reflection our views are applied to the contemplative monastic life.

Structuring surroundings for meeting the Creator

By its very nature the profane world is a *"pro-fanum,"* i.e., the foreground for our meeting with God. Since it is created, its dynamics move us toward the Creator. Since, however, sin came into the world, our approach tends to be self-centered. The more man develops knowledge and sensitivity to values the more he is tempted to listen to things one-sidedly, seeking in them a means to his own development, power or sensorial satisfaction. This attitude leads to a culture which is rather a sort of curtain that veils God's creating presence and smothers his call.

Because of this, in civilizations with a wide-awake religious sense there have always been people longing to live, as it were, beyond this curtain. They gather together to live at a distance (both materially and spiritually) from society, away from its clamors, from the noise of its self-centered thinking and feeling. Thus, as Lacordaire said, "Monks and oaks are perpetual." Following this attraction to external withdrawal, Christian monks achieve in a radical form the spiritual withdrawal the Church continually needs in order to keep in touch with the living God. Religious withdrawal enables one to penetrate into reality at the level where it touches eternity, to listen more fully to what things and facts reveal on behalf of the divine Creator at work in them at every moment.

The law of *silence* proper to contemplative communities is intended to foster the inner silence required for a contemplative attitude. It does this by reducing the heart's tendency toward continual self-utterance which covers reality with its own troubled thoughts and feelings. Silence rightly practiced enables us to speak words to God and to brothers and visitors which raise up all things and happenings to the level of eternity.

Withdrawal and silence are the basic requirements for a contemplative community. But for uniting with one another under these conditions and going unanimously in the same direction (a contemplative fraternity being more than a co-operative for withdrawal and silence) recurrent conversation is required. The brothers should have the opportunity to converse about their understanding of faith, their experience in seeking God, and their interpretation of today's world. At times of change, when spiritual approaches can be so confused and over-all reformulation is needed, meetings for exchange should naturally be more frequent. But they will be fruitful only insofar as they are fed by an intensive prayer life and recollection, and insofar as they have matured in a spiritually poor heart, meekly submitted to God and to the other.

According to Margaret Mead withdrawal into a totally religious community is a response to the change in the modern world which is as urgent as its complement, a far-reaching participation in that world.[9] Anthony, withdrawing into the desert at the beginning of the Constantinian era, and Benedict going out of the emergent medieval society are archetypes for the Christian monk at the time of transition such as the one in which we live.

Stressing structures which make the Mysteries of salvation present

The framework of contemplative life is much more than an openness to the divine. In Christian monasticism, which is not the case in the monasticism of the eastern religions, this openness is also a way of entering into the movement of history. Monastic structures point in so clear-cut a way to the Mysteries of Salvation that they are quite naturally experienced as the primal reality. This is one of the essential means monastic life has for making community.

9. M. Mead, "Cultural Man" in *Man in Community*, ed E. de Vries (New York: Association Press, 1967).

In daily life the central place is taken by the celebration of the sacred liturgy which embraces the whole day. *Lectio divina* and mental prayer develop further this spiritual thrust into the mysteries of faith. The monastery, centered around the church, is adorned with Christian symbols and images. Contemplation however demands that both ceremonial and decoration should be transparent and therefore sober in style.

In a special way at a time when society is becoming thoroughly secularized, many Christians need, and in fact look for places where the totality of the structures which support the community make palpable the movement from Christ toward man and from man toward Christ.

The vows, structures of religious life, which foster its integration into the Church

For the monk it is not enough to sift the voices and images which come from the world and to stress those evoked by Christ. He also feels the need to foster the purification of his own heart in a very special way. He chooses to live according to the so-called "religious vows."

Here also the starting point and the developed structures are basically the same as in the monasticism of the Eastern religions. There is nothing surprising in this because in both cases the inherent ambiguity of the human heart and of civilization is actually the reason for living so expressly in a state of chastity, poverty and obedience.

How human nature is actually at the basis of such a life is put in relief by the German psychiatrist Schultz-Hencke. He states, quite in the line of Freud, that the renouncing of the main objects of man's basic tendencies (toward sexual intercourse and family life, toward the domination of material goods, toward independent planning) is the obvious way to draw one's energies up to a higher spiritual level. The monks have seen this clearly, he says.[10]

10. H. Schultz-Hencke, *Lehrbuch der analytischen Therapie* (Stuttgart, 1951), p. 40.

But the dynamics the Christian monk develops within these same structures are thoroughly different. For the monk of the East these renunciations are means of achieving the extinction of every desire and liberation from every particular reality. For the Christian monk these renunciations are an answer to Christ by which he offers him his heart and his whole life to be redeemed and transfigured by him, to be brought to love through conversion, and to share his Resurrection through the cross. In this way he also hopes to enter more consciously into the fraternal community, considered as a lasting good in Christ.

These two ways—toward nirvana and toward total love—are the only ones in which life according to the vows is viable. As soon as the motivation loses it purity, the way of the vows also loses its spiritual functionality as history shows. In the last centuries religious life in the Western Church has suffered from an increasing ambiguity in its motivation.

In a first phase there was the hidden influence of a closed humanistic sense, finding expression in a self-centered search for spiritual perfection. This loss of authenticity in the matter of motivation disturbed the "sublimation" of the tendencies renounced by the vows, damaging the integration of personality and the smooth building up of community. In a second phase, which is still going on, there exists a resentful reaction to these diminutions of man. This too often results in the rejection of all ascetical and even of contemplative structures, instead of the purification of the motives for which one undertakes them. The claim was made that this way of resolving the problem is justified by the necessity of revalorization of earthly values and of restoring a well-incarnated sense of fraternity.

However, at the very moment when personal love of the Lord is no longer considered the chief reason for the renunciation of such precious human things and, consequently, prayer-life is neglected, religious life becomes inviable. This finally leads to unbearable tensions and to the disintegration of the community as well.

This fact must not be made a pretext for overlooking the importance of the attention paid today to the social meaning of the vows: obedience to the common goal and to one's brothers, affective availability to every person, fraternal sharing of goods. But this "horizontal" motivation for living the vows must be thoroughly inspired and absorbed by the supreme motivation of the love of God.

The role of obedience in the making of a contemplative community

Monastic community united under the restored image of God as Father: Because of the very meaning of original sin, every disturbance which is caused by the ambiguity in our hearts ultimately expresses, to a certain extent, the image we have of God. Now, Christ came and restored the true image of God: a Father whose authority is totally penetrated by love and mercy. In this way Christ in fact also restored the primacy of "transcendent commitment" in human life, animated by "obedient love."

It is a most important element in the contemplative community's vocation to show contemporary man that making a true community is not primarily a matter of skilful organization nor of a firmly maintained juridical order nor even of suitable social structures, but of finding one another within an "obedient love" to a God who is experienced as Father. This above all must be expressed in the structures of the monastic community. This gives us an understanding of the true function of the abbot.

The function of the abbot: The abbot must first of all represent Christ as the image of the Father, the good shepherd "who knows his own" and is known by them. As the good teacher, he hands on the Word of Christ. This is the abbot's first function, and takes precedence over ensuring the good order and the administration of the house. Here we may learn from the Oriental Church where the Bishop, much more than in the West, is first of all the father and spiritual guide of the faithful even at a personal level. In our day we have to take great care to avoid the danger of material or financial administration becoming a burden which weakens the spiritual leadership of the abbot.[11] Constitutions have to take this problem

11. Cf. Thomas Merton, *Monastic Renewal—A Memorandum* (mss.).

into consideration by regulating the distribution of responsibility within the abbey.

Adequate representation of the Father by the abbot demands that he should be the authority in the house in the full sense of that word: a reflection of the divine transcendence which "overarches" the human community. We should not forget either, that the exercise of personal authority is demanded by the vow of obedience which cannot be reduced to simply the common goal or to decisions made in common. Vowing obedience, the monk ultimately wants to submit his own will to the personal will of the abbot when the latter exercises authority. From this submission the monk expects the elimination of the most hindering stumbling block on the way to the Father and to true community: self-will. This vow is an expression at a social level of one's desire for the restoration of divine authority in man's life.

Overcoming crisis in exercising authority: The idea of personal authority in religious life has been discredited in the recent past because of a previous overstress which had reduced to the extreme limit the margin of individual decisions and common deliberations. Here too a one-sided reaction is leading everywhere to the dissolution of religious communities. Monks are called to go ahead in the Christian harmonization of authority and fraternity. This presupposes, among other things, that they should develop their structures in line with the Church's structures. The latter, as we have seen, inspired by the Spirit, reveal our awareness that we need purification by obedience if we want to become charismatic people. Because of the same need of purification in the religious community the authority of the Superior should be maintained, even though in certain matters common decisions are accepted.

Noteworthy in this matter are the reflections made by Roger Schutz in his comments on the Rule of Taizé. The prior often needs the opinion of his brothers to whom the Spirit speaks, he says. But he should remember that the voice of the Spirit is not guaranteed by absolute majority in a democratic vote. Moreover, if he lets decisions depend on a majority of votes, the less purified who are generally the most vocal immediately begin to agitate and to exercise pressure on the general atmosphere, impeding in this way those who are more open to listening to the voice of the Spirit. At the end of the discussion the prior should not make his decision in the presence of the brothers because he too, being only a man, could be insufficiently independent at that moment to discern in all that has been said what is of the Spirit. He should withdraw and decide after prayer in calm and reflection.[12]

An urgent mission of monastic communities: Since so many people today suffer from an inner disintegration because they never knew that fatherly authority which, in a climate of love and trust, acquaints one with the holiness of life's basic structures, opportunities to experience the life of an abbey of Benedictine origin could play an increasingly important role. There indeed people should discover how the representation of the divine Father in the person of the abbot can assure a valuable freedom, a well integrated community and a climate of profound peace. This experience should put them on the road toward the Father in heaven and help them to live with him already while here on earth.

An allied problem: spiritual guidance of monks

Reflecting on the role of the abbot in the making of a monastic community one has to deal also with an allied problem, namely that of the role of the personal spiritual guide. The problem is becoming more typical since we have more frequent contacts with monks of the Oriental Church, and also with those of Eastern religions. There obedience is much more concerned with one's relationship with an imposed or chosen spiritual guide than with a superior.

There are valuable advantages in giving more scope to the role of a personal guide. It accentuates the fact that obedience and spiritual growth are primarily a question of listening to the Spirit within us and only in the second place one of obeying rules and commands. It makes it possible to adjust not only guidance but also the regime of strict obedience to the spiritual needs of the individual

[12]. R. Schutz, *Living Today for God* (Baltimore: Helicon, 1962), c. "Accepting an Authority." pp. 115-120.

so that constitutions and observances can be simplified without weakening the ascetic value of obedience.

However, in the last analysis, abbeys of the Benedictine tradition would seriously weaken their specific function, so needed today, if they reduced obedience and guidance too much to fidelity in following a personal guide. If this were done, the abbot would be hindered in his representation of the divine Father, becoming either a ruler or administrator. It would be best, it seems to me, if private guidance, whose revalorization is urgent indeed, were conceived as a sharing in the spiritual leadership of the abbot, approved and controlled by him in a general way.

To find the right solution it may be useful to remember that, if the crisis in the matter of spiritual guidance is as serious in the Church as that of authority, it is because both are rooted in one and the same crisis: the impact on so many of that anthropocentric exaltation of personal fulfillment and of the demand for an unrestricted authenticity, from which attitudes Christ came to free us. Because of these trends spreading all over the Church, it may still be problematic whether we are yet ready to realize—in line with the Oriental Church—the decisive part of obedience to the will of another in the purification from self-will. Insofar as we do not realize this, the call to put the stress on private guidance could too often veil a tendency to replace rule and authority by a counsellor freely chosen and freely followed.

Virginity of heart and fraternity

As regards the vow of chastity we will confine our reflections to the present-day concern about forming a truly human community united by affectionate love. We already mentioned the present trend to found religious communities on the basis of mutual choice of members (in the sense that a mutually affectionate group either start a community or break away from an existing one). Here we would like to emphasize the incompatibility of this approach with virginity of heart.

A religious community on the basis of mutual choice? It seems to me that mutual choice in establishing relationships as is the case in marriage and friendship, when it does not express the reality of ultimately "finding" one another within the transcendent perspective of the human or Christian vocation, proves to be still subject to a passion which is not purified. On the other hand, a perpetual bond of life between people, understood as mutual right and duty, seems to be meaningful only in two cases: that of marriage and that of the religious community. In both cases it is not the mutual choice which is at the root of the relationship but a transcendent element: in the first, the transcendent order of procreation and education (leading to the duty and right of mutual assistance and to the daily renewed mutual choice), in the second, the transcendence of the Lord and of his Kingdom.

True and sound friendship by its very nature allows friends to be free at every moment to continue the mutual relationship. It may show its worth by being in fact lasting. However, when friends demand perpetual fidelity, they are, to the extent this is so, moved by unpurified sexual needs, at least at the unconscious level.

The theme is delicate, but it seems to me that the tendency to consider mutual choice or acceptance of the members as the basis of community-life, and even the tendency to consider community as the basic element of religious life (to the detriment of the vows) are remote offshoots of the same sexually conditioned attitude toward affective fulfillment. The ultimate root is a thirst for self-experience which, like the corresponding need for self-development, makes one ignore the call to true transcendent commitment.

A most grave danger for contemplative life to be overcome by virginity of heart: All this is extremely important for the monastic community. First as regards the personal choice which creates the community. It is an essential part of the vocation of monks that they should prove, before the People of God, that the choice of the Lord in love is able indeed, even more than anything else, to bring people together and to make a deeply human community.

More important are the consequences to contemplative life. We stated that as soon as one experiences affective togetherness, albeit at an unconscious level, as the first reason which motivates him toward the religious community, the need of self-experience becomes the final moving cause. Such experience can be sought in two directions. The search can be restricted to a merely horizontal togetherness, which is given an evangelical label, or it can reach even to the level of contemplation. When this happens, because thirst for self-experience is the motivation, God will not be sought in himself as he is known by faith, but he will be sought rather as an opportunity to experience absorption by the "cosmic abyss." This means that the search for contemplation comes to share those qualities of decadent religion which are so abundantly illustrated in the final stages of ancient Greek and Roman culture. The search becomes dilettante and eclectic, and the seemingly higher, strikingly contemplative levels reached (cosmic communion, the experience of the "great void," ecstatic communion in the group, etc.) are only illusory forms of self-transcendence. The search of self-experience makes contemplation lose its openness to the God we should meet. Ruusbroec rightly calls it a sort of spiritual unchasteness.[13] There is no virginity of heart.

By vowing chastity we intend to develop a virginity of heart which will penetrate our whole personality, freeing it from all searching after self-experience or spiritual sensation. This spiritual purity allows us to listen to God with that most complete transparency of our whole being, which is proper to prayerful contemplation. It also leads us to experience the truth that pure love of God makes us love the brethren wholeheartedly for God's sake in such a way that they are more and more loved for themselves.

Through history with the Church

Religious life has to contribute in a decisive way to the Church's involvement in Salvation History, above all as regards the basic attitude of "open fidelity."

As for the monastic community, it is a part of its vocation to confirm in a special way the *bond with the eternal* as enlightening the fulfilling life on earth, and therefore also the bond *with constitutive*

---

[13]. J. Ruusbroec, "Die geestelike Brulocht" in *Werken* (Tielt, 1944), I:228-30.

Christian truth and experience perduring through history. In assuring this bond with tradition the monastic community has always conditioned, to a large extent, the way in which the Church co-exists with the world at the level of what we called the "macro-dynamics" of history. Because of its belief that every period of history receives its ultimate meaning from its relationship to eternity (based on its being created and pointed toward the Kingdom of heaven) the monastic community has to contest nowadays in a most decided way the radically evolutionary view of history and human progress propagated by Marxists.

The bond with the past which has to be cultivated by the monk primarily concerns *tradition in its divine sense:* the deposit of God's Word in Sacred Scripture and in other Christian writings insofar as their pneumatic value has been authenticated by the Church. It is because of this that *lectio divina* and the study of the Fathers are so important in the monastic community. This is the privileged milieu where tradition should be perpetually alive and people able to go from it again and again toward the present-day world.

However, we always have to live guided by tradition in a basically free way. It must not be fidelity because of spiritual inertia or because of a desire for self-preservation, but because of a deeply-rooted respect for God, for what he has revealed and achieved in his Church, a respect flowing from the inner experience of tradition's value acquired from living with it.

Tradition could be a dead weight paralyzing one's steps as one goes through history. This is especially the case when it is used by an abbey as a mark of good standing. Monks should be able to live with spiritual and even cultural riches in a very poor way. In the future, furnishing abbeys with artistic productions which do not have much relevance for the preservation of true Christian tradition should be reduced to a minimum. This is necessary if the monks want to ensure the religious transparency of their life with its truely contemplative nature. Likewise we might mention the necessity of renouncing every naive display of the *gloria ordinis*. Modesty about the past (not ignorance!) is inseparable from a climate of spiritual poverty.

A testing-station in the Church for Christian acculturation

Being charismatically deeply rooted in tradition the monastic community may act as a testing-station in the Church for an acculturation in each new era of what is valuable in the eyes of the Lord. *A new synthesis* can be developed there at the level of life as well as of doctrine. It is to a large degree a question of a reflection which is purified from self-centered aims and from the sensational. The spiritually poor monk is intellectually independent from the times, being free from that minority complex which makes one run after the most recent author, relying blindly on him because of his intellectual skill and fame. The poor monk's thinking is not determined by the rulers of "intellectual consumption."

A renewal of contemplative life which is rooted in spiritual poverty should create room for trends of spiritual thinking which would draw their certitude from the Lord himself with whom they live. It should illustrate in this way the view of Newman according to which any valuable intellectual synthesis of authoritative tradition and new ideas depends finally on first principles, ultimate intuitions which can only spring from a heart that is converted and poor. The Church is in extreme need of centers where this insight which has been so sadly neglected might again become a common conviction.

Following the same line of thought we can conclude that for monks *theological study* cannot be in the first place a matter either of erudition or of critical thought. It should rather bring us something much more important but not always appreciated: an organic unification of the new insights with the lasting truth of Scripture and Tradition, in which a simple expression of profound intuition is more important than the technical set of concepts and the learned language in fashion. Maybe changes in methods of education will have to be developed in order to achieve this.

Similar observations could be made about *the renewal of monastic life* itself, which has also to take the way of open fidelity, free from every attachment to the past, independent in the face of current trends, as ready to change immediately as to wait a long time. The poor man is aware that he cannot know the hour of the Lord merely by human calculations but that he has to learn it from the Spirit. Hence also, his use of science and techniques, of psychological and sociological helps toward renewal is a "poor" one. He is always mindful that the Lord does not bless the People of God as long as they rely in the first place on "horses and chariots."

The way of obedient commitment

It should also be stated that in no other form of Christian life is obedient commitment to faith and to the Church's authority so necessary. The reasons for this are:

1. Because the viability of Christian monasticism depends so utterly on true faith and humble obedience, abbeys are the first to reach a crisis and to scatter when the Church as a whole is wavering in this matter.
2. The charismatic nature of renewal will depend all the more on the unrestricted acceptance of the same prerequisites, the more the aims of the renewal concerned are deeply religious.
3. The Church rightly reckons in a special way on monastic communities for assuring her fidelity to faith and authority, which is most critical and even the most decisive point in a time of change. Because of their life totally consecrated to the search for God, monastic communities are in the most privileged position for remaining faithful to this point.

These reasons become more cogent in a larger and more existential context. Salvation History again and again brings the people of God into situations in which they must choose the Lord in a clear-cut way: "He who is not with me is against me" (Mt 12:30). At critical times of history this choice demands embodiment in an historical option for the faith and for the Church's authority. This is manifestly the case nowadays. Hence, the question may be raised whether Christian groups in general, and religious communities in particular, can reach true renewal unless they take a stand unanimously, as a group, as regards the situation in the Church. This may be the unambiguous expression of fidelity which the Lord is finally demanding in our day from those who will survive.

Spiritual implantation in an emergent world

The vocation of the Christian monk has to be found at the heart of this new emerging civilization. Here we can learn from Herbert Marcuse. Both his criticism of modern times and the solution he announces contain a lot of truth to enlighten us in this.

Marcuse's criticism of modern society

Herbert Marcuse is indeed right in saying that modern times are drawing to a close. The civilization now emerging will be characterized by a major shift at the level of its deepest aims and forces.

In recent centuries the dynamics of civilization have been moved and steered by a will to dominate, to achieve, to excel. To this end life was submitted to reason and to technical power to an extreme degree. All this led to the suppression of every kind of spontaneity, and hence to the disruption of man's inner bonds with reality at all major levels:

—with one's instinctive roots (leading to disturbance of inner balance);
—with one's fellow men (inability to achieve affective communion);
—with nature (a thoroughly technically-sensitized man spoiling his natural environment);
—with the transcendent cosmic frame (the loss of the sense of contemplation).

All this is true, but the ultimate explanation he gives calls for discussion. According to Marcuse, the origin of all these evils is the imposition of the observance of sacralized, and hence absolute and lasting, rules and norms—a remnant, he says echoing Marx, of the former period of socio-economic development.

The root of our evils as seen through the monastic experience

To this interpretation the monks may oppose their own experience of the last centuries, which represents in a well-defined way the experience of the Church as a whole.

In actual fact they suffered to some degree from exactly the same difficulties as those formulated by Marcuse. But today the revival in the Church of the call for spiritual poverty (from which monasticism sprang) allows them to realize what the origin of these difficulties is, the fact, namely, that they had lost this very sense of spiritual poverty. Even when they consciously aimed at humble abandonment to the God of Redemption, their spontaneous reflexes were very often conditioned at the unconscious level by the totally opposite "sensitivity" and climate of modern times: a desire for the self-realization and rational achievement denounced by Marcuse. This sensitivity itself stems from something more profound which true Christians and monks have never shared: a return, in principle, to an anthropocentric approach to life, with a spirit of absolute autonomy.

If this is true, then the difficulty of preserving in monastic life the inner bonds of reality (the integration of instinct, the integration of community, the sense of nature, the natural sense of contemplation) is not due to living in submission to transcendent reality experienced as holy and as regulating life by sacred norms. Rather it is due to the fact that the way one lived out this submission was penetrated by a hidden sense of self-centeredness and an unperceived contamination by an anthropocentric and irreligious world.

In short, it was not religion but the lack of a spontaneous religious spirit which was at the root of the difficulty. This was the reason why we did not get sufficiently positive results from living in a dedicated seclusion, in the presence of the Christian mysteries, and with structures ordered to a life of prayer.

Toward a new community beyond anthropocentrism

The way out of the impasse is obvious. To a certain degree it is the way Marcuse has shown: renouncing the attitude which aims above all at systematic achievement and re-establishing the primacy of love. But, in doing this, the Christian goes in the opposite direction.

Marcuse in fact only replaces the idol of self-realization by its counterpart, the idol of self-experience. In both cases sinful identi-

T

fication with the unconverted heart continues. The results to say
the least are questionable, as is proved by the development of the
hippie movement and all that it means.

The Christian renounces the primacy of every anthropocentrism,
either at the level of self-realization, or at that of self-experience. He
goes the way of the poor. The love whose primacy he must restore
is not that of unpurified spontaneity or Eros (characteristic of "the
man of the flesh"), but that of the self-transcending commitment of
"the spiritual man" who has accepted the contestation of his
spontaneous tendencies.

In the face of the wild urge for self-experience, and the consequent
tendency to reject every law and lasting norm, in the face of the
"great refusal" of the establishment, the monastic community
should represent the Christian response in its purest form.

It should express the Christian "great refusal," that is the refusal
of sin as embodied in the trend toward self-realization as well as in
that toward self-experience. It should prove by its own concrete
development that, once liberated from the contamination of the
spirit of "modern times," obedient love frees us from the evils
described by Marcuse and re-establishes the all-embracing integration he announced. It should show how humble entrance into a
respectfully accepted order of things and the performance of daily
duty may be more fulfilling for man than the repeated experience
of creativity; how the mortification of one's personal needs and the
experience of a marginal lack of authenticity can do no harm as
long as we are authentically grasped by love and inserted by this love
into an all-embracing communion with God, with men and with
the world.

In the life of the Christian monk, after the re-birth of spiritual
poverty, it will become manifest that meeting with the living
Christ leads to a contemplative life which is more simple and human
and even infinitely more worthwhile than anything the techniques
of cosmic meditation can offer. Only by going straight along the
way of Redemption by Christ, can these techniques be approached
with the discernment required.

It will be most important to show that this contemplation is not an escape from the world and from the establishment. The Christian monk may contest society, its policies and its structures, but, in the line of Reinhold Niebuhr[14] and Thomas Merton,[15] he warns against the tendency to attribute all our sufferings to insufficiency of structures and to the faults of past generations, escaping in this way from confrontation with the ultimate source which is sin. By this approach and by the sense of organic growth in renewing structures the monk shall present a quiet contradiction to the spirit of Marxism which all over the world is influencing the way in which men are coping with historical change.

The whole of this witness—and we have only sketched some of its major themes—will be given to the world by a community which is also seen to be thoroughly free from the tyrannic impact of the consumer society. There the contemporary world should experience how transparent all things are, how pure the atmosphere we breathe when sobriety of life springs from a humble heart, when the use of things and meeting with people are taken up into the holy sphere of creation and of new life in Christ.

I profoundly believe in the future of a monastic community which takes this line, and in the force of its appeal to the world of today. Its message will not need either the support of the press or orchestration by the mass media. The decisive messengers of the future could well be those who out of poverty of spirit have remained out of the limelight. They will be "discovered" by a generation which is starving because of the absence of God.

Valentine Walgrave OP

Ghent, Belgium

---

14. R. Niebuhr, *The Nature and Destiny of Man,* vol. 1 (New York: Scribner, 1941), ch. 4: The Easy Conscience of Modern Man.

15. Cf. Thomas Merton in *Blessed are the Meek: The Christian Roots of Nonviolence* (Nyack, NY, 1967).

CONTEMPLATIVE COMMUNITY

David F. K. Steindl-Rast OSB*

COMMUNITY IS ALWAYS POISED between two poles: solitude and togetherness. Without togetherness community disperses; without solitude community collapses into a mass, a crowd. But solitude and togetherness are not mutually antagonistic; on the contrary, they make each other possible.

Solitude without togetherness deteriorates into loneliness. One needs strong roots in togetherness to be solitary rather than lonely when one is alone. Aloneness is neutral; loneliness is aloneness which is cut off from togetherness; solitude is aloneness supported by togetherness, "blessed solitude."

Togetherness without solitude is not truly togetherness, but rather side-by-sideness. To live merely side by side is alienation. We need time and space to be alone, to find ourselves in solitude, before we can give ourselves to one another in true togetherness.

A particular balance between solitude and togetherness will characterize a particular community. But by "balance" we mean more than the "ratio" between time spent alone and time spent with one another; we mean an inner relatedness of solitude and

*Br. David Steindl-Rast, a monk of Mount Savior Monastery, is co-founder and chairman of the Center for Spiritual Studies established by Buddhists, Hindus, Jews and Christians. He holds degrees from the Vienna Academy of the Fine Arts and the Psychological Institute. He received his Ph.D. degree in experimental psychology from the University of Vienna. He has published many articles and lectures widely.

togetherness to one another which makes each of them what it is in a given case.

On one end of the spectrum lies a type of community in which togetherness is the goal that is sought above all, a particularly close-knit family, for example. We may call this type togetherness-community. On the other end of the spectrum lies a community totally oriented towards solitude, for instance a community of hermits. Let us call this type solitude-community. Since in either case both solitude and togetherness are essential for true community, the difference is one of emphasis.

The spectrum is continuous, but the distinction is clear: in togetherness-community, togetherness is the measure of solitude; the members have a right and a duty to get as much solitude as they need for deep and strong togetherness. In solitude-community, solitude is the measure of togetherness; here the members have a right and a duty to get as much togetherness as each one needs to support and enrich solitude.

Man cannot survive without community. Nor can he be truly happy unless he find the particular type of community that will fulfill his needs for solitude and togetherness. The process of matching one's personal needs with a particular type of community within the wide spectrum of possibilities is an essential part of "finding one's vocation." (Note that we bracket here the question of "temporary vs. lifelong vocations"; "vocation" in our context means merely what one feels called to choose at a given time.)

Contemplative life as a "vocation" means a particular form of life in which, ideally at least, every detail of daily living is oriented toward recollection. By recollection we mean mindfulness, ultimately unlimited mindfulness, the inner attitude by which we find meaning. Contemplative life in this sense is a form of life designed to provide an optimum environment for a radical search for meaning.

Meaning and purpose are not identical (it is possible, for instance, to accomplish a purpose that has no meaning). Two different inner gestures of man correspond to purpose and meaning. When we comprehend the purpose of a given thing or action we "grasp" it, we are in control. When we want to understand the meaning of a given thing or situation, it must "touch" us. (How does this "grab you?" as the young people say). We are responsive, but no longer in control.

By grasping purpose we gain knowledge; by allowing meaning to take hold of us we gain that wisdom which is the ultimate goal of contemplative life. The two are mutually complementary; we must distinguish without separating them. The openness for meaning is joined to the pursuit of purpose through leisure.

Leisure is not the opposite of work (we should be able to work in leisure). The opposite of work is play. Work is something we do to accomplish a purpose which lies outside the activity itself; once the purpose is accomplished, the activity ceases. (We shine shoes in order to have them shined, not in order to shine them; once they are shiny, we stop.) Play is something we do because we find meaning in it, an activity which has all its purpose within itself. (We sing in order to sing, for its own sake, not in order to have sung.)

Leisure introduces into every activity an element of play, an element of doing whatever it be also for its own sake, not only to get it done. Thus leisure provides the climate in which man can be open for meaning. Contemplative life as a form of life molded by a radical search for meaning will necessarily be a life of leisure, ascetical leisure.

It seems possible to gain some insights into the ascetic elements of contemplative life by an analysis of the so-called Peak Experience. This term denotes a deeply personal experience of meaningful insight, often in a flash, always in a moment of leisure. The experience itself is totally unreflexive, but later reflection finds in it a series of paradoxes.

What takes place in the Peak Experience is paradoxically both I lose myself, and yet I am in this experience more truly myself than at any other time. (Expressions one uses afterwards to describe what happened may include: "I was out of myself"; "I was simply carried away"; "I completely lost myself in . . ."; and yet "I was more fully alive, more truly myself than ever.")

Another paradox of which one becomes aware in the Peak Experience is the fact that one is at the same time alone (not lonely) in a profound sense, and yet deeply one with all others present or even absent. Often a Peak Experience occurs during a moment of solitude, out in nature for instance, but even when I am in the midst of a large crowd, say, in a concert hall, this one passage of music which touches me deeply seems to single me out, as if it had been written and performed especially for me. On the other hand, even on the mountain top or on a lonely shore my heart expands in the Peak Experience to embrace earth and sky and all living creatures. The paradox is simply that I am most intimately one with all when I am most intimately alone.

There is a third paradox implicit in the Peak Experience: in a sudden flash of insight everything makes sense; everything, life and death and the whole universe; but not as if someone had given us the solution to a complicated problem; it is rather that we are reconciled with the problem. For one moment we stop questioning and a universal answer emerges; or rather, we glimpse the fact that the answer was always quietly there, only our questions drowned it out. When I stop asking, the answer is there.

The three paradoxes with which we are confronted in the Peak Experience provide a key for the understanding of contemplative life; they are like seeds out of which the most universal ascetical practices of contemplative tradition grow. Out of the paradoxical insight that I am most truly myself when I lose myself grows the ascetical practice of detachment. Poverty or detachment aims at more than giving away what I have; I must ultimately give away what I am, so as to truly be.

The experience of being alone when one is one with all provides a key for the understanding of celibacy. The monk (the *monachos*, the "lover" whom everyone calls "brother") sustains the paradox which others experience only in a brief moment. He is alone so as to be truly one with all; or one could also say he is so deeply united with all, that solitude is paradoxically the only adequate expression for this unity.

Ascetical obedience is also rooted in the Peak Experience, in the insight, namely, that everything makes sense the moment I stop questioning, the moment I listen. Learning to listen is the heart of obedience; following someone else's commands is merely a means to this end. In last analysis, we have only the choice between absurdity and obedience. *Ab-surdus* means "absolutely deaf"; *ob-audiens* denotes the attitude of one who has learned to listen thoroughly, to listen with a heart attuned to the deepest meaning.

The Peak Experience is a moment in which meaning strikes us, takes hold of us. Contemplative asceticism serves to support the monk's wholehearted search for meaning. It makes sense, then, that the structural paradox of the Peak Experience should provide a clue for understanding the paradoxical structure of ascetical practice. Contemplative life is basically the attempt to expose oneself to the meaning of any given moment (through detachment, celibacy, obedience) in unlimited mindfulness.

Contemplative community in the strict sense will be a community of people who support one another in that radical search for meaning which finds expression in ascetical tradition. However, solitude is an integral part of this tradition in all its forms. An emphasis on solitude is implicit even in the disengagement characteristic of detachment and in the silence characteristic of obedience; in celibacy solitude becomes explicitly a key element of contemplative life. Contemplative community is solitude-community.

This means that in contemplative community the members live in community so as to protect one another's solitude both from deteriorating into loneliness and from being infringed upon by misguided togetherness. If there is one lonely monk in the community, the others must ask themselves: "Have we supported this aloneness by the togetherness he needed?" Yet, each one must also ask himself again and again: "Have I respected the solitude of my brother? Have I protected it against my own whims of togetherness?" Monks are the guardians of one another's solitude, to the left as well as to the right.

Solitude, however, is not an end in itself. The end is a community supportive of the ascetical quest for meaning; and this is to say that the end is a community of leisure, for through leisurely living alone can we find meaning. The very reason why people join to form community of this kind is the mutual help they can give to one another in creating an environment in which leisure is possible. The leisure of which we are speaking is not the privilege of those who have time, but the virtue of those who take time. Contemplative community is solitude-community for the sake of leisure. To live leisurely means to take things one by one, to single them out for grateful consideration. And this is the essence of celebration. All other aspects of celebration are optional, but when everything is stripped away that can be stripped away, these two elements remain. Wherever someone singles out something (or someone) for grateful consideration, we have a little celebration. Celebration cannot and need not be justified by any purpose; it is ultimately meaningful. To live leisurely means to celebrate every moment of life. Contemplative community is solitude-community which provides leisure to celebrate life.

David Steindl-Rast OSB

Mount Savior
Elmira, N.Y.

ME PSYCHOLOGICAL DIMENSIONS OF THE CONTEMPLATIVE COMMUNITY

Dominic H. Salman OP*

THE PSYCHOLOGICAL STRUCTURES of any community are complicated and many-dimensional. Those of specifically religious communities obviously raise special problems, that make them more difficult to understand; they have, moreover, been far less studied than the more ordinary secular groups of common social life. The psychological features of contemplative communities have been even less investigated, and they no doubt remain the least understood of them all. This report will therefore be of a very preliminary nature. It makes no claim for theoretical authority or practical finality. Its only intention is to stimulate productive thinking by providing discussions on a certain number of apparently relevant themes, thus encouraging a more explicit awareness of the factors involved. It is concerned with general problems, rather than with concrete solutions that will always depend upon peculiar circumstances in specific cultural environments. Even when particular attitudes or rulings are suggested, they are only proposed to high-light the importance of a significant factor, that must somehow be recognized and safe-guarded. The whole concern of this report is with relevant variables that deserve to be considered. It gladly leaves the responsibility of wise and prudent decisions to the appropriate authorities, guided by

*Fr. D. H. Salman is a professor in the Department of Psychology at the University of Quebec at Montreal. He is a member of the Ecumenical Institute of Spirituality.

experienced counselors, and advised by well-inspired communities. The only purpose of this paper is to provide food for thought.

An attempt has been made to reduce the theme to more manageable proportions by considering only one form of contemplative community, the masculine, Christian, Benedictine, Cistercian species of a much wider genus. This will allow the elimination of many irrelevant questions, a more immediate approach to significant problems, and a more concrete discussion of the possible solutions. It might however prove useful, at some future date, to reflect upon peculiarities of the Cistercian tradition, and upon the principles that justify them. There is no better method than this comparative approach to establish the nature of a corporate identity, and to confirm a sense of one's individual vocation.

The problems discussed in this paper have been grouped under three headings, related respectively to the ecological environment, affiliation to the community, and communication within it.

THE ECOLOGICAL ENVIRONMENT

The contemplative community is the cultural environment within which the contemplative religious normally lives and moves and has his being. It helps him to grow and to develop within his chosen vocation in many ways, the first and most fundamental of which consists in the provision of an appropriate physical setting. For this bodily environment should at all times remind him of his condition and of his purpose: that he is an ordinary man living a human life with other like-minded individuals, that he has renounced the world, and is decided to live really separated from it though not unmindful of its spiritual needs; and that he is mainly concerned with the presence of God, the worship of his glory and the quest for a greater knowledge of his truth and a deeper love of his goodness. These far too general principles need of course to be spelled out in more exacting detail.

Enclosure

A first concern would be for a proper separation from the world, as organized by the time-tried rules of enclosure. A physical separation would seem essential, by walls or fences or the sheer distance of empty spaces. But the separation must be effective and rigorous, if singleness of purpose is to be maintained in the pursuit of a truly contemplative life.

Guests and visitors will always remain a problem, as will letter-writers and senders of gifts. One might at least try to remember basic principles, and to judge concrete solutions accordingly. The first principle would state that all these persons are outside the contemplative community, and so a potential disturbance and distraction that should as far as possible be minimized. The second principle would recognize that all these outsiders provide opportunities for service and stimulations towards a more apostolic life. The real problem would therefore be to decide whether the community as a whole thinks fit to lead a more apostolic life, if it has the men available to carry out such pastoral functions, and if it thinks appropriate to apply these men to such tasks. The answer will of course depend on many things, but not least on the notion the contemplative community has of its own vocations within the Church.

Modern mass-media raise other problems. It would not seem sufficient to consider only radio, television and the movies, magazines and glossy weeklys and daily papers. For the ever-increasing flood of semi-scientific ecclesiastical publications is now just as dangerous for the life of the mind, not to mention that of the spirit, of any unprotected reader, with its devastating catalogue of new recipes in catechetics and homiletics, in pastoral work and counseling, in pop-liturgy and inspired prayer-meetings, in social reform and revolutionary economics. Here again, I would suggest, two contradictory principles must be simultaneously maintained. On the one hand, the torrent of senseless and soul-destroying "information" must be firmly excluded. For truly the medium is the message, and any systematic exposure to it is bound to destroy all possibilities of contemplative life. On the other hand, some contact must obviously be maintained with the Church militant without the monastery walls, and the human culture within which it is rooted.

And some communication must therefore exist with the outer world. Until now, such relations between the contemplative community and the Church at large and the world seem to have been haphazard and unorganized. It might be useful to recognize that a major problem is involved. What knowledge of this sort is necessary to the contemplative monk? What is useful, in relation to his level of literacy, his socio-religious function, his personal vocation. What type of information, and what form of presentation, are conducive to contemplative prayer? Which, on the other hand, lead to distractions, to worldly passions, to dissatisfaction, to anxiety? A great deal of reflection, and a still greater amount of experimentation by trial and error, will be needed, before any confident answer can be given to these difficult questions. In the meantime, precautionary measures could be taken. It would seem essential to prevent the flow of unalloyed poison, and therefore exclude direct access to radio and television, to the daily and to the weekly press, and to the bulky trash of illiterate and incompetent ecclesiastical publications. Important information should be filtered out and then assimilated by religious personalities of sufficient theological and spiritual judgment. Only then should it be communicated to the contemplative community, in a manner that would serve its purpose and not destroy its form of life. Both the written text and the spoken word could serve in this connection, and either community leaders or masters from without could fulfill this important function. What is essential, however, is to know that a deliberate policy is required, that it must be worked out, and that it must be applied. A contemplative community must be protected from the destructive impact of the mass-media; but it must also be helped to remain in touch with the evolution of the Church and the World. Specific methods and institutions will have to be worked out to carry out these functions of defense and assimilation, methods and institutions that did not exist before and indeed were not needed. But they are now absolutely required, in our present secular world of mass-persuasion (or is it mass-perversion) through electronics, publicity and propaganda. The future life of contemplative communities depends upon their capacity to adapt to this new and more difficult cultural environment, by creating more effective organs of defense and communication.

Buildings

A second concern would be related to the physical environment within which the contemplative community lives and operates. A church is obviously necessary, within which the community as a whole can decently foregather and perform its solemn worship. A chapter is likewise required, and a refectory, if their respective religious functions are to be properly fulfilled. Sheltered cloisters are needed at all times to walk in and to meditate, but even more in the cold of winter or the heat of summer. If private cells are frowned upon, semi-isolated booths at least should be provided for personal reading or private prayer. For how can one expect the development of autonomous religious personalities, if no privacy is allowed to individual monks? A library is more than ever essential, in this our time where a growing proportion of the population has become effectively literate. Buildings for work are no less essential, so that it may be properly carried out when it is accomplished and safely left aside when it is finished. An infirmary must be provided, a guest-house, a kitchen and a dozen other services that should be convenient to the users while causing the least possible disturbance to others. And so each individual, each group and the community as a whole need their proper buildings and spaces if life is to develop peacefully and organically. The physical organization of the monastery is both an expression of and a positive factor in the life of the contemplative community.

All this is classic and would hardly bear repeating if there was not a trend opposed to the establishment (!) of well-organized monasteries. Enthusiasts of such persuasion are not content with stark simplicity, virile austerity, unadorned purity of architectural forms and rigorously functional choices in the organization of the physical environment: all of which could be readily and indeed gladly accepted, as corresponding to authentic traits of Cistercian tradition. They would go much further, in wanting small priories, mean buildings, multi-purpose assembly-halls, a precarious economy, a life of constant work. Now it is a fact that there are at present a number of deeply religious men dedicated to such ideals of religious life. Their vocations must be respected, and their quest permitted or even encouraged. Yet it would also seem important to clarify the exact nature of their calling, and its precise relation with the contemplative life of the more classical monastic community.

In such small pioneering communities, there is obviously much more scope for independence and responsibility. But this is strictly in the field of practical life, not at all in the realm of contemplation. Much more time and effort will also have to be given to daily chores and the work of subsistence, and this will necessarily reduce the time available for organized prayer and *lectio divina*. Public worship will in any case be curtailed, for lack of men, of space, and time. And so the whole balance of life will be shifted to the operative prayer-by-action pole of monastic life at the expense of the complementary worship and *lectio divina* pole. This corresponds to a perfectly respectable religious vocation. It might even claim to be authentically contemplative. But it would surely approximate the lay-brother type of contemplative life rather than the choir-monk variety. An explicit and deliberate choice would have to be made if a whole community decided to live in that very distinctive way.

Another point should be made in this connection. Small communities are not demographically viable in the long run. It is easy enough to find a group of six to ten like-minded men of comparable ages, say twenty-five to forty-five. But if they remain a small group, they will be thirty years later a group of old and ailing dotards. If they attract vocations, they will automatically increase in numbers, and their style of life is bound to change. Only a reasonably large monastery can maintain a steady state by evening out randomly fluctuating arrivals and departures, and so achieving the permanent organization of a well-structured contemplative community. Only such a large community can provide for the variety of contemplative vocations that is normally attracted by a well established monastery. But there will be independents and originals, anxious to do their thing in their own peculiar way. They might well be encouraged to do so, at their own risk, rather than have them remain and trouble a peaceful community.

Icons

A contemplative community needs to be protected from the world without, and it must live at ease within its own buildings and inner spaces. But it must also establish and maintain the quality of its inner environment. It must therefore help its members to remember that they constantly live in the presence of God. There was a time when this seemed obvious to all concerned, and all religious houses were provided with an abundance of crosses and statues and paintings and carvings. The situation has now changed completely, and we find ourselves in the midst of the most savagely iconoclastic period the Church has ever experienced. I am sure this is not only a theological but also a technical mistake. Man is an embodied spirit, he perceives through his senses, and responds deeply to the shapes and colors that act upon him. Images of realities unseen awaken his attention, and remind him of the objects of his faith. It is normal and useful for him to people his environment with images and emblems of his deepest concern, and any community dedicated to a religious life should build up an appropriately decorated environment. Everything should be done to maintain all concerned at the level of an active faith and a burning concern for the love of God. *In conspectu angelorum psallam tibi, Domine* is a permanent theme, which one should not be able to forget in a properly appointed monastery.

Now it is obvious that saintly discretion is as necessary in the field of religious decoration as in all other fields of endeavor. Quiet simplicity, chaste propriety, gracious dignity, delicate restraint, are much to be preferred to the blatant vulgarity of so many barbaric outpourings of unregenerate pseudo-artists. These are matters of taste upon which no private individual can legislate, and in which each community will perforce have to reveal the quality of its esthetic culture and of its spiritual sophistication. My main psychological concern here is to insist upon a minimum of figurative or

V

representational decoration, that will make the monastery into a house of God dedicated to prayer. It should not be possible to mistake it for a farm or a factory, a dance-hall or a bus-station.

Misunderstandings in this field are so great that one more point must be made. Some recent reformers have not only done away with recognizable representations of Christian belief and devotion, they have innocently introduced a certain number of other objects, to stimulate the imagination of their fellow-religious. But they appear extraordinarily unaware of the real effect produced by the introduction of such extraneous material. Three very different examples of this aberration, which I have personally observed, may help to clarify the issue. The first concerns a religious house which happened to possess a rather nice cloister surrounding an inner courtyard well planted with shrubs and flowers. There was nothing in these neutral surroundings to remind one of one's Christian beliefs; but it was barely possible to pray, if one's faith, hope and charity were sufficiently activated from within. A nature-loving brother now introduced two squirrels into the courtyard and he soon gave them a cute little house in the best Disneyland style. This changed the setting in the most radical way. Every passer-by would stop with great benevolence to watch these nice little animals. But I doubt if one in a hundred thought to relate them to the Maker of all creation and so return to his religious quest. With the best of intentions, silliness and childishness and irresponsibility had brought distractions into the community, instead of positive incitations to deeper prayer and to greater love.

My second example is that of a religious house in which a long corridor led on each side to a certain number of rooms. No religious decoration was provided, not even a bare cross or a text from the Gospels, so that one might have thought oneself in army barracks, in a hospital or in a prison. Some bright young reformers now sought to improve the situation by decorating the walls with travel-posters. Their choice was morally unimpeachable and esthetically competent. Yet the effects in the mind of the beholder were no doubt those intended by the travel-agency: muted dissatisfaction with present drab surroundings, a wild desire to wander carefree in the blue yonder, vain dreams about bright seas and sandy beaches, silvery lagoons and the perfume of delightful bowers. None of this would seem conducive to more fervent prayer or a better-integrated contemplative life. It brings into the community the deliberate seduction of undisputable distractions. Yet it was all done with the best of intentions, and with the quiet satisfaction of progress achieved. Lord, forgive them, for they know not what they are doing.

My third example is somewhat more subtle. It concerns a monastery whose cloisters and inner courtyards were also bereft of all trace of Christian symbolism. But they had been beautifully disposed according to the most rigorous canons of Zen Buddhism: exquisitely-raked stretches of sand, cleverly assembled blocs of age-worn rock, strangely contorted pieces of driftwood, etc. The esthetic effect was overwhelming, and the spiritual effect no doubt deeper. But *what* is the spirit that is here inspired, by these symbols that are as typical of Mahâyâna Buddhism as the Fish was of primitive Christianity and the Last Judgment of medieval belief? Is it not the void emptiness of Sunyatâ, rather than the concrete fullness of Jesus Christ, true man and true God, dying upon the Cross and risen from the dead? And will these utterly un-christian symbols lead to the personal God who has revealed himself through the Bible and the life of Christ? Surely it is folly to refuse sacred symbols when they are Christian, and then to borrow the alien symbols of false beliefs from the most atheist of Eastern traditions.

For images are normally required for embodied men who lead a social life in a physical environment. Christian images are recommended for a contemplative community of men who serve and seek a Christian God. It is true, of course, that sacred images raise problems of their own that would deserve to be discussed in due time. But more urgent questions must first be settled. We must restore images destroyed by angry iconoclasts; we must get rid of profane distractions; and we must remove the false symbols of alien beliefs. When these fundamental corrections will have been made and order restored, there will be time enough to discuss the finer points of icon-devotion.

AFFILIATION TO THE COMMUNITY

A Cistercian monk is by his very nature the member of a community. He belongs to this contemplative community, which provides him a home and family and the necessary spiritual environment for his growth and development in his chosen vocation. But such a community and the mode of his belonging are of a peculiar type, that would require more explicit description. An attempt will be made here to formulate the situation under five headings: affiliation, identity, belonging, concern and intimacy.

Affiliation

A monk is a man who has left his family, his parish and all the social groups of his natural origins to become a voluntary member of a new community. A radical break is involved, by which such an individual is uprooted from his early environment, to be replanted in a new soil to develop a different and more spiritual form of life. This is quite different from the many other sorts of voluntary commitments possible to man, such as marriage, joining a profession, or becoming member of a political party. For all these are additional involvements that are grafted on to earlier commitments to extend them, they do not renounce the past (as far as humanly possible) in order to build a new future. A religious vocation absolutely requires this initial sacrifice, by which one *leaves* one's family and the world. A clear break, and a new start, are required. It is one of the essential functions of the noviciate to provide this experience of death and renewal, of disappearance of old habits and structures and identities, and their replacement by new realities. If the novitiate does not achieve this initiation into a new form of life, it has failed its primary purpose. It may educate respectable and pious laymen; it will not have created authentic religious, who have renounced the world to follow Christ.

A minor practical problem might be mentioned in this connection, one that has caused some hesitation in recent years. It concerns the permission now given to visit dying parents, and the attitudes to be taken to this new permissiveness. I would suggest that it all depends on the level of spiritual education of the laymen concerned. It would be a tragedy, and a scandal, if parents and friends were to believe that because a son has given his life to serve the Lord he has ceased to love his parents and become indifferent to their fate. If such were to be their interpretation, a timely and if necessary prolonged visit home would surely be required. But if a true understanding of the contemplative life were to prevail, if dying parents could be happy and proud of their sons, unavailable in the flesh but close in the spirit of faith, who are praying for them more effectively as death approaches because of the sacrifices they have both accepted, then it might be good for all concerned not to leave the monastery even though the legal possibility exists. It all depends, in other words, on the quality of people's faith, and their ability to understand the notion of sacrifice. Neither will appear overnight, and both will need a long education.

Affiliation to a community of course requires mutual acceptance. After a time of trial and mutual accommodation, the voluntary association is then made final. Vows are pronounced, that seal reciprocal responsibilities, and membership until death is thus assured. The final nature of these vows would seem more important than the particular content (stability, obedience). For no serious commitment can be undertaken by gyrovague wanderers who roam fitfully from one house to another, in search of more personal self-expression rather than a more steadfast quest of God.

Identity

A new identity is acquired by membership in the religious community. One's birthplace and family and secular accomplishments are no longer significant factors of one's religious personality, but rather one's recognized affiliation as an accepted member of a chosen monastic group. One's conception of oneself is transformed, and with it one's ideal-self with all the strong motivational factors it involves. One's new identity is to belong to this group, to participate in its quest, to imitate its best models, to learn from its examples, to enter into its tradition so as to emulate its finest accomplishments.

This identification with a group of like-minded companions has always been important, but it is far more urgently required in these our present times. For it is far more difficult now than it has been for the last thousand years for the isolated individual to obtain a social validation of his faith. The sociology of knowledge shows that very few of one's beliefs are acquired through one's personal experience. Most of them are learned through a slow process of socialization and acculturation, and therefore received from other men and groups already present in the social environment. At the same time, they are easily accepted because they are so widely believed. Such beliefs take on an aura of credibility and of obviousness because they are taken for granted by the population as a whole. They have never been denied, and therefore do not need to be proved. Private beliefs, that are different from (or opposed to) those of the social environment, are in a far less favorable condition. They are much harder to acquire in the first place; they are far more difficult to maintain; and they always remain vulnerable to the relentless pressure of the teeming masses who do not share them. Such beliefs are therefore very dependent upon the support they can get from small groups of like-minded companions. All this would be true of any socially-shared conviction, but it applies even more to ideological beliefs of a systematic nature, that are more remote from ordinary experience.

Now it is a fact that modern man is isolated in his religious faith. He is acutely aware of the prevalence of other cultures, of other ideologies, of other beliefs, not to mention the wide variety of agnostic or atheistic disbeliefs. He knows that many around him are completely uninterested in all forms of religion and indifferent if not inimical to its manifestations. Moreover, this concerns immediately relevant value-judgments in social and moral matters, as well as the more difficult and apparently more remote theological issues. A modern Christian is therefore very conscious of his minority status, in a universe of other convictions opposed to his own. His faith will be qualified by its exceptional and in fact even marginal nature, for he is constantly aware of other people in his environment, who are decent and honest and respectable and perhaps even gifted and intelligent, but who share neither his beliefs nor his convictions concerning the Revelation of God and the destiny of man. It will be very difficult for such a Christian to sustain his faith, and to live by it; and it will only be possible if he can find a community that will comfort his convictions, encourage his hope and nourish his love.

All the foregoing remarks apply thrice compounded to the monk with a contemplative vocation. Opposition to his beliefs and condemnation for his life will come not only from unbelievers but from other Christians and indeed from eminent representatives of his own Church. For many he will be an object of derision and contempt. And even high-placed prelates will consider that he is wasting his life in idle ignorance when he might so usefully be employed in rural missions or inner-city parishes. It is therefore essential for him to discover a group of like-minded men, who share his values and accept his priorities, who by their very life and their example validate his vocation and bear witness to its utter significance. It is the community which by its very existence shows that a contemplative life is possible and that it is good. This similarity in purpose and dedication is a major factor in any contemplative life. It could of course be further strengthened by wisely measured relations with other communities with cognate spiritual vocations.

Identity, of course, is not only given by affiliation with the presently existing community. It is also given by the past history of this community, by its origin, by filiation from earlier monasteries, and so by the whole tradition of one's order. In this way, by joining a contemplative community one enters into a living tradition. The contemplative life is not only a theory, it is also a practice; it is in fact a life which can only be learned by actual experience. It develops far more easily and more normally if the example of life-long practitioners and the guidance of experienced elders are available. An immense amount of spiritual culture is thus transmitted to the neophyte, giving content and structure to his feeble attempts, and slowly making him into a living link in the chain of a distinctive tradition of contemplative life. No man stands alone in this field of spiritual endeavor; and the most creatively original are usually those who have grown the deepest roots in the tradition from which they spring. It behooves each individual to become humbly grateful to his community for the riches which it bestows upon him, and to assimilate this heritage to the best of his abilities. But it would also be proper for each community to consider if it is successfully handing on the treasures of its tradition, and if it is providing adequate guidance and examples to its junior members. If not, appropriate corrective measures should be applied.

Acceptance

A community is more than the sum of its individual members. It includes a "we-feeling," by which each individual shares in the trusting knowledge that all are accepted members of the group, and that they all securely belong to the community. Acceptance is of course tentative at first, since no one knows initially how a postulant will succeed in the new life he is attempting. Yet even the postulant should feel that all hope for him and in him, and that if he fails it is not because the group was unwilling. In due time, acceptance will become explicit in the shape of mutually binding vows. And then more than ever unconditional acceptance, based upon a mutual choice, and founded in identical shared convictions and aspirations, should be the basic attitude of the community towards its members. This should of course apply to all concerned, including the least gifted, the least educated, the least useful, the least advanced on the path to perfection. For by the bounty of the Lord they have been accepted in a merciful (if perhaps unwise) community; and they will not be abandoned. The community is and remains glad to have them, and it would be dismayed to see them abandon their generous attempt to lead a contemplative life.

A community should also be permissive and approving toward its individual members. Each one should feel gloriously free, to be and to live, to grow in the service of the group and to develop in his quest for God. Each individual should feel that his contribution is acknowledged, that his presence is recognized, that he is approved as a deserving member of the community who operates to the best of his abilities in the group effort. More important still, he should feel that all are concerned with his vocation, and that all rejoice in his progress. This common attitude of good-will and encouragement is of particular importance in this spiritual field, where all growth is based upon private motivation. For one cannot force such a development, one can only encourage it when it already exists. Yet such rewarding approval, with its blend of unselfish love and more socially embodied in-group affection, can be an important factor in the religious life of the contemplative community.

At this point of the discussion, it might be useful to inject a word of caution. The sort of community we have described, that is accepting and permissive and approving, will prove to be a helpful and healing environment. To the individual, it gives a feeling of full security. He feels protected, he can relax, he feels less inclined to mobilize his defense-mechanisms and his no less rigid and defensive character-traits. Fears and anxieties slowly decrease, and the more healthy and positive aspects of his personality can more readily develop in a trusting and loving environment. Moreover, the individual becomes more easily aware of the needs of his brethren, and of the necessities of a well-ordered community life. In this way, he develops his personality in a new and effective way, by becoming a better-adjusted and more fully-functioning member of the community. This is an essential component of personality development, that can only normally occur within a community, but that will spontaneously take place if a healthy community spirit makes it possible. It might be useful to add that this type of growth by socialization is as important in a cenobitic contemplative life as in any other quest for maturation or perfection.

A good community therefore has obvious and undisputed therapeutic qualities. This is a useful and indeed beneficial property, for which we should all be thankful. But it would seem important to recognize categorically that therapy is not the principal intention or purpose of the contemplative community, or for that matter of any religious association. There is an essential difference between therapeutic communities and a widely varied group of other social groups which I shall provisionally call educational, among which we would classify both religious communities in general and contemplative communities in particular. The difference lies in the fundamental emotive-affective attitudes involved. The therapeutic community is concerned with weak and ailing personalities, it seeks to decrease all possible frustrations, so as to minimize pathological defences and encourage spontaneous growth. The educational community is not unmindful of these factors, but its main purpose is directly opposite. It presents demanding standards, compelling requirements and arduous ideals. It sets up challenges, that have to be faced and overcome. It seeks to invigorate, in a virile and unflinching spirit, not to relax in an overly permissive and protective environment. All these factors are characteristic of any educational community. But they are more typical still of a religious community whose aim is to seek perfection, and a contemplative community whose sole purpose is to know and to love God, and God only. Hardship is then willingly accepted, sacrifice is of the essence of a vocation that is wholly marked by the sign of the Cross. Truly this is not an enterprise for the slow healing of weaklings, but rather an establishment for the training of strong and vigorous men. No contemplative vocation is conceivable without a strong streak of obstinate singleness of purpose, and such forceful personalities need the challenge of highly demanding social environments rather than the soothing and sedative atmosphere of therapeutic communities.

It is therefore important to think clearly about the purpose of a contemplative community. Its intention is to provide the invigorating environment that will encourage growth in the face of deliberately accepted hardships and sacrifices. It is not, as some ill-informed and badly-tutored readers of popular psychological books have believed, to provide a comforting form of group-therapy for the delicate souls of fragile personalities. Objective norms will have to be served, trials and frustrations will have to be accepted, unpalatable decisions will have to be obeyed (without the anodyne, at times, of group-discussions and "participation"). For the contemplative life is a serious enterprise that accepts unavoidable hardships joyfully in the hope of things to come.

Mutual concern

As any other religious association, the contemplative community should include a significant factor of mutual concern, mutual care and mutual responsibility. There is a need in every human individual not to remain alone, but to be related to other familiar persons whose life and fate he somehow shares. For people who live in the world, the family, the neighborhood and the profession have traditionally served this purpose. For members of a religious institution, the function will be accomplished by one's brethren brought together in an organized community. A same dwelling-place, shared meals, common worship, will be its most visible signs; showing concern and care in all the trials of life, in illness and old age, its most obvious manifestations. In this way, the fundamental aspects of Christian life expressed by fellowship and love of one's neighbor will fulfill their much-needed function in the development of a well-balanced religious life.

All these factors are most beneficial for a contemplative life. By providing trust and security, they liberate the individual and allow him to pursue his single-minded quest untrammelled by inopportune anxieties. On the other hand, the moral efforts required by the social responsibilities we have mentioned should develop the religious personality, purify it of its worst failings, and so prepare it to a better life of prayer and worship. Yet, and no matter how valuable and indeed indispensable all this may be, it finally remains secondary and peripheral and inessential. For the primary purpose of the contemplative is to seek God, and God only, in solitary encounter. It is not to lead a virtuous and satisfying common life of mutual help and loving concern. This may be a condition and a necessary preliminary for a successful cenobitic contemplative life, it does not in itself or by itself determine such a life. And great care should therefore be taken to restrain the impact of communality, to limit social interactions to the extent required by true mercifulness and authentic charity, but not to allow it to encroach upon that part of the individual's life that is reserved for his intimate life with God alone. Brotherly love and mutual concern may be essential foundations and necessary means in a contemplative

community, they are neither its primary intention nor its fundamental purpose.

Intimacy

All men live in social groups, and this general rule also applies to
religious persons living within their own associations. However,
the situation of the cenobitic monk residing in a contemplative
community is of a rather special kind, that would deserve further
study. For these group relations are significant factors in the
development and the organization of the personalities of individual
members.

Three main forms of group interactions can be readily and
usefully recognized. The first concerns *intimates,* such as a Father or
a Mother, a Brother or a Sister, a Husband or a Wife, or a Child;
and also, if the local social culture accepts their existence and
encourages their development, a Friend. Each individual only has
a small number of such intimates, but he meets them frequently in
close encounter and they influence the whole of his life.

A second type of group interactions concerns *familiars.* These are
well-known social partners one meets in frequent face-to-face
encounter. Their number, though greater than that of intimates,
cannot be unduly extended. Their presence and their actions result
in a social control that influences the whole of one's behavior and
life. Yet no intimacy is necessarily involved, no private exchanges
are required, no actual conversation is really needed. Such was the
situation of traditional man, in a village environment or a small-
town neighborhood, in a self-contained city borough or a well-
defined social class. Such can also be the case in relation to the
categories of people we had mentioned as possible intimates. For
while it is possible and perhaps desirable to be intimate with one's
parents or spouse or children, there is no guarantee that this will
actually be the case. Many potential intimacies remain unrealized
in the barren womb of mute and unformulated familiarity.

The third type of group interactions concerns mere *acquaintances.*
Modern man has many such relationships. But their interactions
are often functionally impersonal, as with the sales-lady or the bank-

cashier, the taxi-driver or the news-vendor, the gas-station attendant or the waiter. Or they concern persons in sharply-defined roles, who are moreover classified in numerous segregated groups: in the work-group and in the political party, in the supporting association and the hobby-group, in the benevolent association and in the parish, in home and family or away on a vacation, etc. Such acquaintances can only have a limited influence on one's personality, and a sharply restricted impact on one's behavior. For interactions with them are linked to particular situations, they are related to special fields of behavior, they affect only a narrow sector of one's life.

What now is the condition of the cenobitic monk within his contemplative community? He has practically no acquaintances, for persons outside the community, who come to lecture or to preach are usually too infrequent visitors to become significant social partners. All the members of the community, on the other hand, are familiars, whose constant presence powerfully conditions his individual life. A very few, finally, could become intimates, if it were thought proper and useful to promote them to that privileged status. Both of these last two categories deserve a word of comment.

All the members of the contemplative monastic community are familiars for one another, and we have already described the enormous importance of their attitudes and of their manner of life. But all this is perfectly accomplished by the performance of daily tasks with patient regularity and loving concern. It does *not* require prolonged conversation, far less public discussion, and not at all the emotional encounters of group-dynamics. Moreover, there is no reason why the latent factors of inter-personal dynamics should be brought to the awareness of the people concerned, and there is less reason still to make them the public objects of group-discussion. People cannot comfortably live together if they spend their time analyzing one another's hidden motivations. Familiarity in the context of a religious community should therefore lead to easy acceptance and willing co-operation, to spontaneous service and loving concern, to mutual service and shared joy. It should not lead to futile attempts to achieve insight therapy with discussions and explanations that are only useful for college graduates with great verbal facility who can afford the long-term entertainment provided by a gifted psychoanalyst. Familiarity is a condition that must be lived in daily encounter, not one to be explained in frequent discussion. It can lead to closeness and deep social understanding, it has no necessary relation with intimacy. Indeed true familiarity should be respectful of the other's privacy, it should leave him perfectly free to lead his own life and pursue his own quest. This reason is even more compelling in the present context, since the main purpose of the contemplative's vocation is to seek God, and surely no one would want to disturb him from that avocation. In the last resort, one would wish for trusting and understanding familiarity, together with a total respect for one another's privacy. Intimacy is another subject altogether, that requires separate discussion.

Is one to seek intimates in the contemplative community? The answer is not obvious, since one might think that the contemplative's essential concern would be to become intimate with God and God only. This would not however entirely solve the problem. And the question will be discussed at greater length in the third part of this report, in the context of a more general inquiry into the quality of interpersonal relations in the contemplative community.

COMMUNICATION

Man is a social animal and it is generally recognized that his personality can only develop through the process of interpersonal encounters. Communication with other persons is therefore essential at all stages of his growth, in the adult phases of his evolution toward religious maturity and spiritual perfection as well as in the early phases of childhood and adolescent personality formation. This would seem to raise particular problems for members of a contemplative community, who by choice and by tradition are wedded to a rule of silence. What forms of interpersonal encounter do remain available, in this rather special social situation? I shall try to show that many different types of significant personal relations are possible, and have in fact been traditionally used. But it would seem important to become explicitly aware of their existence, to make sure that they are effectively used, to measure their possible effects, and to evaluate their relative importance in the conduct of a well-ordered contemplative life.

We shall consider three main types of interpersonal encounter, subdivided into a total of eight distinct forms. The first concerns the private encounters of the individual contemplative with the Lord he serves, and with the witnesses of Christian tradition who reveal him. The second concerns the public social relations within the organized community, which though apparently external remain exquisitely interpersonal and deeply affect individual personalities. The third is related to personal I-and-Thou encounters, various forms of which will be considered. The discussion as a whole should clarify the factors involved and the values to be considered, thus preparing more lucid choices and wiser decisions by the persons involved.

Communication with the Lord

The most basic and most fundamental interpersonal encounter in the life of the contemplative is the one in which he meets his personal God. In more explicitly Christian terms, this encounter establishes a direct relationship with the three persons of Holy Trinity, the Father, the Son and the Holy Spirit. This encounter takes place every day and many times in the day: in silent prayer and private meditation, in brief devotions and public worship, in positive effort and in trusting abandon, and still more perhaps in the constant awareness of an ever-active Presence of the divine. It is in these meetings with the living Lord that all the fundamental developments of a spiritual life take place: a discovery of oneself and of one's fundamental sinfulness, a discovery of the Lord and of his saving grace, the slow and painful realization of one's utter unimportance, and the gradual revelation of the infinite sanctity of God.

All this is excruciatingly difficult, for it takes on all the appearances of a one-sided operation. God is invisible, and he long remains a silent partner, reached only in the mute and inconclusive darkness of faith. Yet one soon learns that a real interpersonal encounter does actually take place. One should know that all essential spiritual developments are completed in the crucible of this experience, and one should never forget that this interpersonal encounter alone and no other is typical of the contemplative life. Its unique importance should therefore be recognized, it should be faithfully practiced, and no other activity should ever be allowed to jeopardize its dominant position in the contemplative life.

At the same time, it must be admitted that other forms of personal encounter are normally required, and are in fact usually provided. The contemplative therefore is not left entirely alone, in the terrifying presence of a transcendent God. But meet his Savior he must, if he is ever to fulfill his vocation.

Lectio divina

A second private way to achieve interpersonal encounters is to communicate with the great representatives of the apostolic tradition. By slow and prayerful reading of the Bible in general and the New Testament in particular, of the Fathers of the Church and its approved spiritual masters, one can develop a close familiarity with these major witnesses of Revelation. One can know their minds and their hearts, one can participate in their experience of the ways of God, one can question their options and compare their choices and evaluate their attitudes and reconsider their solutions. A real dialogue is thus established, a virtual discussion, in which one actually confronts these very personal representatives of the teachings of Revelation. An active process of reflection and meditation is thus set up, that should lead to gradual transformation and growth, and eventually to true conversions.

This type of process is no doubt less intimate and ultimately effective than a direct encounter with the Lord. But it does take place in the presence of God, in a spirit of faith and hope and charity, and therefore in a context of saving grace. On the other hand, it does have the immense advantage of an explicit formulation in human language of the treasures of divine Revelation. God speaks to us here, abundantly; and it is therefore easier for us to respond, and to establish with him a more explicit communication. *Lectio divina* therefore allows us to operate on two levels simultaneously. On the one, we communicate with our fathers in the faith and in the life of the spirit, and so enter into our heritage of Christian devotion; on the other, we encounter God, who speaks to us in more accessible terms, and so helps us to answer him more easily. Both are forms of interpersonal encounter, and both lead to essential developments in the contemplative life. Normally they complement each other, in the well-ordered life of the contemplative community.

Social life in the community

In an earlier part of this study, we have discussed the emotional-affective atmosphere of the contemplative community, as a general environment for the individual monk. We shall now consider the same community from the point of view of the social interactions which life together necessarily entail. For these encounters also are personal interactions between familiars, and they have a decisive impact upon the development of individual religious personalities. Let us first consider the daily round of regular life, with its duly appointed public worship, its common meals, its well-organized work-schedule, its monastic observance. All this requires an immense amount of mutual adjustment: of exactness and regularity, of acceptance and docility, of patience and generosity, of attentive care and willing service. This constant adaptation to the realities of the social order is an excellent school for the practice of all the moral virtues, and at the same time it helps to develop the social maturity of the religious personalities involved. All this, moreover, can be accomplished in total silence. If words are occasionally used, they can be restricted to the objective needs of information concerning organizational requirements. And in this way, an immense amount of mutual education by interpersonal encounter can be effectively accomplished, through the normal operations of community life, without any verbal communication relative to people's inner life. It would seem that this is a distinctive and significant factor of spiritual growth, that is always available in the contemplative community.

It is however obvious that other more openly verbal forms of social communication are also required. One obvious and valuable traditional institution is available in the *chapter*, where problems of common life can be explicitly recognized and formulated, discussed and acted upon. One classical form of chapter has perhaps become somewhat obsolete, where individual members could only accuse themselves and then accuse others, while an all-knowing and omnipotent presiding Prelate pronounced oracular judgments. This was only acceptable when humility seemed more important than truth, and dependent submission better than a lucid and courageous opinion. Under present circumstances, it might be better to seek a more objective justice: to allow a defense of the accused by favorable witnesses, as well as blame by critical ones; and perhaps even at certain times an explanation if not an excuse by the accused himself might be thought acceptable. All this, of course, under the watchful control of a moderating Superior. In any case, some such form of open discussion would seem useful, if group pressures are to socialize too individualistic bachelors, whose peculiarities and idiosyncracies might otherwise become a nuisance to the community. From another point of view, the public airing of private dissatisfactions will certainly help to relieve tensions, and will thus restore peace in the community. In any case, the regular meetings of a well-organized community chapter should provide valuable occasions for interpersonal encounter, and so become important factors in the development of religious personalities. It would be essential, however, to respect the strictly public character of the subjects discussed. Such a chapter concerns public actions and behaviors, public failings and disorders. It does not pretend to discuss or to evaluate the inner life of individuals, their motives or their intentions, their vices or their sins.

Relations with the Abbot

Two important forms of interpersonal relations have already been considered: the private ones a contemplative entertains with his

God and his Fathers in the Christian tradition, and the social ones he enjoys in the group-life of the community. In their very different ways, both are essential. Yet more is needed to initiate beginners into the process of spiritual growth and to help them along on the path to perfection. Some deeper and more personal forms of human encounter will be required, with more intimate and there- fore more demanding types of interaction. For it is by the practice of such human confrontations, lived in faith in the presence of the Lord, that one learns to establish deeper and more authentic inter- personal relations with one's God. Such more intimate forms of human encounter have always existed in traditional monastic life, though they seem to be neglected by many communities, who only practice them in a desultory and half-hearted way, because they are unaware of their meaning and of their functional role in a healthy contemplative life. We shall consider at least four typical forms of such encounters, the first of which concerns the individual monk's spiritual relations with his Abbot.

In any form of Benedictine or Cistercian monastic life, it will be essential for each individual to come to terms with his abbot, a towering figure of legitimate pre-eminence, who as the Father of his community is the true image and representative of God. Under modern conditions, the abbot will not usually be the spiritual director of the majority of his monks. Nor need he be a paternalistic father-figure whose overwhelming power dominates the infantile and dependent child-personalities of his subordinates. For he will know that even when first they joined the community as mere beginners in spiritual life they already had adult personalities on the socio-psychological level. He will also know that on the spiritual level also they should be helped to grow into a condition of full and mature autonomy, though always docile and deferent in relation to his legitimate authority. Finally, he will be aware of his own failings and incapacities, including his unavoidable inability to inspire confident trust and spontaneous attachment in *all* the members of his community. Yet he will strive to foster proper attitudes, effective relations, and the required quality of interaction, with each and every one of his subordinates.

What then is required and what should the individual monk try to achieve with the help of his abbot who is his necessary social partner in this form of interpersonal encounter? Not necessarily, I would suggest, an intimate friendship, nor a close relationship, nor frequent personal exchanges, nor a mutual (or one-sided) dependency, nor an emotional-affective infatuation. But rather a certain basic ability to face one another in the presence of the Lord, in the stark simplicity of an attitude that recognizes their mutual goodwill and desire to serve in the relative and contrasting positions in which Providence has placed them. They may not actually encounter one another on this level more than a very few times a year. But the capacity, and the willingness must be there at all times, with the mutual awareness of its availability. In this way, they will both know that in times of need they can communicate at this essential level, that they can overcome all obstacles, and that they can operate with some confidence and facility at this fundamental level of their common vocation.

All this is difficult. It may require a long schooling, persistent efforts, excruciating trials, and a major purification of individual attitudes. Yet it is essential to the psychological maturity of the human person, and to the spiritual perfection of the cenobitic monk in his contemplative community. Moreover, such developments are entirely based on the infrequent but soul-searching personal encounters of the individual with his abbot, and the abbot with his individual subordinates, in the living presence of the Lord.

Spiritual guidance

A second type of intimate personal interaction that should help the individual monk toward religious maturity is provided by his encounters with his spiritual guide. Or such would be the case if spiritual guidance were seriously practiced in a productive way. But does effective guidance really exist in contemporary religious life? Novice-masters are everywhere present, of course, as institutionally required by Canon Law and Monastic Rules. Regular confessions are likewise organized and spiritual guidance is universally recommended. But do all these institutions really operate in an effective way? At what level of authentic intimacy does the postulant or novice or young professed really communicate with his novice-master? Do the older religious really reveal their innermost problems to an attentive and concerned spiritual director? Can such wise and helpful and trustworthy guides be easily found, in the average community? Circumstances no doubt vary. But I do not think that in these our times spiritual guidance is widely practiced in an effective way.

It may be useful to describe the nature of this rather special type of inter-personal encounter. It is, first of all, an essentially asymmetrical process. The disciple opens his heart, he reveals his innermost secrets, he discloses his most intimate problems. The director remains shrouded in total privacy: he does not normally talk about himself, far less does he confess his personal trials and tribulations. It is only by his attitude and his questions, his advice and his encouragements, that he shows himself to be a valid partner in dialogue, who is worthy of trust, deserves to be consulted, and can reasonably be believed. As a result, and although two concrete personalities are here in face-to-face interaction, their concern is entirely focussed on the condition and progress of the disciple. A second characteristic of such relations is the narrow scope of their theme, which is strictly limited to the field of spiritual growth and development. For nothing should be discussed in such encounters that is not relevant to better prayer and more loving service, to greater love of God and one's fellow-men.

The inter-personal relations thus practiced therefore concern a rather narrow field of action. Yet they include the most essential concerns of the persons involved, and they are enacted in the presence of a divine witness that compels absolute honesty and total dedication. They should therefore provide opportunities for valuable forms of intimate interpersonal encounters, and so contribute to the growth and maturity of the religious personalities of both individuals involved. Many capacities typical of spiritual perfection will obviously be required: lucid insight into one's attitudes and motivations, ruthless honesty, total trust, great inner security rooted in faith and hope, easy docility based on secure autonomy rather than stubborn resistance based on weak and anxious dependency, and many more of a similar nature. All these accomplishments are possible, and they should normally emerge. But they will only develop if the interpersonal encounters required for authentic spiritual guidance are really practiced in a sustained effort of continued generosity. Serious commitment to spiritual guidance should therefore be encouraged by the appropriate authorities: by explicit teaching concerning its necessity and its value, by the provision of an adequate number and variety of directors, and by a discrete supervision relative to its practice and effective functioning.

Colloquia

A third form of interpersonal encounter that should be available in a contemplative community would occur in the context of social gatherings leading to group discussions. Such meetings, however, raise several problems that deserve to be explicitly discussed.

The first problem concerns the legitimacy of group discussions within the Cistercian tradition, which at least in post-Lestrange times has not seemed overly favorable to such forms of social communication. But we now know through the writings of the great medieval authors that *colloquia* and *collationes* were a normal feature of twelfth-century Cistercian life. We also know that the monks were allowed and indeed encouraged to discuss spiritual themes related to the meanings of Scripture, the problems of religious life, the joys of contemplation, and the raptures of eternal bliss. Meetings of this type are therefore acceptable, in principle, providing they serve the essential purpose of contemplative vocations.

There is, however, an obvious danger of wasting time on concerns irrelevant to the primary purpose of the contemplative life. Commenting on the quality of such discussions in the twelfth century, Dom Knowles calls attention to a deeper and more insidious peril of such activities. At that time, discussions were often more Platonic and scholastic then specifically religious. Moreover, monks steeped in Cicero and Augustine, not to mention the new spirit of Arthurian romance, "had much to learn and to leave before they could follow Aelred with the fourth gospel of the Cross." Similar problems would surely arise under modern conditions, with such doctrines as Marxism and psychoanalysis as background inspiration, and minds more attentive to the teachings of Nietzsche and Heidegger, or Teilhard and export-Zen, than to the Scriptures or the Fathers of the Church.

It would therefore seem necessary that such meetings be somehow controlled and guided by the wisdom of appropriate religious leaders. Either, as has been suggested, by an appointed spiritual guide, with some recognized experience of God and the ways of God in contemplative prayer or by a team of *two* such discussion leaders, who while usefully different are deeply in mutual understanding, and so able to tolerate each other's interventions, and therefore also capable of sharing the task of leadership. This is a most effective way to lead discussion groups, for it allows one leader to sit back, attentive but relaxed, and so ready to take over effectively when the other gets entangled in irrelevant argument, or too involved emotionally to retain proper control of the proceedings. Such dual leadership has another advantage, in that it appears less openly authoritarian than that of a single appointed discussion leader. In any case, the role of such leaders would be to maximize participation by attending members and only to speak up to guide, to stimulate, and to add their personal testimony to the contributions of the group. The result would be a process of mutual enlightenment and edification, rather than deliberately imposed teaching.

The possibilities of spiritual exchange within such groups seem obvious and no doubt deserve to be more fully used. But it would seem just as important to be concerned with the necessary limits of this practice so as to make it truly subservient to the essential purpose of the contemplative community. Spiritual discussions are only useful if and when they improve the quality of one's prayer and the unselfishness of one's love. They will become at best a distraction, at worst a positive hindrance, if they do not in fact serve this intention. For some individual monks at all times, and for some periods at least in the lives of all contemplatives, there will be neither a need nor a desire to participate in such gatherings. Provision should certainly be made to protect such members of the community from what are to them irritating and harmful distractions. Some may wish to share silently in such meetings without feeling obliged to participate in open discussion. This desire should also be respected, though the motives for the individual's limited public involvement might usefully be discussed by him in private with his spiritual father. The frequency of discussion meetings will also have to be controlled so as to maintain a proper balance between the essential activities and the ancillary or instrumental ones. I have no authority to impose regulations, but I would venture to suggest that one (or at most two) meetings a week should prove sufficient to stimulate the spiritual life of even the most slothful of monks. Special care should also be taken to ensure the ultimate privacy of each individual's intimate and personal life with God. No one should be allowed, far less encouraged, to make a public confession of his inner experience. Nor should one be subject to "personal appeals" that require the indecent revelation of intimate involvements. The only public commitments a monk should be called upon to make are the confession of his faith and the proclamation of his vows. All the rest is essentially private, and should remain inviolate.

A technical problem must now be considered, which concerns the number and size of such discussion groups in the monastic community. Very small groups, with from two to half-a-dozen members, are no doubt possible. But they entail special problems, which will be discussed further along in this paper in the context of friendship relations. Discussion groups are most effective when they contain from twelve to sixteen members, or up to twenty if a number of silent participants are included, as might well here be the case. Several such groups will of course be required in the monastery, and it would seem reasonable to allow them to be different according to individual needs, vocations, levels of literacy, phases of spiritual development, etc. All groups should be open, in principle, so that none develops into an exclusive sect or a closed and potentially factious clan. Some group of this type should be available to anyone who needs that form of help. It might therefore seem appropriate to conceive the community as a whole as an interlocking network of spiritual discussion groups, for the abbot and his counselors to provide the necessary institutional guide-lines, and to be concerned with their effective operation. Just as, in another connection, it might be useful to conceive the total community as an interlocking network of individual spiritual directors linked with the individual monks they usually guide.

Other groups

Spiritual development by meaningful interpersonal encounter can therefore be fostered by the provision of appropriate *colloquia*. It would seem important, however, not to confuse this type of mutual enlightenment and edification in the contemplative life with other, apparently similar, but in fact very different, forms of group discussion. And I may be forgiven if I explicitly mention some of those other forms of social encounter, which might also exist in a monastic community, but which should be evaluated in a quite different spirit.

A first type would concern educational discussion groups, in the realm of theology or other fields of religious learning. Such meetings would appear quite legitimate and useful for all those who need such studies: monks who prepare for ordination, literate choir monks learning to abide by *lectio divina*, other monks both choir and lay, as they develop their knowledge of Christian doctrine in proportion to their legitimate individual wants and social needs. Such learning would of course be essentially theological, and so based upon and developed within, a fundamental attitude of faith. It would also presumably take the shape of that sort of theology-for-Christian-life that has been called monastic, rather than the more technical theology of the great speculative system-builders. It would therefore provide valuable foundations for the spiritual develop-ment of those who learn to appreciate it and to live by it. Yet, though useful and commendable as a widening and a deepening of one's more articulate faith, such learning does not automatically ensure authentic spiritual growth. Theological education is a separate and distinctive undertaking. Theological discussion groups may therefore find a legitimate place in the life of the contemplative community. But they should be judged on their own educational merits. They should not be conceived as immediate and infallible factors of spiritual progress. Nor should such meetings be confused with the spiritual *colloquia* we have described as typical and important features of the well-tempered contemplative community.

A second type of non-spiritual discussion groups would be related to the various problems of local government within the monastic community. In the Church in general, and in monastic circles in particular, there is at present an immense and somewhat adolescent concern for organizational principles, which is too often couched in such unreligious terms as democracy and autocracy. On the social level, there is much talk of dialogue and participation, of delegation of authority and subsidiarity. On the individual level, the fashion is to discuss initiative, creativity and responsibility, not to mention job-satisfaction and meaningful work. An unconscionable amount of time and effort has been wasted in the discussion of such problems, by people who honestly believed that they were essential to spiritual renewal. I would like to suggest a rather different view.

It should be remembered, first of all, that most of these themes are largely irrelevant to the individual's growth in spiritual life. If one is assured of silence and enclosure, if one can enjoy daily worship and *lectio divina* and regular work, one is endowed with all the essential conditions of a contemplative life, no matter what the social organization. The greatest danger in such matters is to pervert one's scale of values, to lose one's peace of mind, to be distracted from one's overriding quest for God. No doubt, one must also bear a measure of responsibility for the life and structures of the community. But these are relatively minor issues, for a contemplative whose essential concern is God and God only. It would therefore seem expedient to reduce such socio-organizational activities as much as possible, to introduce changes slowly and peacefully, to seek stability and continuity rather than constant innovation. Above all, it would seem important to remain detached, to retain a sense of humor, to be aware of the relativity of all possible solutions, and to be convinced of the ultimate unimportance of all such concerns. Surely there is a great danger in our times of thinking that renewal means external transformation rather than inner conversion, and changing the lives of others rather than improving the quality of one's own commitments.

On the personal level, moreover, there seems to be some confusion concerning the purpose of contemplative life. It is of course possible to achieve personal development through meaningful work, just as it is possible to obtain personal satisfaction and major enhancement of self-esteem through success in responsible leadership and effective job-performance. But these otherwise perfectly respectable gratifications are typically those of the man of the world leading an *active life*. They are not in any significant way those of contemplatives, whose overriding concern is the quest for God, and whose identity and self-esteem are established through their personal relations with the divine Persons. Even the unavoidable functions of administration and government, of study and teaching, should always remain subordinate to the essential search in prayer and meditation that leads to loving unity with God.

It would therefore seem a mistake to spend overmuch time or effort on the discussion of community organization and government. It would be a more grievous misunderstanding still to believe that such discussions have any necessary connection with contemplation.

A third form of non-spiritual group encounter deserves to be mentioned, because it is completely different from the other ones we have already considered, and because it is being increasingly used in various places in a sometimes inconsiderate manner. In this type of meeting, the monastic community (or a portion thereof) is assembled to hear a distinguished guest. The visitor gives a talk, and then he usually answers questions put to him by members of the assembly. The impact of such encounters on the contemplative life of the community will of course depend on the subject of the communication, and on the quality of the presentation. If the subject is directly relevant to the life of the spirit, and if the speaker is both technically competent and personally experienced, such meetings may help individual monks and the community as a whole in their contemplative vocation. But even then care should be taken not to perturb the slow and peaceful process of spiritual development by an overabundance of disturbing outsiders who by their sheer number and tiresome frequency may become a hindrance rather than a help in the religious life of the community. Such encounters will therefore prove more effective if they are wisely limited and if leave of absence is given to those whom they may distract or disturb rather than stimulate.

The situation is quite different when the distinguished visitor comments upon subjects less relevant to contemplative life. Even when the talk concerns the life of the Church, the information received and the reflections they lead to may all too easily become distractions which turn the monk away from his essential contemplative quest. Has he not renounced the world so as to be free to live and pray unimpeded in the living presence of the Lord? Some contact with a constantly evolving culture should no doubt be maintained, if only to understand the postulants who join the monastery and the guests who visit it in search of spiritual sustenance. Some knowledge of the condition of the world is also required in a contemplative life of prayer that is organically joined with the universal Church and so radically concerned with the ills of mankind and the redemption of all men in Christ. Yet none of this justifies an abundance of lectures on a variety of subjects that can so easily become a serious obstacle to a life of contemplative prayer. There is great danger here of encouraging idle curiosity, excessive concern for the inessential, exorbitant interest in the transitory, inordinate involvement in the superficial, etc. This is a difficult problem, for which I can suggest no other solution than judicious ascetic restraint. One should at least remember that brilliant lectures by eminent prelates and laymen of great renown do not necessarily enhance the spiritual life of a contemplative community; they may in fact cause great harm.

A fourth form of non-spiritual group encounter must now be considered, if only to recognize this other and very different type of monastic social interaction that should not be confused with spiritual discussions in *colloquia* and *collationes*. It may be quite justified, perhaps, for a gathering of monks to relax in the shade with a can of beer; or in other climates or seasons to assemble around a comforting fire with a mug of hot cocoa or a toddy of rum. Such convivial assemblies would no doubt generate affable companionship and jovial conversation, and there may well be a place for meetings of this type in the life of the monastic family. But such encounters are obviously related to relaxation and recreation rather than to the positive practice of contemplation and they should therefore be evaluated with those factors in mind. They do not directly provide the interpersonal encounters that lead to spiritual growth, though they may usefully improve the spirit of brotherly love in the community if they are exceptional rather than frequent and decently restrained rather than boisterously vulgar.

Friendship

So much for non-spiritual forms of group encounter, all included in the third type of communication within the monastic community that we had undertaken to discuss. One last type of spiritual interpersonal relation that can occur in the contemplative community must still be considered, which is generally known by the name of friendship (*amicitia*). Friendship obviously promotes intimate relations of a most demanding nature and so contributes to the development of the personality involved in such a relationship. If the friendship is also of a religious nature, it should likewise help in the maturation of the religious personalities. Both the theory and the practice of this form of interpersonal religious behavior are well-attested in the monastic tradition as is obvious in the writings of such men as St Bernard and Aelred. Yet both raise difficult problems, which will have to be at least briefly touched upon before the place of friendship in the modern contemplative community can be reasonably assessed.

The practice raises problems, because of doubts concerning its extension in the early Cistercian tradition. St Bernard surely entertained friendship relations, but apparently with people outside the monastery more often than with his brethren within. Aelred certainly had several intimate friends within his community, but he apparently felt the need to promote them to official functions (such as prior) to allow the full flowering of the relationship. All this concerns abbots and prelates, for there seem to be no documents relative to friendship in the lives of ordinary monks, nor are institutional provisions apparent which could favor their existence or encourage their development.

The theory of friendship also raises some problems. Initially based on Aristotelian and Stoic materials reformulated in Cicero's treatise, the theory had been extended under the influence of St Augustine to become a doctrine of universal friendship founded on divine grace or the similarity of all men to God. In a Cistercian environment this led all too easily to a notion of monastic friendship uniting brethren who live together in charity under a common rule in the service of the same Lord. There can be no objections to such speculations which in their own context are no doubt valid and stimulating. But they fail to discover the essential nature of authentic friendship which rests on the two notions of selective choice and reciprocity. Selective choice, first of all, because one singles out a very particular person as the object of one's friendship and the partner of one's choice. This is not based on the other's proximity, similarity or intrinsic worth, but only on the spontaneous growth of an attitude over which one has little control and by which one expresses the most creative and unselfish aspects of one's unfettered ability to love. It is moreover typical of such preferential involvements that one chooses one specific person as friend, while remaining completely indifferent toward other and perhaps better men who stand beside him. Reciprocity is the second distinctive factor of friendship and it is no less essential. For friendship requires mutual choice, mutual acceptance, mutual love. No one can decide on a friendship by solitary decree, no matter how great one's unrequited love, and so one always depends on the spontaneous willingness of the other person concerned. Nor should one forget that true friendship is of necessity a slow process that over the years leads to ever better and greater understanding and trust. The whole operation is therefore a difficult and somewhat improbable achievement. Not everyone has known this experience to a significant degree or in a lasting way. And even the luckiest should be content to have enjoyed it a very few times, and for limited periods, in the whole of their lives.

Is there room for such friendships in the modern contemplative community? I would think so, providing essential safeguards are provided. Intimate interpersonal relations within a true friendship between contemplative monks should be beneficial for the development of their religious personalities and the growth of their contemplative vocations. But if they are to remain faithful to their authentic calling, such friendships should always be lived in the active presence of the Lord, they should always concern the pursuit of a better life of service and worship, they should jealously exclude all distractions from the quest of God. All this is difficult. But it is because it is so hard and because it requires such deep purifications that it can be useful and indeed extraordinarily valuable for the growth of true charity. All mundane interests should of course be eliminated, all petty ambitions and social advantages, all selfish exclusiveness and jealous possessiveness. The quality of the feelings involved in such a human friendship would obviously require constant purification and renewal.

On the other hand, it might be useful to recognize the possibility of many rather different forms of religious friendship within the monastic community. The intense and rapturous friendships described by the extant medieval texts, with their mixture of sometimes questionable passion and doubtful rhetoric, do not represent the only possible model of amity between virtuous adult men. One could imagine more temperate forms of spiritual friendship that could normally lead to helpful and productive encounters. Nor are frequent meetings usually necessary, nor for that matter are they necessarily useful. It is often quite enough to know that a friend is available to whom one can easily and trustingly appeal in time of need. Friendship in the monastery is not an end in itself, that should be sought for its own sake; it is a merciful blessing, that should only be used as a help toward a more dedicated search for God.

If friendships are to be accepted within the monastery, it would seem expedient to recognize their existence in community life, and to control their operations by appropriate institutions. A time might be set aside for such encounters, that break the otherwise fundamental law of silence; a limited time at not too frequent intervals. Individual monks addicted to the practice might be asked to discuss this significant feature of their religious life with their spiritual directors, so as to learn to use it wisely and effectively. The abbot might sometimes think of his community as an interlocking network of friendships of varying types and strengths, and this would seem better to give open recognition to the existence of such amical relations, and so use them virtuously, than to feign to ignore them, and let them proliferate, indiscriminately promiscuous and chaotically uncontrolled.

The most typical friendships link together two persons only, in an intimate relationship. But it is also possible, in principle, for three or four or some such small number of individuals to be likewise united by bounds of deep understanding and mutual trust, based upon similarities of temperament, of education, of past experience, of values or of purpose. Such very small clusters, however, prove intrinsically unbalanced, unstable and prone to division. Even-numbered units tend to separate into rival couples, odd-numbered units try to enlist the non-paired individual into competing coalitions. The only mini-group of this size that has proved viable is the nuclear family, based on the sex-difference of the two leading members, and their spontaneous ascendancy on their much younger children. Even this unit of course is fragile; and it is soon dissolved by the increasing independence of growing offspring.

However, it is barely possible that loose friendship associations of this type could prove useful in the development of religious personalities and the progress of individual contemplative lives. But they might also, and much more easily, turn the monk away from what should be his overriding purpose and his paramount quest. For most of the varied and complex natural feelings involved in such relations will tend to distract him from the essentials of his contemplation. It would therefore seem prudent to curtail such involvements rigorously, and to use them most sparingly in the social organization of contemplative communities. The best evaluation of such friendship groupings is of course provided by their effects on the growth of individuals toward perfection and on the peaceful piety of community life. It is by their fruit that they will be judged.

Conclusion

To include this over-long section on interpersonal relations within the contemplative community, it may be useful to reformulate the fundamental principles involved. The first concerns the essential encounter of the contemplative with his God, for it is this constantly evolving inter-relationship, served by private and public readings and regular preaching, that is central to his life, and that at all times remains the primary factor of his spiritual development. The second is related to the daily round of ordinary monastic life, regulated by chapter and obedience, that provides the essential socialization of each individual monk. All this, it will be observed, can take place in absolute silence. Verbal interaction, however, also remains important, and we have seen that it is available in many different forms: with the abbot, with the spiritual director, in spiritual discussion groups, and in friendship relations. The possibilities for deeply religious human encounters are obviously there, in dangerous abundance. It would be a serious mistake not to make full use of them, of those in particular that are by their very nature most immediately related to spiritual progress. But it would be disastrous to use them carelessly, those in particular that might by their intrinsic structure lead to human involvements and secular distractions. The purpose of the contemplative community is to foster individual growth, not to provide a satisfying social life. The purpose of the contemplative monk should be to be alone with his God, though he recognizes that as a human being he needs an appropriate community and indeed depends on it for the fulfillment of his purpose. Social interactions therefore should only be accepted insofar as they are instrumental in achieving the overriding purpose of contemplative life.

D. H. Salman OP

Montreal, P.Q.

X